ADVANCES IN MOTOR DEVELOPMENT RESEARCH

BOARD OF REVIEWERS

Suzette Blanchard
University of Maryland

Martin E. Block
University of Maryland

Allen Burton
University of Minnesota

Graham E. Caldwell
University of Maryland

Joan Duda
Purdue University

Gail Dummer
Michigan State University

Sarah Erbaugh
Wayne State University

Larry Forrester
University of Maryland

Barbara Hart
University of Wisconsin, Milwaukee

Kathleen Haywood
University of Missouri, St. Louis

Claes von Hofsten
University of Umea (Sweden)

Jody L. Jensen
Indiana University

Stephen Langendorfer
Kent State University

Ann Lanphear
University of Maryland

Doug Larish
Arizona State University

Karl Newell
University of Illinois

Sally J. Phillips
University of Maryland

Mary Ann Roberton
University of Wisconsin, Madison

Esther Thelen
Indiana University

Terry L. Truly
University of Maryland

Beverly Ulrich
Indiana University

Maureen Weiss
University of Oregon

Jill Whitall
University of Wisconsin, Madison

Kathleen Williams
University of North Carolina, Greensboro

Craig Wrisberg
University of Tennessee

ADVANCES IN MOTOR DEVELOPMENT RESEARCH

Volume Three

Edited by

Jane E. Clark

and

James H. Humphrey

AMS PRESS
New York

Advances in Motor Development Research, 3

ISSN 0888-2990

Copyright © 1990 by AMS Press, Inc.

International Standard Book Number
Series: 0-404-63450-8
Vol 3: 0-404-63453-2
Library of Congress Catalog Card Number: 86:47829

All AMS books are printed on acid-free paper that meets the
guidelines for performance and durability of the Committee on
Production Guidelines for Book Longevity of the Council on Library
Resources.

AMS Press, Inc.
56 East 13th Street
New York, N.Y. 10003

MANUFACTURED IN THE UNITED STATES OF AMERICA

RJ 133
·A35
Vol.3
copy 1

About the Editors

Jane E. Clark, Associate Professor of Physical Education at the University of Maryland, conducts and directs research in motor development. Her major research interest is in the area of motor control and coordination. Currently she is focusing on the development of locomotor skills.

James H. Humphrey, Professor Emeritus at the University of Maryland, is the author of over 40 books and 200 articles and research reports. He is perhaps best know for his work in child learning through motor activity. In recent years he has been exploring the area of stress in childhood with reference to its influence on child development.

CONTENTS

vii

CONTRIBUTORS

Chantal Bard
Human Motor Performance Laboratory
Laval University, Québec, Canada

Janette B. Benson
Psychology Department
University of Denver, Denver, Colorado
Geoffrey D. Broadhead
School of Health and Physical Education
Kent State University, Kent, Ohio

Graham E. Caldwell
Department of Physical Education
University of Maryland, College Park, Maryland

Gabie E. Church
The Cleveland Clinic Foundation
Cleveland, Ohio

Jane E. Clark
Department of Physical Education
University of Maryland, College Park, Maryland

Michael E. Crawford
Department of Recreation
University of Missour–Columbia, Columbia, Missouri

R. E. A. van Emmerik
Department of Kinesiology
University of Illinois, Urbanb-Champaign, Illinois

Michelle Fleury
Human Motor Performance Laboratory
Laval University, Québec, Canada

Marie Gagnon
Human Motor Performance Laboratory
Laval University, Québec, Canada

Norma S. Griffin
Department of Physical Education
University of Nebraska, Lincoln, Nebraska

Carol France Haller
Department of Physical Education
University of Maryland, College Park, Maryland

Kathleen Haywood
Department of Physical Education
University of Missouri– St. Louis, St. Louis, Missouri

Jürgen Konczak
Motor Development and Child Study Laboratory
University of Wisconsin– Madison, Madison, Wisconsin

Stephen Langendorfer
Department of Physical Education
Kent State University, Kent, Ohio

K. M. Newell
Department of Kinesiology
University of Illinois, Urbana-Champaign, Illinois

David Niles
Department of Psychology
Indiana University, Bloomington, Indiana

Esther Thelen
Department of Psychology
Indiana University, Bloomington, Indiana

Beverly D. Ulrich
Department of Physical Education
Indiana University, Bloomington, Indiana

Ann VanSant
Department of Physical Therapy
Temple University, Philadelphia, Pennsylvania

Kathleen Williams
Department of Physical Education
University of North Carolina–Greesboro, Greensboro, North Carolina

PREFACE

Advances in Motor Development Research presents original research and reviews on contemporary problems of interest to scientists studying human motor development. Research in this volume, the third in the series, stretches across the lifespan from infancy to old age and includes a variety of approaches to motor skill development. Except for the Review Section, all papers represent original research.

It is the purpose of the editors and AMS Press, Inc., to provide motor development researchers with an annual series reporting original research and review/theoretic articles on current issues in motor development. All papers in this volume have been reviewed by at least two scholars from our Board of Reviewers. *Advances in Motor Development Research* should supplement and support journals and annual reviews on similar topics. However, to the best knowledge of the editors, this series is the only publication devoted specifically to research in motor development.

Motor development has evolved into a complicated and complex subject involving, among others, biological, behavioral, and biomechanical considerations. The scholars who have contributed to this volume represent the field well, and we extend our gratitude to them for their contributions. In addition, we wish to thank the members of the Board of Reviewers for giving of their time and talent in evaluating the manuscripts.

A volume of this nature could serve as a basic and/or supplementary text in motor development courses. It also could serve as a reference for motor development specialists as well as scientists investigating similar topics.

PERCEPTUAL DETERMINANTS OF ACTION: STAIR-CLIMBING CHOICES OF INFANTS AND TODDLERS

Beverly D. Ulrich

Esther Thelen

and

David Niles

ABSTRACT

Adults use perceptual information to make accurate body-scaled judgments of the affordances offered by objects in their environment, such as whether they can climb onto an object or pass between two objects without turning their shoulders. Little is known about how this ability is acquired. In this study we asked if children, who were beginning independent locomotion, would perceive differences in the affordances offered by three sets of stairs of varied riser heights. Our results suggested that younger infants perceived primarily the small and medium steps as climbable, and that their choices were related to the experiences of walking and climbing. Older subjects perceived that all sets afforded climbing and play. These results suggest that very young children make distinctions among the affordances offered by objects in their environment and that their motor abilities and experiences are related to their perceptions.

Virtually all action choices are shaped by perceptions of what the objects, surfaces, and other animals in the environment will allow. J. J. Gibson (1958, 1977, 1979, 1982) referred to these aspects of the environment as affordances. Affordances are the functional utilities of an object. They are specific to the animal and take into account the properties of the object as well as those of the animal (Turvey, Shaw, Reed, & Mace, 1981). For a bird a tree affords habitation, whereas for a horse it affords merely temporary shelter from the sun. To an adult human a stick may afford utility as a lever for moving a large object. A young child, however, may not perceive the stick as a lever but may perceive that it affords splashing in a puddle. That is, affordances exist whether or not the perceiver is aware of them and perceptions of what an object affords can change.

Animals are highly accurate in perceiving the affordances of relevant objects in their environment. In visually guided jumping, frogs decrease their attempts to jump through an aperture when the aperture's width is decreased to nearly their head size, that is, when it becomes impassible (Ingle & Cook, 1977). Mantids seldom miss when striking at prey, in part because they seldom attempt distances they cannot reach (Maldonado, Levin, & Barros-Pota, 1967). Apparently, mantids use visual information to classify the continuum of distances from their prey into distances that require a lunge and strike, those which require a strike without a lunge, and those which are too distant to reach.

Adult humans are also adept at perceiving affordances for action. Warren (1984) found that college-aged males of a wide range of statures could, by visual inspection alone, determine which in a series of stairs of varied riser heights afforded bipedal climbing and which was most energy efficient. Individual choices varied but were body-scaled; subjects' choices were the same mathematical function of leg length, regardless of stature. Similarly, when Warren and Whang (1987) asked adults to walk through apertures of varied widths, these subjects turned their shoulders in order to pass through when a precise ratio of aperture to shoulder width was reached or exceeded. Subjects' perceptual judgments of passability without rotation, based on visual inspection of the apertures alone, corresponded closely to their actions.

How do humans acquire the ability to perceive the affordances in the environment accurately when initiating actions? Is this an ability that is available without direct practice so that trial and error is not necessary when moving in a varied and changing environment? Do changes in movement goals, body dimensions, and physical abilities affect the affordances perceived? Although J. J. Gibson did not address these questions in his formulations of affordance theory, others (Gibson, 1969; Gibson & Rader, 1979; Neisser, 1976) have suggested that experience is important in perceiving affordances. Experience includes acting on objects and developing expectancies. More important it includes extracting information about the object from sensory sources (visual, tactile, auditory, etc.), which indicate characteristics of objects in general, such as texture, rigidity, and mass. The amount of experience necessary for an animal to perceive accurately the affordances an object or set of circumstances provides may vary across animals and by circumstance. Changes in body dimensions and physical abilities inherently affect the object-animal fit.

Accuracy implies making choices that accomplish the animal's goal. Inaccurate perceptions would result in a trial and error approach, unsuccessful attempts, and inefficient actions. Action choices that provide an appropriate fit between the objects in the environment, the animal, and the task or goal suggest that the animal responds to the affordances offered.

Researchers who have examined aspects of perception and action in human infants have found that, in general, functionally appropriate perceptions of what an object affords emerge as the physical capacity to perform that function or task emerges. Studies of reaching movements clearly indicate that by three months infants discriminate between objects that are and are not graspable and that they are not likely to reach for objects too far away or too big to grasp. By five months infants adjust arm and hand actions to accommodate variations in object distance and size (Bruner & Koslowski, 1972; Field, 1977; von Hofsten, 1980).

Gibson and Walk (1960) demonstrated that by the time babies are able to crawl, most will perceive an apparent sudden drop-off of the crawling surface, or "visual cliff," and avoid it. Results of a subsequent study suggested that the perception that the "visual cliff" did not afford crawling emerged at a developmentally appropriate time. Campos and colleagues (Campos, Hiatt, Ramsay, Henderson, & Svejda, 1978) observed that nonlocomotory babies, when lowered into the drop-off area next to the "cliff," did not perceive it as unsafe (as measured by changes in heart rate). Instead their heart rates decreased, which has been associated with focused attention in infants. For infants still dependent on others to move about a room, the need to perceive such affordances is irrelevant; relevance emerges as the child becomes independently mobile. Palmer (1989) found that young walkers use visual information to adjust their actions prior to and during attempts to pass through apertures. These infants acted differently when approaching and passing through apertures that were narrow (8 or 12 inches wide) versus wide (16 or 24 inches). Actions chosen by expert walkers also differed from those of novice walkers who were of the same chronological age.

The purposes of the present study were, first, to extend aspects of Warren's (1984) study of perceived affordances of stairs of varying heights by adults to relatively inexperienced locomotors and climbers (i.e., infants and toddlers). In addition, we were interested in determining if developmental shifts in perceptions were identifiable. We specifically asked, if children were given a choice among three sets of stairs of varying riser heights, would they perceive one of these sets as more affordable for climbing than the others. If so, were there measurable variables that related to their choices. Due to the obvious limitations in infants' abilities to communicate, we had to infer from their chosen pathways to equally motivating sets of toys which sets of stairs were perceived as most desirable.

Affordances require an appropriate animal-environment fit, but they may exist without being recognized or may be perceived incorrectly. A set of stairs that affords climbing for an adult may not for a toddler or crawler. Leg length, muscular strength, and postural control may be constraints that preclude some riser heights from affording climbing for the young child. If objects in the environment (such as stairs) differ in their affordance of actions (e.g., climbable vs. not climbable) and the actor perceives these affordances accurately, then he or she should demonstrate a preference for objects that afford the action they desire to make. Initial choices should, therefore, not be randomly distributed or unsuccessful. Subsequent choices may vary more, as satisfying curiosity or alleviating boredom may become the goal, rather than simply using the stairs as a pathway to toys.

STUDY 1

Method

Subjects

Subjects were 22 normal infants (13 females, 9 males) within the age range of 8 to 17.5 months representing developmental levels in˜which experience in independent locomotion was low but increasing. We defined normal as free from complications during birth and without diagnosed visual or motor deficits. We recruited subjects by telephone from published birth announcements. Table 1 presents a description of age, experience, and anthropometric data for the subjects.

Experimental room

The experimental room was 8 ft by 11.25 ft and contained three sets of stairs that were arranged in parallel (see Figure 1). We chose to limit the number of sets of stairs to three and to provide large differences among them in order to be

Table 1
Subject Characteristics—Study 1

	M	*SD*	*Range*
Chronological Age	13.3 mo	2.24	8.0–17.5
Walking Experience	2.48 mo	1.73	0.0–5.0
Stairs Experience	0.41	0.45	0.0–1.0
Stature (crown-heel)	76.3 cm	4.98	68.0–85.0
Shoulder-Elbow	14.6 cm	1.50	11.5–16.9
Rump-Knee	21.0 cm	1.60	19.0–25.3
Weight	9.8 kg	1.51	7.5–13.0

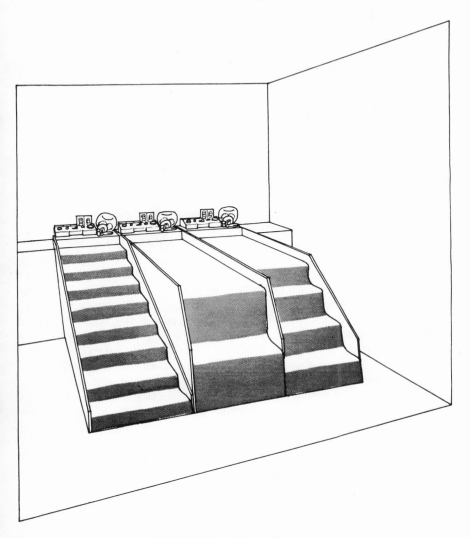

FIG. 1. Experimental room.

conservative about whether or not infants can make affordance distinctions. Sets varied in riser height (*S*mall = 3 in, *M*edium = 6 in, and *L*arge = 12 in) with a uniform tread depth of 9 in. We included a 6-in riser height to represent stairs common to the child's environment. It was possible that children might choose stairs most similar in size to those with which they are most familiar. The top of each set was two feet high. Uniform depth was attained by extending the top step of the *S*, *M*, and *L* sets 12, 48, and 66 in, respectively. We placed a set of identical brightly colored toys (9 in high and 12 in deep) on the back edge of the platform of each set, and randomized the arrangement of the stairs across subjects.

Procedure.

Upon arrival at the laboratory, babies were given an adjustment period of approximately 10 min during which they played with toys and interacted with experimenters. Subsequently, parent (mother or father) and child entered the adjoining experimental room. Parents oriented their children to the room by placing them (a) in front of each set of toys for 20 s, allowing them to touch the toys, (b) in front of each set of stairs for 5 s, drawing their attention to the stairs, and (c) by holding them as they walked in a circle around the free space in the room. Twelve test trials followed. At the start of each trial, parent and child sat on the floor opposite the stairs. Parents allowed their children to explore the room (and the trial began) when the experimenter said, "Let him/her go." Each trial ended when the child touched the toys or when one minute elapsed. We used three starting positions, left, center, and right, changing them with each test trial. Starting positions were randomized across children and counterbalanced with arrangement of the stairs. Parents interacted with their children as they would at home, encouraged exploration if needed but did not point to the stairs or toys. After the first 6 trials (set one), parent and child returned to the waiting room while experimenters rearranged the stairs (average elapsed time was 4 min). Parents did not repeat the orientation procedures at the start of the second set of 6 trials. All trials were videotaped. We mounted a camera on a tripod positioned behind the starting position in an adjoining room. This resulted in a view of the child from the posterior while he or she climbed the stairs. After the test trials, we took anthropometric measurements and asked parents to recall when their child attained specific motor milestones and the extent of their experience with stairs.

Anthropometric measurements

Parents removed their children's clothing for measurements of body size. The first author, who has extensive experience in anthropometric assessment techniques, collected these data. We placed the children in a reclining position on a measuring table to take crown-heel and crown-rump measurements. A single section of a Martin-type sliding anthropometer was used to measure limb (shoulder-elbow, elbow-wrist, rump-knee) and trunk (shoulder-rump) lengths. To measure skinfolds (subscapula, triceps), we used a Lange skinfold caliper, and to measure weight, a Healthometer pediatric scale. Same day test-retest reliability of the measurements, based on 6 subjects, ranged from 0.82 to 0.99 for the 7 items and averaged 0.92 across the items. Ponderal Index scores were derived from the values for length and weight (Bayley & Davis, 1935).

Motor milestones

Parents recalled for us when their child was first able to sit alone, crawl (on hands and knees), stand alone, walk with support, and walk alone (e.g., walk across the room from one adult to another, 5 to 8 ft). In addition, they indicated the extent to which stairs were available to their child. We assigned a value of 1 to this variable if the child had unrestricted access to stairs on a regular basis (at least three times a week), a 0.5 if access was limited but available, and a 0 if stairs were not available in the child's normal environment.

Treatment of the data

The videotape of each trial was coded individually, on a playback unit that has frame-by-frame capability. Variables coded included:

1. Method of locomotion (crawl or walk)
2. Set of stairs *(S, M, L)* child attempted to climb on initial and subsequent attempts within the trial (attempt defined as any effort to raise any part of the body onto a step)
3. Whether the attempt was successful
4. Any loss of postural control during initial attempt to climb
5. Whether child reached the toys
6. Actions other than attempts to ascend directly to the top of the stairs:
   a. climbed from one set to another while ascending
   b. turned around in a full circle on the stairs
   c. descended (on hands and knees) without reaching toys
   d. descended (walking) without reaching toys
   e. climbed a second set of stairs
   f. miscellaneous
7. Was set chosen closest to child's starting position

We calculated interobserver reliability as percent of agreement between data coded independently by 2 observers for 6 randomly chosen subjects (72 trials). We used the formula: number of agreements divided by the number of agreements plus the number of observations seen only by observer *a* plus those seen only by observer *b*. The range of values we obtained was 0.88 to 1.00 with a mean of 0.98.

Results

We reasoned that if infants were not able to perceive the affordances offered by the stairs, their initial choices would be randomly distributed among the sets. Ther choices, however, were not random. Of the 22 subjects, only 1 chose the L set initially while 7 chose the M set and 14 chose the S set [$X^2(2) = 8.01, p < .02$].

We tested the possibility that initial choices were a function of proximity to subjects' starting position. Ten subjects chose the set closest to them while 12 did not, resulting in a nonsignificant chi-square [$X^2(1) = 0.68$].

Because their initial choices were primarily S or M, we used a discriminant function analysis to determine if any known descriptors could account for the variation between the infants who chose the S set and those who chose the M set. Discriminant function analysis is essentially a form of multiple regression analysis and therefore is subject to problems of multicollinearity. To reduce the size of the data set and the difficulty in interpretation due to multicollinearity among the dependent variables (Gordon, 1968; Klecka, 1984), we generated an intercorrelation matrix. Based on the resultant correlation coefficients, we selected variables to represent body-build and motor milestones that minimized the intercorrelation among the variables. The variables we chose for inclusion in the discriminant function analysis were chronological age, walking experience (defined as number of months since the child began walking independently), stair-climbing experience, stature (crown-heel length), and shoulder-elbow and rump-knee lengths.

A significant discriminant-function equation resulted [Wilks' Lambda = 0.595, X^2 (2) = 9.33, $p < .009$]. Only two variables were included in the equation, walking experience and stair-climbing experience. The resultant standardized discriminant function coefficients were 0.90 and 0.46 respectively. Group mean values for these variables suggested that those children who were walking longer and had more experience with stairs were more likely to pick the M than the S set. Examination of the method used to approach the stairs (walk or crawl) further supported the relation between the child's capacity for independent locomotion and stairs' choice in that all those who initially crawled to the stairs ($n = 5$) chose the S set.

Most children chose a set of stairs they could climb on their initial attempt and did so while maintaining control of their actions. Only 1 of 22 subjects was unable to climb the set initially chosen; 3 additional children slipped or fell forward on the steps as they began to climb.

Parents of 11 subjects reported that their infants did not have stairs available in their normal environment, yet 10 of the 11 chose a set initially that they could climb (1 unsuccessfully attempted the L set). Of the successful ones, 8 chose the small set, apparently without benefit of experience climbing stairs.

In subsequent trials most infants displayed some variation in their choices (though the L set comprised only 2% of choices during the first set of trials, and 6% over all trials). The majority of subsequent choices, however, matched their initial choices (see Table 2).

Behaviors exhibited by subjects while on the stairs across all trials indicated that on most trials subjects chose to climb directly to the toys at the top of the stairs (187 of 232 trials, 81%). Nine children (41%) climbed straight to the toys on all of their attempts, while 13 varied their pathways at least once. Those children who varied their pathways did so an average of 5.2 times. For each variation coded, an average of 27% (6 children) chose to move in that manner. The actions chosen, sample distribution, and mean frequency for each action are shown in Table 3.

Discussion

The results of this first study suggest that these infants (aged 8 to 15 months) not only perceived some stairs as more climbable than others but that their choices were related to their locomotor capacities. In speaking of affordances, Gibson (1958) stated, "Depending on the locomotor capacities of the animal, [the] terrain provides definite possibilities or impossibilities for crawling, walking, climbing and the like. . . . If the animal can discriminate the textured variables it can discriminate among potential paths for locomotion . . . the kind of locomotion for which the animal is equipped" (p. 192). Apparently these infants perceived with some accuracy the affordances of these sets of stairs relative to the kind of locomotion for which they were equipped.

Based on the results of study 1, we decided to extend the upper end of our age range to include children with greater experience walking and climbing stairs

Table 2
Distribution of Choices of Subjects in Study 1 on all Trials as a Function of Initial Choice

	All Choices*					
	Set 1 (6 trials)			Both sets (12 trials)		
Initial Choice	S	M	L	S	M	L
S (N = 14)	77%	20%	3%	61%	34%	5%
M (N = 7)	31%	69%	0%	39%	52%	9%
L (N = 1)	71%	14%	14%	38%	54%	8%

*All Choices combines initial stairs choice in a trial plus subsequent attempts to climb a set of stairs within the same trial. Some infants climbed more than one set per trial; some did not attempt to climb during a trial.

Table 3
Variations in Stairs Activity—Study 1

Action	Number of Children (%)	M Number of Times
1. Crossed over to another set	5 (23%)	1.6
2. Crawled back down	8 (36%)	2.3
3. Walked back down	5 (23%)	2.2
4. Attempted a second set of stairs	7 (32%)	3.1
5. Turned around in a full circle on a step	5 (23%)	1.4
6. Miscellaneous	2 (9%)	1.0

(i.e., ages 17.5 to 25 months). If, as affordance theory suggests (E. J. Gibson, 1969, 1982; J. J. Gibson, 1977, 1982), one learns to perceive affordances (which requires time), to explore, and to seek out appropriate perceptual information and if the affordances offered by an object are specific to the characteristics (size, shape, strength, capabilities, etc.) of the animal, then older children who have had more time to learn and who have different capabilities may perceive different affordances for the same three sets of stairs.

STUDY 2

Our questions for study 2 were twofold. First, we asked if older children were given the same three sets of stairs of varying riser height would they perceive a set(s) as more affordable for climbing than others. Second, we asked if older children's choices would differ in comparison to those of the children in study 1, i.e., a developmentally younger group.

The methods used were identical to those in study 1. A description of the subjects by age, experience, and anthropometrics is presented in Table 4.

Results

Unlike Group 1, these children did not choose the S and M sets to the exclusion of the L set. Their choices were more evenly distributed, with 6 choosing the L set initially, 10 the M set, and 9 the S set $[X^2 (2) = 1.02, p < .60]$.

Chi-square analysis was used to examine the relationship between subjects' starting position in the room and set chosen. Twelve chose the set closest to them, 13 did not, resulting in a nonsignificant chi-square value $[X^2 (1) = 1.11]$.

While the distribution of their choices may be interpreted statistically as

Table 4
Subject Characteristics—Study 2

	M	SD	Range
Chronological Age	20.5 mo	2.30	17.5–25.0
Walking experience	8.75 mo	2.56	5.0–15.0
Stairs experience	0.66	0.37	0.0–1.0
Stature (crown-heel)	84.3 cm	4.22	76.5–92.5
Shoulder-Elbow	16.4 cm	1.30	13.5–19.3
Rump-Knee	24.6 cm	1.90	20.5–28.3
Weight	11.6 kg	1.51	8.1–15.9

random, as in study 1, we applied discriminant-function procedures to the data. The same variables used for Group 1 were included to determine if those who chose one set differed in a measurable way from those who chose different sets. The results of this analysis failed to produce a set of variables that could be used to distinguish among children based on their initial choices (Wilks' Lambda = .70, $X^2(4) = 7.6$, $p < .11$].

All children were able to climb the set of stairs initially chosen. Three of 25 (12%) slipped or fell forward onto the steps as they began to climb.

On subsequent trials subjects showed a preference for, though not an adherence to, the stairs initially chosen. Overall, an average of 51% of their choices were distributed between the other two stair sizes. Table 5 presents the distribution of choices in set one and both sets, relative to initial choice. Once on the stairs, subjects were likely to choose to vary their actions on at least one trial; only 4 (16%) did not. Children who varied their actions did so an average of 8.3

Table 5
Distribution of Choices of Subjects in Study 2 on all Trials as a
Function of Initial Choice

	All Choices*					
	Set 1 (6 trials)			Both sets (12 trials)		
Initial Choice	S	M	L	S	M	L
S (N = 9)	53%	27%	20%	50%	28%	23%
M (N = 10)	25%	49%	26%	35%	36%	29%
L (N = 6)	27%	19%	54%	31%	18%	51%

All Choices combines initial stairs choice in a trial plus subsequent attempts to climb a set of stairs within the same trial. Some infants climbed more than one set per trial; some did not attempt to climb during a trial.

times during their 12 trials. During 69% of all trials in which an attempt to climb was made (202 of 294 attempts) children's initial stair choices resulted in progression directly to the top. For each of the five specific variations coded, at least 28% displayed that action; across all variations an average of 46% of all subjects chose that action at least one time.

Discussion

In this study experience walking and climbing stairs was not related to infants' choices. This suggests that when infants gained some level of experience or ability in these activities, the stair heights no longer represented constraints on their actions. In this environment, for these children, all three sets of stairs provided potential paths for locomotion. Further, subsequent choices for the older children were more likely to differ from their initial choices than were those of the younger children (see Tables 2 and 5).

Children's behaviors after mounting a set of stairs provide further evidence that the affordances perceived by older children differed from those of younger ones. Once on the stairs children had the option of proceeding directly to the top (where toys were located) or performing other play actions such as crossing from one set to another or turning around in a circle on a step. Of the 22 younger children, 9 (41%) chose to climb straight to the toys on all attempts. Of the 25 older children, only 4 did so (16%). Of those who varied their pathways, the number of times they did so was also greater for the older children than the younger children, 8.3 and 5.2 times respectively (see Tables 3 and 6 for types of variations used and occurrences by group).

GENERAL DISCUSSION

Both the younger and older groups of infants were confronted with the same environment, but their perceptions of the affordances offered by objects in that environment were different. The younger infants perceived only the small and medium steps as climbable, while all three sets afforded climbing and play for the older group. What characteristics then, of the infants and/or their experiences, account for this developmental shift?

Warren (1984) observed that adults accurately perceive affordances offered by stairs of different riser heights in relation to their own body size. Subjects consistently perceived the cut-off point at which riser height no longer afforded upright locomotion as 0.88 of leg length. This value closely approximated the ratio Warren predicted by a biomechanical model. Similarly, subjects' identification of the set that was most efficient was 0.25 of leg length, which corresponded to the ratio determined by a direct test of minimal energy expenditure (ratio was

Table 6
Variations in Stairs Activity—Study 2

Action	Number of Children (%)	*M* Number of Times
1. Crossed over to another set	16 (64%)	2.9
2. Crawled back down	12 (48%)	3.1
3. Walked back down	7 (28%)	3.6
4. Attempted a second set of stairs	14 (56%)	3.4
5. Turned around in a full circle on a step	8 (32%)	1.9
6. Miscellaneous	4 (16%)	1.8

0.26). He suggested that the origin of the ability to perceive the environment in such a body-scaled and energy efficient manner may be in normal exploratory activity. Unknown is whether adults could perceive so accurately throughout earlier periods of development.

For Warren's subjects growth was stable or nearly stable, and we can infer that they would have had extensive experience with bipedal climbing on stairs and other objects of varied heights. In contrast, our younger subjects were in a stage of rapid change in body dimensions and with more limited experience, both in time and variety of objects. Nonetheless, children in study 1 appeared to make some a priori distinctions among the affordances offered by the 3 sets in that 21 of 22 ignored the large set on their initial attempt. That their choices were functionally appropriate is suggested by the fact that all but one (the only one whose initial choice was the *L* set) were able to climb the set they chose. For only three infants, the actions used to mount the first step resulted in an observable loss of postural control, e.g., fell forward onto step or foot slipped off step.

Variations in body build did not account for variations in their choices as it did for adults (Warren, 1984). One might argue that the set not chosen *(L)* was ignored because the infants' legs were too short to afford climbing that riser height. However, 5 children proceeded to climb the *L* set successfully at least one time during the remaining trials, demonstrating that it was possible, if not easy, for at least 23% of them.

Children in study 2 distributed their initial and subsequent stairs choices more evenly among all three sets than did those in study 1. Further, the actions they chose while on the stairs varied to a greater extent. Their choices, like those of younger infants, were unrelated to their body size. Unlike younger infants, choices were not distinguishable by walking or stair-climbing experience. More of the older children apparently perceived that the stairs afforded a variety of actions.

Perhaps concepts of affordances develop as a continuum of levels and transitions. At each point on the continuum the perception of what an object affords the perceiver emerges based on the interrelationship of multiple dynamic and interrelated elements. When viewing a set of stairs the elements that may affect a child's perceptions may include leg strength, limb lengths, locomotor abilities, experiences with stairs, and previous opportunities to explore climbable objects. Thelen and Fogel (1989) suggest that these contributing elements may develop at different rates. Thus any one element may be rate limiting or facilitate the emergent behavior, in this context, perceived affordances. For children at the younger developmental level (study 1), given these sets of stairs, leg length was not the rate-limiting factor in their choice between the S or M set, but locomotor abilities and opportunities to explore climbable objects were. For children in study 2, who were at a higher level developmentally, all of the elements may have been developed sufficiently to provide the perception that each not only afforded climbing but also a means for exploring variations in their climbing behaviors.

REFERENCES

Bayley, N., & Davis, F. C. (1935). Growth changes in bodily size and proportions in the first three years: A developmental study of sixty-one children by repeated measures. *Biometrika, 27*, 26–87.

Bruner, J., & Koslowski, B. (1972). Visually prepared constituents of manipulatory action. *Perception, 1*, 3–14.

Campos, J. J., Hiatt, S., Ramsay, D., Henderson, C., & Svejda, M. (1978). The emergence of fear on the visual cliff. In M. Lewis & L. Rosenblum (Eds.), *The development of affect* (pp. 149–182). New York: Plenum.

Field, J. (1977). Coordination of vision and prehension in young infants. *Child Development, 103*, 48–57.

Gibson, E. J. (1969). *Perceptual learning and development*. New York: Appleton-Century-Crofts.

Gibson, E. J. (1982). The concept of affordances in development: The renascence of functonalism. In W. A. Collins (Ed.), *The concept of development* (pp. 55–81). Hillsdale, NJ: Erlbaum.

Gibson, E. J., & Rader, N. (1979). Attention: The perceiver as performer. In G. Hale & M. Lewis (Eds.), *Attention and cognitive development* (pp. 1–21). New York: Plenum.

Gibson, E. J., & Walk, R. D. (1960). The visual cliff. *Scientific American, 202*, 64–71.

Gibson, J. J. (1958). Visually controlled locomotion and visual orientation in animals. *British Journal of Psychology, 49*, 182–194.

Gibson, J. J. (1977). The theory of affordances. In R. E. Shaw & J. Bransford (Eds.), *Perceiving, acting, and knowing* (pp. 67–82). Hillsdale, NJ: Erlbaum.

Gibson, J. J. (1979). *The ecological approach to visual perception*. Boston: Houghton-Mifflin.

Gibson, J. J. (1982). Notes on affordances. In E. Reed & R. Jones (Eds.), *Reasons for realism* (pp. 401–418). Hillsdale, NJ: Erlbaum.

Gordon, R. A. (1968). Issues in multiple regression. *American Journal of Sociology, 73*, 592–616.

Hofsten, C. von. (1980). Predictive reaching for moving objects by human infants. *Journal of Experimental Child Psychology, 30*, 369–382.

Ingle, D., & Cook, J. (1977). The effects of viewing distance upon size preference of frogs for prey. *Vision Research, 17*, 1009–1019.

Klecka, W. R. (1984). *Discriminant Analysis.* London: Sage Publications.

Maldonado, H., Levin, L., & Barros-Pita, J. C. (1967). Hit distance and the predatory strike of the praying mantis. *Zeitschrift fur Vergleichende Physiologie, 56,* 237–257.

Neisser, U. (1976). *Cognition and reality.* San Francisco: W. H. Freeman.

Palmer, C. (1989). Infants' perception of aperture affordance for locomotion. Manuscript submitted for publication.

Thelen, E., & Fogel, A. (1989). Toward an action-based theory of infant development. In J. Lockman & N. Hazen (Eds.), *Action in social context* (pp. 23–63). New York: Plenum.

Turvey, M. T., Shaw, R. E., Reed, E. S., & Mace, W. M. (1981). Ecological laws of perceiving and acting: In reply to Fodor & Pylyshyn (1981). *Cognition, 9,* 237–304.

Warren, W. H. (1984). Perceiving affordances: Visual guidance of stair climbing. *Developmental Psychology: Human Perception and Performance, 10,* 683–703.

Warren, W. H., & Whang, S. (1987). Visual guidance of walking through apertures: Body-scaled information for affordances. *Journal of Experimental Psychology: Human Perception and Performance, 13,* 371–383.

AUTHORS' NOTE

This study was supported by National Science Foundation grant BNS 85-09793 and NICHD RCDA HD-00492 to E.T. We thank Lynne Covitz, Melissa Hestin, and Darla Kroft for their assistance with data collection.

2

MOTOR-TASK GOAL AS A CONSTRAINT ON DEVELOPMENTAL STATUS

Stephen Langendorfer

ABSTRACT

Newell (1986) suggested that organismic, task, and environmental factors all may influence developmental change in motor performance. Previous studies examining the influence of organismic and environmental factors have shown little effect on developmental status. The present study examined the effect of task demand and changing the goal of a throwing task from accuracy to force on the developmental status of the motor pattern. Two groups of subjects (34 young adults; 43 nine- and ten-year-olds) performed trials of overarm throwing under different goal conditions. The adults performed trials for accuracy and for force; the children threw using accuracy, force, and combined force-accuracy goals. The videotaped sideview recordings were categorized using Robertson's developmental component category checklist for the overarm throw. Modal values of trials were analyzed using nonparametric Friedman planned comparisons. Males, both children and adults, significantly improved the developmental status of movement components when throwing for force compared to an accuracy goal. The more primitive developmental status of the female subjects and the thrower-to-target distance appeared to require them to treat all conditions as forceful, preventing them from shifting developmental status.

There is ample evidence throughout the motor development literature demonstrating that motor tasks change across time and age. While product or performance scores of tasks have been the most typical means of noting developmental change (Eckert, 1987; Roberton, Halverson, Langendorfer, & Williams, 1979), developmental sequences recently have become more popular measures to describe changes in the qualitative aspects of motor tasks (Roberton & Halverson,

16

1984). Studies have suggested that motor tasks change in relatively regular and invariant sequences across age (Halverson & Williams, 1985; Langendorfer, 1987b; Roberton, 1977, 1978; Roberton & Langendorfer, 1980; Williams, 1980). Theories for explaining these regular ordered changes have not been evident.

Roberton (1984, 1987) noted that motor-development researchers have been so intent on describing the changing movement characteristics of their subjects that often they failed to consider the influence that a variety of other factors may play on those changes. She argued that motor-development researchers need to focus more effort on studying the effect of environmental variables on the development of motor skills as a means for explaining the determinants of developmental change. In an effort to address the question of environmental influences on developmental status, Roberton (1987) manipulated the kinematic characteristics of a throwing target for young children (3 to 8 years) using Gentile's closed-open skill paradigm. She found that, with the exception of the velocity of a ball thrown at an unpredictably moving target, the subjects' accuracy, developmental status, and velocity were unchanged across environmental conditions. Similarly, Langendorfer (1987b) asked children to strike a suspended ball under both stationary (closed) and moving (partially closed) conditions. He found that the developmental status of the movement components for striking largely was unchanged and relatively robust across conditions for most subjects. While these studies demonstrated the robustness of developmental status, they were unable to offer significant insight into explanations for developmental change.

Recently, Newell (1986) presented a triadic model for classifying factors that may influence developmental change. He argued that organismic, task, and environmental factors interact to constrain the control and coordination of motor tasks. He suggested that developmental sequences probably are artifacts of changes in object-to-body size relationships (body scaling) that have been unobserved due to the lack of focus on organismic and environmental constraints. His approach deviates substantially from more traditional developmental views, which hold that maturational, experiential, or motor program determinants act as the primary cause of developmental movement change. Although his paper primarily addressed body scaling and gravitational influence on movement, he did suggest that task-specific constraints may include the goal of the task, performance rules, or implements which control motor task performance. Consequently, he claimed that the interaction of constraints from the three areas control the development of movement coordination, thus altering the order and robustness of traditional developmental sequences.

Along Newell's suggested line of inquiry, Davis (1984) had investigated the way that visual information may directly and unconsciously alter the performance of a motor task. He reported, however, that changes in visual target conditions alone were not sufficient to significantly alter accuracy scores of throwing by adults. Similarly, Davis and Langendorfer (1985) found that children's throwing accuracy did not change when subtle differences in the precision and location of visual target center conditions were introduced. Coincidently, in these studies, definite shifts in ball velocity were noted that coincided with shifts in the task demands or goals (Davis & Langendorfer, 1985).

Langendorfer (1985, 1987a) explored the notion that body scaling relationships influence changes in the developmental status of motor skills. However, standard anthropometric measures such as limb lengths accounted for less than 10% of the explained variance in the developmental status of fourth-grade children throwers. Apparently, traditional measures of assessing body size provide little information about how a person will use his or her body to perform a motor skill.

In sum, previous efforts to alter specific environmental variables or to examine organismic relationships have not indicated that these factors produce or explain qualitative developmental shifts in performance. Previous studies have not provided substantiation for Newell's coordination model for development. In fairness, however, little attention has been given to the effects of varying the task demands themselves or to the interaction of the three areas. The purpose of this study was to determine the influence of the goal of a motor task on the developmental status of performing that task. Specifically, the study investigated whether shifting the goal of an overarm throw from accuracy to force altered the developmental status of movement components of the throwing motor pattern.

METHOD

Subjects

Two separate groups of subjects were used in the study. First, 34 young adults ($n = 17$ males, $n = 17$ females), ages 19–25 years, volunteered from several university classes. Subjects were predominantly university physical education majors. The second group consisted of 43 fourth-grade children ($n = 23$ males; $n = 20$ females), ages 9 and 10 years, selected from several classrooms of a single elementary school. All subjects were nonhandicapped volunteers in good health.

Procedures

As previously reported in Davis (1984) and Davis and Langendorfer (1985), all subjects performed a series of overarm throwing trials at an 8-ft diameter circular target suspended vertically against a wall. The adult subjects threw from a distance of 10 m while the children threw at the target from only 6 m. Adult subjects threw tennis balls a total of 55 trials at the target as reported in Davis (1984). From among these trials, one block of 10 trials of throwing for accuracy was selected and 5 previously unreported trials of forceful throwing. Similarly, each child threw tennis balls for a total of 85 trials over two days from which blocks of trials for three conditions of (1) accuracy (10 trials), (2) accuracy *and* force (10 trials), and (3) force alone (5 trials) were selected (Davis & Langendorfer, 1985).

Under the accuracy condition for both groups, subjects were instructed to "hit the center of the target," which was marked by a small red circular dot. Under the force condition, subjects were told not to worry about hitting the target but simply to "throw the ball as hard as you can" or to "crash the ball against the wall or target." Under the combined accuracy-force condition for the children, subjects were instructed to "hit the center of the target, but throw as hard as you can."

For adults, the sideviews of the first five trials of the selected accuracy goal condition and all five trials of the forceful throws were recorded by a Sony color video camera on a Sony SLO-326 cassette recorder (½" Beta format) operating at a scan rate of 30 Hz. The adult subjects had 340 videotaped trials available for use in the study. For the children's group, the sideviews of the first five trials of all three selected conditions were recorded using the same equipment and similar procedures. A total of 645 videotaped trials of children were used. A total of 985 videotaped trials were available for use in the current study.

Data Reduction

All trials of the overarm throw were played back in slowed and stopped action on the videocassette recorder and classified using the Roberton developmental movement component category checklist for the overarm throw (Roberton, 1977, 1984; Roberton & Halverson, 1984; Roberton & Langendorfer, 1980). The movement components for backswing, stepping action, trunk action, humerus action, and forearm action were each considered separately (see Roberton, 1977, 1978, 1984, 1987; and Roberton & Langendorfer, 1980, for descriptions of the movement component sequences). The data were summarized across trials by calculating the modal or most frequent response for the five trials in each condition. This modal value was used in the subsequent statistical analysis.

Previous studies (Roberton, 1977, 1978, 1982; Roberton & Langendorfer, 1980) have demonstrated that the Roberton checklist exceeds 80% exact agreement for both intra- and inter-observer objectivity. In addition, the instrument typically classifies trials within the modal trial 90% of the time. The current study demonstrated similar objectivity and reliability for movement component sequences, exceeding 80% exact agreement and 90% across trial consistency, despite using videotape instead of 16-mm film.

RESULTS

Friedman's planned pairwise comparisons tested the ranked modal values of the ordinal movement component data for differences between movement conditions for the adult subjects. Significant differences at the $p < .01$ level existed for males between accuracy and forceful trials on the developmental levels within stepping and trunk action component sequences (see Table 1). The differences between humerus and forearm action components for males were significant at the $p < .05$ level. In all cases where significant differences were noted, the forceful throwing condition resulted in the more advanced mean movement pattern than the accuracy condition.

No significant differences between accuracy and forceful trials for any of the females' movement components were observed (see Table 1). Descriptively, the changes in mean categorizations for females also demonstrated that forceful throwing produced more advanced movement patterns than for accuracy throwing. Differences between the backswing patterns were not significant for either gender.

Friedman's planned pairwise comparisons also were used to examine the paired rank differences across the children's movement conditions. Significant

Table 1
Mean Values for Throwing Developmental Status across Goal Conditions for Adult Subjects

Males	Goal Conditions	
	Accuracy	Force
Backswing (4)[1]	3.6	3.8
Stepping Action (4)	3.2**	3.9
Trunk Action (3)	2.2**	2.9
Humerus Action (3)	2.5*	2.9
Forearm Action (3)	2.4*	2.9
Females		
Backswing (4)	3.4	3.5
Stepping Action (4)	3.3	3.6
Trunk Action (3)	2.0	2.1
Humerus Action (3)	1.9	2.2
Forearm Action (3)	1.9	2.2

[1]Numbers in parentheses indicate number of developmental steps within component sequence and maximum mean value.
*Indicates a significant difference exceeding $p < .05$.
**Indicates a significant difference exceeding $p < .01$.

differences existed for the boys between the accuracy and the forceful trials on the developmental levels within stepping, trunk, and humerus action sequences ($p < .01$) and in forearm action ($p < .05$). The mean category values are listed in Table 2. Additionally, there were significant differences for boys between accuracy only and the accuracy + force conditions in stepping and trunk-action components and between the combined accuracy-force and force conditions for trunk action ($p < .05$).

The girls demonstrated a significant improvement ($p < .01$) only in stepping action levels between force and accuracy conditions. No differences were detected between any conditions for the backswing component for either gender. As with the adult data, where differences in developmental status were detected, the most advanced level was observed during the forceful trials.

DISCUSSION

Major findings

The important findings resulting from the study can be summarized with four points. First, the results confirmed an observation that should be obvious even to

Table 2
Mean Values for Throwing Developmental Status across Goal Conditions for Children Subjects

Males	Goal Conditions		
	Accuracy	Acc + Force	Force
Backswing (4)[1]	3.7	3.8	3.8
Stepping Action (4)	3.3**	3.7	3.8
Trunk Action (3)	2.0**	2.3*	2.6
Humerus Action (3)	2.3**	2.5	2.7
Forearm Action (3)	2.3*	2.4	2.7
Females			
Backswing (4)	2.7	2.8	2.9
Stepping Action (4)	3.0**	3.0**	3.3
Trunk Action (3)	1.8	2.0	2.0
Humerus Action (3)	1.7	1.7	2.0
Forearm Action (3)	1.7	1.7	1.7

[1]Numbers in parentheses indicate number of developmental steps within component sequence and maximum mean value.
*Indicates a significant difference exceeding $p < .05$.
**Indicates a significant difference exceeding $p < .01$.

casual observers: some throwers use different patterns to achieve different throwing goals. Specifically, this study demonstrated that subjects throwing for accuracy on the average used more primitive patterns than when they threw with forceful intent. In fact, when subjects' data are examined one-by-one, those throwers who did change their throwing pattern always improved one developmental level when shifting from an accuracy goal to a force goal. It also should be noted that not all subjects changed their pattern in response to the altered goals.

Second, and surprisingly, only males changed their mean throwing pattern significantly. Female subjects, whether child or adult, showed only a descriptive improvement from accuracy to force except for girls in stepping action (see Table 2). In other words, the female throwing patterns demonstrated relatively little change across task-goal conditions.

Third, when asked to use accuracy and force simultaneously, boys used very similar patterns to the ones they used to throw for force alone. The only significant changes between the combined accuracy + force and force conditions came in the trunk-action component. Apparently, more boys began using differentiated trunk rotation under forceful throwing than had when still trying to maintain some accuracy along with force.

Finally, there were surprisingly few age differences. The children's responses to shifting the goal from accuracy to force were in the same direction and same size, descriptively, as the adults'. The throwing distance and number of conditions under which the children threw were different, but it is unlikely that these influenced the similar results. The only apparent descriptive differences were in the mean developmental level used, and these were surprisingly similar between the 10-year-olds and adults within gender.

Implications

These findings have several implications for motor development researchers. First of all, evidence that the mean developmental status changed contrasted with several previous studies that had not demonstrated motor pattern shifts in children. The previous studies (Langendorfer, 1987b; Roberton, 1987), however, had manipulated variables which Newell (1986) classified as environmental since the skills shifted from closed to open skills. The present study changed task demands (i.e., goal) rather than the immediate environment. Apparently, task demands produced a stronger influence on shifting developmental status.

Second, since the goal or task demand that researchers impose on subjects is clearly an important consideration, Roberton's (1977, 1978; Roberton and Langendorfer, 1980) limitation of studying the overarm throw for *force* seems especially justified. This means, however, that while we know how the forceful overarm throw develops, we do not know if those observations can be extended, for example, to accuracy throwing at targets. Since the current study was not longitudinal or even cross-sectional, the influence of task goal on the actual developmental sequence is left for further study.

Third, since it is not immediately obvious why there was a differential gender effect to shifting goals, further exploration is needed. The most logical explanations for the difference would center not on gender itself but on the differences in experience, skill level, or strength between the males and females. Further study needs to control developmental status as an independent variable rather than age.

Fourth, since not all subjects reacted to the changing goal demands of the throw, it is important to understand why some subjects did or could not shift their throwing pattern. Future study of these individual differences may provide valuable developmental information of both a theoretical and practical nature. Any satisfactory developmental theory must account for these individual differences. At the same time, knowledge of these differences may help clinicians and practitioners provide better learning experiences for all learners.

Finally, the results of this study challenge motor-development researchers to hypothesize a more satisfactory and comprehensive theory for developmental changes and the influence that organismic, task, and environmental variables have on these changes. The only traditional current theory, stage theory, borrows heavily from developmental psychology and depends upon deterministic constructs such as schema. Newell (1986) has argued that these constructs are neither elegant nor parsimonious for explaining the regular ordered changes in motor skills. They also provide little explanatory power for individual differences.

Possible Explanations

Several possible explanations exist to account for the shift in developmental status of the throwing motor patterns resulting from differences in task goal. These include considering constraints on the dynamical requirements of the task itself, hierarchical developmental organization of throwing "options," the most advanced developmental status of which the mover is capable, and the relative contribution of different movement components to the successful completion of the goal.

Dynamical task constraints

Producing a forceful, high-velocity throw is achieved under a unique set of movement characteristics. The spatio-temporal organization is such that maximal object speed is generated by sequentially putting muscle groups under maximal elastic stretch over the longest body axes. These characteristics, most strikingly portrayed by the baseball pitcher, also represent the most advanced level within each developmental component sequence (Halverson, et al., 1982; Roberton, 1977, 1978). The developmental literature indicates that achievement of advanced developmental characteristics of the forceful throw rarely appear in children prior to the age of 10 years, almost never is demonstrated by females, and usually is associated with extensive practice (Halverson, et al., 1982). The current study also demonstrated that males did not produce the movement organization characteristic of high-velocity forceful throwing when accuracy was emphasized. Previous deterministic explanations (e.g., maturation, learning) intended to account for observed developmental and gender differences fail to explain why goal changes also affect the developmental status of throwing.

Consider the case of throwing for accuracy over a short distance with the intent of precisely hitting a target such as in a dart throw. Typically, the thrower organizes the throwing act much differently than when the goal is to throw for speed or force. The thrower "freezes" body parts such as the feet and trunk and brings arm segments closer to the midline of the longitudinal body axis (Halverson, 1966; Roberton, 1987). By thus constraining movement degrees of freedom to those which contribute mainly to producing a linear object propulsion, two things are accomplished. Extraneous, potential sources of error are minimized and the person solves the movement problem in an efficient and cost-effective manner. Such movement organization also is characteristic of the most rudimentary development status most often used by young and/or inexperienced throwers.

In the current study in the accuracy condition, throwers were required to use a moderate amount of force due to the thrower-to-target distance (10 m, or 33.9 ft, for adults and 6 m, or 20.3 ft, for children). They demonstrated an interesting combination of the two previous movement organizations. There was a step, but it was shorter than the one used under forceful conditions. The trunk action used only block rotation. The humerus laterally rotated and horizontal abducted, but these actions occurred earlier in the throwing motion than the 50 ms before ball release that characterized the high-velocity throw. For forceful throws, such movement patterns are usually classified as developmentally intermediate in status.

If the previous descriptions for movement patterns associated with task goals were ordered from most accurate to most forceful, the sequence of changes would mimic those of the robust developmental sequences for forceful throwing previously described as age related (Roberton, 1978; Roberton & Langendorfer, 1980; Halverson, et al., 1982). The parallel in descriptions may simply be coincidental. They also may give insight into the developmental process. Apparently developmentally primitive throwers constrain their movements in much the same way that more experienced throwers, such as the subjects in this study, constrain their movements to achieve accuracy. One observation is that a primitive or accurate throwing pattern requires dynamic coordination of fewer limb and joint actions. Such constraints on the degrees of freedom may aid the inexperienced thrower in coordinating the task in much the same way that they aid the more advanced thrower trying to be more accurate.

Hierarchic developmental organization

The previous explanation fails to address the developmental observation of sequence order. Acquisition of motor skills appears to be structured in a hierarchic fashion that overlays other dynamic coordination constraints. With the forceful overarm throw, this sequential organization manifests itself as an ordered series of movement states. From a Piagetian stage perspective, advanced throwers actually have developed this hierarchic repertoire of movement organizations in a step-by-step process. Previously mastered movement organizations can be selected that best meet certain demands or conditions.

Drawing from the previous section, constraining certain "degrees of freedom" (Newell, 1986) may be one dimension along which movement change is organized. Primitive movers organize a throw by reducing the number and types of degrees of freedom to a minimum to achieve the task. Throughout the developmental course of a skill, degrees of freedom are expanded until a maximal number are available and able to be coordinated. Since this process is hierarchic and cumulative, more advanced throwers "regress" and use more primitive "options" when the goal of the task permits more latitude. It is highly improbable that primitive throwers can coordinate the elaborate degrees of freedom and constraints characteristic of an advanced throw and therefore it is rare for them to attempt such options. When they do, they are probably unsuccessful and consequently do not attempt them again. This speculation is one way that dynamical constraints can be integrated with a stage perspective.

Developmental status of the throwers

As hypothesized above, the most advanced developmental status that a person has achieved interacts with the adaptations which they can make. For example, Roberton (1987) noted that her preschool subjects failed to adapt their movement organization to accommodate changing environmental conditions. Langendorfer (1987b), also noted that his children did not accommodate the striking pattern with movement changes of the ball. Roberton (1987) suggested that the primitive or novice movers appear to lack the "options" to accommodate the throwing pattern to changing constraints.

In the current study, the failure of females to adapt their throwing patterns as the males did may have resulted from a similar constraint due at least in part to the study's methodology. Recall that all subjects, regardless of gender or developmental status, were required to throw the same distance. For a subject whose throwing skill was less well developed, the 10-m distance for adults and 6 m for children may have represented a difficult task that required near maximal force demands. In effect, the subject-to-target distance, especially the 10-m distance for the adults, constrained the females to throw forcefully just to reach the target even under conditions of accuracy. This view was supported by Davis & Langendorfer (1985) when they observed that the female subjects improved a much smaller percentage from accuracy to force than did the adults. Since females as a group use more primitive motor patterns and throw at slower velocities, they, like younger children, did not have the same "options" to accommodate to changing environmental constraints.

The thrower-to-target distance phenomenon may provide an interesting experimental protocol for exploring how task constraints interact with developmental status, strength, and perhaps gender. By extending thrower-to-target distances in a systematic manner until maximum velocity is achieved, one may discover how force production constrains the development of throwing and other motor skills without verbally changing the goal of the task. Interactions between strength, developmental level, and gender could clarify some of the dynamics for producing forceful movements.

Relative contribution of movement components

The relative contribution of joints and limb segments appears to be specific to the task goal requirements. For example, the backswing action, which is essentially preparatory to the projectile act, did not demonstrate significant changes between conditions for either the children or adults, males or females. On the other hand, for the male subjects, movement components such as stepping, trunk, humerus, and forearm actions involved in the projectile phase of throwing did demonstrate changes when more forceful conditions were required.

Under conditions of accuracy requiring substantial force production (i.e., throwing distances of 10 and 6 m, respectively, as in these experiments), the contribution of some movement components (e.g., trunk action, stepping) appear to become more important than others. Stepping action, for instance, significantly changed for adult males and for all the children. Apparently, however, the accurate throwing goal was achievable with less tightly constrained actions by some movement components than was forceful throwing. While some subjects used the same movement patterns under both conditions, some subjects reduced the length of the step and type of trunk action while attempting to throw accurately. Anecdotally, many subjects were observed to reduce the overall range of trunk rotation in order to maintain visual contact with the target during accurate throw trials. They turned farther away when not trying to throw accurately. On the other hand, arm components showed less probability of changing across conditions, even for the males.

The results of children's trials demonstrated that throwers used similar movement patterns to achieve combined forceful *and* accurate throwing as they do with simply forceful throws. Davis and Langendorfer (1985) had reported similar findings with velocity data. There were significant differences between accuracy throwing and both force and force plus accuracy conditions, but not between force and force-accuracy conditions. The implications for a speed-accuracy trade-off in throwing seem to indicate that accuracy is subservient to speed. It could be argued that teachers could require throwers to practice under conditions requiring primarily speed or force first and then add accuracy requirements without sacrificing speed or accuracy.

Conclusion

The present study indicates that motor patterns are not absolutely robust to all environmental conditions, but that some movers can accommodate their movements to shifting environmental constraints. Because differences between goal conditions and genders and among movement components were apparent, there is need for further investigation into the interaction among environmental factors. Newell's (1986) recent triadic model for examining the constraints on action, while not wholly satisfactory, serves to augment stage theory observations in explaining changing motor skills. Together dynamical constraints and a developmental perspective can provide an interesting means for identifying and testing the effects of different variables on the development of motor skills.

REFERENCES

Davis, W. E. (1984). Precise visual feedback information and throwing accuracy in adults. *Perceptual and Motor Skills, 59,* 759–768.

Davis, W. E., & Langendorfer, S. (1985). Speed/accuracy tradeoff in the overhand throw of mentally handicapped and nonhandicapped subjects [Abstract]. *Psychology of Motor Behavior and Sport—1982. Proceedings of the Annual Conference of the North American Society for the Psychology of Sport and Physical Activity* (p. 98). Gulf Park, MS.

Eckert, H. (1987). *Motor development* (3rd ed.). Columbus, OH: C. E. Merrill.

Halverson, L. E. (1966). Development of motor patterns in young children. *Quest, 6,* 44–53.

Halverson, L. E., Roberton, M. A., & Langendorfer, S. (1982). Development of the overarm throw: Movement and ball velocity changes by seventh grade. *Research Quarterly for Exercise and Sport, 53,* 198–205.

Halverson, L. E., & Williams, K. (1985). Developmental sequences for hopping over distance: A prelongitudinal screening. *Research Quarterly for Exercise and Sport, 56,* 37–44.

Langendorfer, S. (1985). *Relationships among body size and motor development measures in the overarm throw for force.* Paper presented to the IVth International Congress on Auxology, Montreal, Canada.

Langendorfer, S. (1987a). Anthropometric correlates of motor development status. *Abstracts of Psychology of Motor Behaviour and Sport—1987,* 37.

Langendorfer, S. (1987b). Prelongitudinal screening of overarm striking development performed under two environmental conditions. In J. E. Clark & J. H. Humphrey (Eds), *Advances in motor development research: Volume 1* (pp. 17–47). New York: AMS Press.

Newell, K. M. (1986). Constraints on the development of coordination. In M. G. Wade & H. T. A. Whiting (Eds.), *Motor development in children: Aspects of coordination and control* (pp. 341–361). Amsterdam: Martinus Nijhoff Publishers.

Roberton, M. A. (1977). Stability of stage categorizations across trials: Implications for the "stage theory" of overarm throw development. *Journal of Human Movement Studies, 3,* 49–59.

Roberton, M. A. (1978). Longitudinal evidence for developmental stages in the forceful overarm throw. *Journal of Human Movement Studies, 4,* 167–175.

Roberton, M. A. (1982). Describing "stages" within and across motor tasks. In J. A. S. Kelso & J. E. Clark (Eds.), *The development of movement control and coordination* (pp. 293–307). New York: Wiley.

Roberton, M. A. (1984). Changing motor patterns in childhood. In J. R. Thomas (Ed.), *Motor development in childhood and adolescence* (pp. 48–90). Minneapolis: Burgess.

Roberton, M. A. (1987). Developmental level as a function of the immediate environment. In J. E. Clark & J. H. Humphrey (Eds.), *Advances in motor development research, Volume I* (pp. 1–15). New York: AMS Press.

Roberton, M. A., & Halverson, L. E. (1984). *Developing children—Their changing movement.* Philadelphia: Lea & Febiger.

Roberton, M. A., Halverson, L. E., Langendorfer, S., & Williams, K. (1979). Longitudinal changes in children's overarm throw ball velocities. *Research Quarterly, 50,* 256–264.

Roberton, M. A. & Langendorfer, S. (1980). Testing motor development sequences across 9–14 years. In C. Nadeau, W. Halliwell, K. Newell, & G. Roberts (Eds.), *Psychology of motor behavior and sport—1979* (pp. 269–279). Champaign, IL: Human Kinetics.

Williams, K. (1980). Developmental characteristics of a forward roll. *Research Quarterly for Exercise and Sport, 51,* 703–713.

AUTHOR NOTE:

This study was supported in part by a Summer Research Appointment from the Research Council of Kent State University. The data for this study were collected as a part of a larger study conducted by the author, Drs. Walter Davis, Robert Stadulis, Mary McCracken, and graduate students from the Motor Behavior Laboratory/Motor Development Center. The assistance of Ms. Sandy Cushing Woods and Ms. Diana Harrod in data reduction especially is acknowledged.

3

MOVEMENT CHARACTERISTICS OF
OLDER ADULT THROWERS

Kathleen Williams
Kathleen Haywood
Ann VanSant

ABSTRACT

Although a great deal is known about the course of change in fundamental movement patterns in children and young adults, almost nothing is known about movement patterns of older adults performing these skills. Most studies of older performers have emphasized functional and exercise-related tasks. The purpose of this investigation was to describe the characteristics of older adults, as they performed an overarm throw for force. This movement pattern was selected because it has an extensive validation history, and because older adults might continue to use overhand patterns. For example, they may play tennis, volleyball, and field sports. Twenty-one adults (16 females and 5 males) between 67 and 77 years of age were videotaped as they made five throws. In addition, each subject completed a questionnaire requesting information about previous experience with overarm throwing and other, related movement skills. In general, all the throwers used moderately advanced movement patterns. Those subjects reporting more experience used more advanced patterns than subjects with less overarm movement pattern experience. Decreased range of motion at the shoulder and hip is discussed as a possible constraint to action.

A great deal is known about the course of change in fundamental motor skills like kicking, catching, jumping, and throwing. Motor developmentalists (c.f., Clark & Phillips, 1985; Langendorfer, 1980; Roberton & Halverson, 1984; Seefeldt, Reuschlein, & Vogel, 1972) hypothesized and validated developmental

29

sequences for many fundamental movement skills. These sequences were identified by observing children and young adult subjects almost exclusively. Very little is known about the movement patterns used to perform motor skills in older adults.

When the activities of older adults are studied, functional aspects of performance typically are emphasized. Concern focuses upon assumed declines in speed and range of movement and the slowing of information processing. The training effects of exercise programs are examined widely, sometimes with the goal of forestalling such declines. Consequently, the relationship between physical fitness levels and psychomotor speed has received attention. Investigations involving subjects over 60 years of age have identified improvements in physical capacity following 10–12 week training programs (see Welford, 1982 for a review). In other studies, fitness levels and psychomotor speed have been highly correlated *and* predictive of longevity (Spirduso, 1980). Researchers have hypothesized that physical activity increases cerebral blood flow, possibly maintaining or improving information processing capabilities.

Another aspect of function, balance ability, has received attention. The assumption is that, with aging, there are changes in postural and balance mechanisms, leading to greater instability (Isaacs, 1982). Neurological changes, related to balance, were documented by Woollacott and her colleagues (Woollacott, Shumway-Cook, & Nashner, 1982, 1986). They found that older subjects (61–78 years) swayed more than younger subjects (19–38 years). Additionally, older subjects were more variable in contraction amplitudes of postural muscle groups. Onset latencies also were longer for distal postural muscles. These types of changes could result in increased instability, or a lessened ability to maintain balance.

Movement patterns of older adults have been studied less often. Walking is of primary interest (Gabell & Nayak, 1984; Murray, Kory, & Clarkson, 1969), because knowledge of how older individuals retain their ability to move around has obvious functional significance. Today, adults remain active for more of the life-span, so examining their ability to perform other fundamental motor tasks takes on added significance. No longer are older adults satisfied merely to "get around." With increased longevity, individuals remain active in a variety of sport-related activities, like bowling, tennis, racquetball, and track and field (Cunningham, Montoye, Metzner, & Keller, 1968; Stones & Kozma, 1981). They attempt maximal performances in age-group competitions like Senior Olympics (Stones & Kozma, 1981). It is, therefore, of interest to examine how older adults perform sport-related movement patterns.

The overarm throw for force was investigated because overhand movement patterns are found in many of the skills older adults perform throughout their lives (in tennis, volleyball, field sports, etc.). In addition, the developmental sequence of the overarm throw has an extensive validation history (c.f., Roberton, 1977, 1978; Robertson & Langendorfer, 1980).

Roberton (1977) hypothesized developmental sequences for the overarm throw, dividing the body into segmental movement components (Table 1). A movement component is a body segment (or segments) that changes at a rate different from other body segments (Roberton & Halverson, 1984). Sequences for each component comprising the overarm throw were validated longitudinally and cross-sectionally using a variety of normal (Halverson, Roberton, & Langendorfer, 1982; Roberton, 1977, 1978; Roberton, Halverson, Langendorfer, & Williams, 1979) and handicapped (Roberton & DiRocco, 1981) populations. With minor modifications, Roberton found that movement components for trunk, humerus, and forearm consistently met intransitivity and universality stage criteria proposed earlier (Roberton, 1978). That is, nearly all the individuals studied appeared to go through the sequences in the hypothesized order. Additionally, subjects in each of these investigations could be described by the existing categories. No new or different actions occurred, demonstrating that Roberton's categories were comprehensive (Roberton, 1978; Roberton & DiRocco, 1981). The leg action component adhered to stage criteria less consistently. A sequence for the arm action of the preparatory backswing was hypothesized and received preliminary validation (Langendorfer, 1980; Roberton & Halverson, 1984).

Because older individuals have not been studied as they perform the overarm throw, it is unknown whether existing action categories for any or all of the developmental movement components adequately describe their movements. For example, older adults may have a smaller dynamic range of motion, particularly at the shoulder (Murray, Gore, Gardner, & Mollinger, 1985) and hip (Murray, Drought, & Kory, 1964; Murray, Kory, Clarkson, & Sepic, 1966). A smaller range of motion used by older subjects could result in movement patterns not seen in younger throwers. Alternatively, it might result in the use of developmentally less advanced patterns.

Aside from purely describing movement patterns used by older performers is the issue of explaining *why* a particular level of behavior is exhibited. Over the years, maturation of the nervous system has been viewed as a primary cause of developmental change. For example, McGraw (1945/1969) hypothesized that maturation of higher cortical centers was responsible for the emergence of progressively more advanced movement patterns in infants. Although possible, traditional notions of nervous system maturation seem an unlikely cause for the varied actions observed in older adults.

Recently, developmentalists have applied principles of dynamical systems theory (c.f., Clark, Whitall, & Phillips, 1988; Thelen, Kelso, & Fogel, 1987) as an alternative to maturationist explanations for changes in movement patterns. In particular, they examine the influence of internal and external constraints on action, like strength, balance or muscular stiffness (Schöner & Kelso, 1988; Thelen, 1988). For example, Roberton and her colleagues (Getchell & Roberton, 1989; Roberton & Halverson, 1988) examined how sequential changes in the hop

Table 1
Developmental Sequences for Movement Components of the Overarm Throw for Force

---

TRUNK ACTION COMPONENT

Level 1. No trunk action action or forward-backward action. Only the arm is active in force production. Forward thrust of the arm may pull the trunk into passive rotation, but no "twist-up" precedes the action. Trunk action, if any, is hip flexion. Preparatory extension may precede hip flexion.

Level 2. Upper trunk rotation or trunk "block" rotation. Spine and pelvis rotate away from the intended line of flight and then simultaneously begin forward rotation, as a unit. Upper spine may twist away, then toward the direction of force. The pelvis remains fixed, facing the line of flight, or may rotate as forward rotation begins.

Level 3. Differentiated Rotation. Pelvis precedes the upper spine in initiating forward rotation. Movement is away from the line of flight; forward rotation begins with pelvis, while upper spine is rotating away.

HUMERUS ACTION COMPONENT

Level 1. Humerus Oblique. Humerus moves forward to ball release in a plane that intersects the trunk obliquely above or below the line of the shoulders.

Level 2. Humerus aligned but independent. Humerus moves forward to ball release in a plane horizontally aligned with the shoulder, forming a right angle between humerus and trunk. When the shoulders reach front facing, the humerus has moved independently ahead of the outline of the body via horizontal adduction of the shoulder.

Level 3. Humerus Lags. Humerus moves forward to ball release horizontally aligned, but at the moment the shoulders reach front facing, the humerus remains within the outline of the body.

FOREARM ACTION COMPONENT

Level 1. No forearm lag. Forearm and ball move steadily forward to ball release throughout the throwing action.

Level 2. Forearm lag. Forearm and ball appear to "lag"—remain stationary behind the head, or to move downward and behind. The deepest point of "lag" is *before* the shoulders reach front facing.

Level 3. Delayed lag. The lagging forearm delays reaching its final point of lag until the moment of front facing.

FOOT ACTION COMPONENT

Level 1. No foot action. Feet do not move throughout the throwing action.

Level 2. Ipsilateral foot action. A step is taken with the ipsilateral (same side as throwing hand) foot.

Level 3. Contralateral foot action, short step. A step is taken with the contralateral (opposite side from throwing hand) foot. Step length is less than half the thrower's standing height.

Level 4. Contralateral foot action, long step. A step is taken with the contralateral foot. Step length is half the thrower's standing height or longer.

PREPARATORY BACKSWING ACTION COMPONENT

Level 1. No backswing. Ball in the hand moves directly forward to release from the arm's original position.

Level 2. Elbow and humeral flexion. Ball moves away from the intended line of flight to a position behind or alongside the head by upward flexion of the humerus and elbow.

Level 3. Circular, upward backswing. Ball moves away from the intended line of flight to a position behind the head via a circular overhead movement with elbow extended, or an oblique swing back, or vertical lift from the hip.

Level 4. Circular, downward backswing. Ball moves away from the intended line of flight to a position behind the head via a circular, down and back motion, carrying the hand below the waist.

Note. Modified from Robertson & Halverson (1984).

---

might emerge as a result of changing body constraints. Roberton & Halverson (1988) discovered that stiffness of knee musculature was less in individuals characterized by more advanced developmental levels in the hop. In a follow-up study, Getchell & Roberton (1989) identified changes in stiffness, which they hypothesized cause performers to use developmentally more advanced patterns. They suggested that developmentally immature hoppers may set stiffness levels too high, resulting in hard landings. As the performer is able to produce more force, there is the risk of injury. To prevent this, the authors hypothesized that lower stiffness levels are achieved by reorganizing the movement to the more advanced pattern.

Actions performed by older performers may be similarly constrained, whether they are walking, swinging a racket, or throwing a ball. In older adults, it is possible that limitations in range of motion (Murray et al., 1985), the ability to balance (Woollacott et al., 1982, 1986) or some other unidentified factor provide critical constraints on patterns used to throw a ball forcefully.

Like descriptions of movement sequences, our knowledge of factors that might constrain movement comes almost exclusively from investigations of infants, children, and young adults. Only recently have theorists (c.f., Schroots, 1988; Yates, 1988) begun to examine the other end of the lifespan from a dynamical perspective. Because we know so little about the performance of fundamental motor skills in older adults, this study will provide an initial description of the characteristics of older throwers, using Roberton's (Roberton & Halverson, 1984) and Langendorfer's (1980) developmental sequence categories (Table 1). This preliminary information can provide a basis for future systematic exploration of constraints that may result in the expression of particular movement patterns.

METHODS

Subjects

Participants in this study were 21 adults, between 67 and 77 years of age, from St. Louis, Missouri. Sixteen women and 5 men took part. Each subject signed an informed consent form before testing.

The average age of the women was 71.3 years (SD = 2.9 years). The average age of the men was 71.6 years (SD = 3.1 years). Subjects were participants in the Active Adult Program at the University of Missouri-St. Louis. Many more women than men are enrolled in the program, contributing to the unequal number of male and female volunteers. This predominance of female participants may be related to gender-specific differences in life-expectancy. Females tend to live approximately 75 years, while males live just over 67 years (Shephard, 1978).

Movement Task and Instrumentation

Subjects were videotaped from approximately 30 ft (9.15 m), using a Panasonic ProCam video camcorder (Model 1954). The camcorder was equipped with a high-speed, 1/1000 s shutter, and recorded movement at approximately 30 fields per s. Sagittal views of each subject's throws were recorded.

After arriving at the test site, volunteers completed a consent form and a preliminary questionnaire about their general activity level. Joint markers were placed at the ankle, knee, hip, wrist, elbow, and shoulder joints. Subjects then were taken to a large outdoor field where five overarm throws were videotaped.

Throwers remained behind pylons to throw so release would occur directly in front of the camera. There was adequate space to walk or run up to the markers, however. Subjects made forceful overarm throws that did not risk injury. They threw a tennis ball as far and hard as they could.

After videotaping, volunteers receive a questionnaire requesting additional information. They were asked about previous experiences with overarm, object projection skills, like tennis and (overarm) volleyball serves, badminton strokes, and field throwing events. All 21 subjects returned their questionnaires.

Data Reduction

The first two authors reduced the data, using the developmental categories hypothesized and validated (Table 1) by Roberton (Roberton & Halverson, 1984) and Langendorfer (1980). Trials were viewed on a NEC DX-1000U VHS deck. Use of this videodeck enabled the investigators to slow the speed of the videotape, as well as to view the movement field by field.

Before reducing the data, an objectivity criterion of 85% exact agreement was established. Both intra- and inter-rater objectivity were examined. One trial from each subject was selected for this phase (a total of 21 trials). Both authors categorized these trials independently; the first author re-viewed the same trials one week later. There was exact agreement at or above the 85% criterion for all movement components. For intra-rater agreement, objectivity levels were 95% for the trunk and foot action, 90% for forearm and backswing components, and 86% for the humerus. Inter-rater exact agreement was similar across the components: 100% for the trunk action, 95% for the humerus, 90% for the forearm and feet, and 86% for the backswing. Because high levels of agreement were reached, the remaining trials were reduced by the first author.

RESULTS

The primary focus of this investigation was to describe the characteristics of older adults performing an overarm throw for force. To begin to examine *why* these subjects threw in the way they did, the amount and nature of previous overhand movement pattern experience of the subjects was examined.

The amount of practice with overhand, object projection activities is hypothesized to influence subjects' level of skill in the throw (Halverson et al., 1982). The possibility that experience would help to differentiate between the older adults was examined by reviewing the information taken from questionnaires returned by each subject. These questionnaires were reviewed blindly. Participants were divided into two groups: one group of 11 (4 males and 7 females), with some background in sport and recreational activities involving overhand object projection patterns, and a second group of 10 (1 male and 9 females), with little experience. Although participants were placed into these two categories, the majority reported that their involvement came in their earlier years. Of the 21 subjects, 13 discontinued their participation in activities involving an overhand object projection pattern by age 40. There was a tendency for those in the limited background group to discontinue their participation in these activities earlier: 5 of 10 reported that their involvement came before age 20. All of those categorized in the more extensive background group reported involvement into their 20s.

Two participants indicated that they took part in Senior Olympic competitions, and three had been employed in sport- or recreation-related fields. Of these, both Senior Olympians and two with job experience were placed in the extensive background group (based on their participation backgrounds). The third indicated that the position involed swimming. This subject was categorized as having limited overhand object projection pattern experience.

In all, 98 trials were available for analysis. Seven trials (all from different subjects) were lost due to experimenter error. As suggested by Roberton, Williams, and Langendorfer (1980), frequency distributions of developmental levels within each movement component were generated from these trials. Each is discussed separately.

All the trials analyzed could be categorized using Roberton's sequences for the overarm throw for force (Roberton & Halverson, 1984). No new or different actions occurred among these older adults that would require formation of new movement categories.

Trunk Action Component

All the trials performed were categorized at the first and second steps within the three-step developmental sequence (Figure 1). Just over 2% of the trials (2

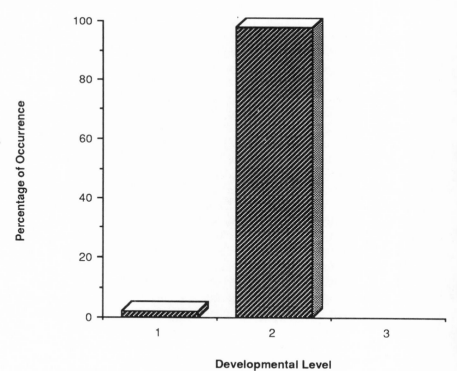

FIG. 1. Percentages of occurrence for each developmental level of the trunk action component. See Table 1 for description of levels within this component.

trials) were placed at step 1 (no action), while 97.9% of the trials (the remaining 96) were categorized at level 2 (block rotation).

The level of trunk-action categorizations did not differ when grouped by amount of experience using overarm movement patterns. In both groups (experience vs. limited experience), one trial (2%) was placed at level 1, while the remaining trials (49 and 47, respectively) were categorized at level 2 (98%).

Humerus

Most of the trials performed by the older adults were placed at the second level of the three-level humerus sequence. Seventy-five percent of the trials (74 total) were categorized at step 2, humerus aligned, but independent (Figure 2). Only 23.5% (23 trials) and 1.0% (1) of the trials were categorized at step 1 (humerus oblique) and step 3 (humeral lag), respectively.

There were clear differences in humerus categorizations, based on the level of experience recalled by the adults in this investigation. "Experienced" throwers

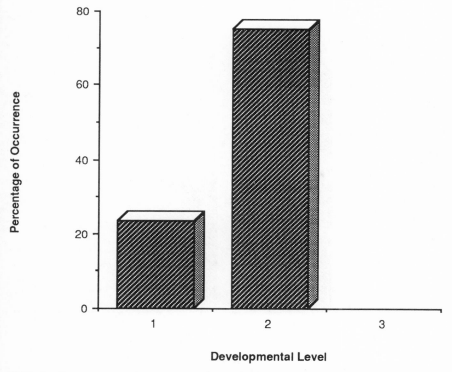

Developmental Level

FIG. 2. Percentages of occurrence for each developmental level of the humeral action component. See Table 1 for description of levels within this component.

were much more likely to use more advanced humeral actions than less experienced throwers. Virtually all of the experienced throwers' trials were placed at level 2 (98%—49 trials). The remaining 2% (1 trial) were categorized at level 3. On the other hand, 47.9% of the less experienced throwers' trials (23) were characterized as level 1 actions; the remaining 25 trials (52.1%) were categorized at level 2.

Forearm

Unlike the categorizations for the first two movement components, most forearm action trials (63) were placed at level 1, no lag (64.3%). The remaining 35 trials (35.7%) were categorized as level-2 actions, forearm lag (Figure 3). No trials for any subject were found to display delayed lag (level 3).

As with the humerus, the forearm action of less experienced throwers tended to be categorized at lower developmental levels than for experienced throwers. Trials for inexperienced throwers were very likely to be placed at level 1 (83.3%

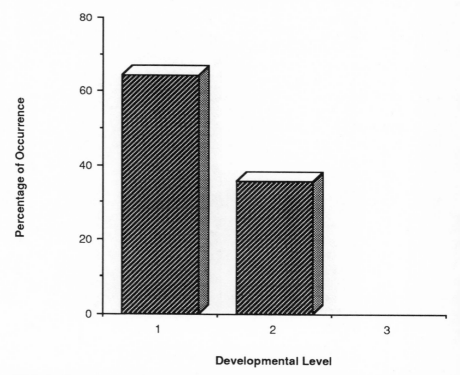

Developmental Level

FIG. 3. Percentages of occurrence for each developmental level of the forearm action component. See Table 1 for description of levels within this component.

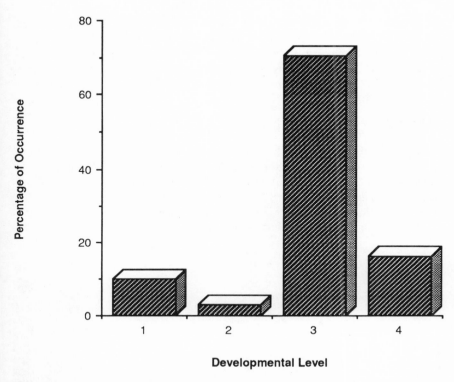

Developmental Level

FIG. 4. Percentages of occurrence for each developmental level of the foot action component. See Table 1 for description of levels within this component.

or 40 trials). The remaining trials were categorized as level 2 actions (16.7% or eight trials). In contrast, experienced throwers' trials were nearly equally divided between these same developmental levels (46%—23 trials—at level 1; 54%—27 trials—at level 2).

Feet

Trials were distributed across all four of the foot-action categories (Figure 4). Just over 10% (10 trials) of the trials were placed at level 1 (no step). Only 3.0% of the trials (3) had charcteristics of step 2 (ipsilateral step). Most performers used a contralateral step, most of the time: 70.4% of the trials (69 trials) were categorized at level 3 (short step), while 16.3% of the trials (16 total) were placed at level 4 (long step).

Categorizations of foot actions were similar for experienced and inexperienced groups—most trials were placed at level 3 (68% for the experienced group—34 trials; 68.8% for the inexperienced throwers—33 trials). For the experienced throwers, however, all remaining trials (32% or 16 trials) were categorized as level-4 actions. In contrast, for the less experienced throwers, 20.8% of the trials (10 trials) were characterized as level-1 actions, 4.2% (two trials) were categorized at level 2, and the remaining three trials (6.3%) were placed at level 4.

Backswing

No trials were described by level 1 characteristics of the preparatory backswing action. In contrast, 8.2% (8 trials) were categorized at level 2 (humerus and elbow flexion); 34.7% (34 total) were placed at the third level (circular, upward backswing), and 55.1% (54 trials) were charcterized by the most advanced movement actions, a circular, downward backswing (Figure 5).

More experienced throwers tended to demonstrate more advanced backswing

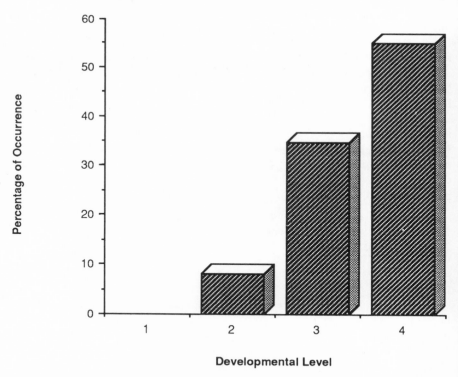

Developmental Level

FIG. 5. Percentages of occurrence for each developmental level of the preparatory backswing action component. See Table 1 for description of levels within this component.

patterns than less experienced throwers. Five trials (10.2%) were placed at level 2, nine trials (18.4%) were characterized by level-3 actions, while the remaining 35 trials (71.4%) were placed at level 4. Three of the inexperienced throwers' trials (6.4%) were categorized at level 2 of the backswing, 25 trials (53.2%) were placed at level 3, and the final 19 trials (40.4%) were described by level-4 actions.

DISCUSSION

There were two primary findings in this investigation of movement patterns used by older adult throwers. First, all the throwing actions observed could be categorized using Roberton's developmental categories for the overarm throw (Roberton & Halverson, 1984). No actions other than those previously described occurred among these subjects. This finding suggests that Roberton's categories are comprehensive descriptions of the actions of older performers. Second, the older adults generally demonstrated intermediate to moderately advanced performances. Most trials were placed at the middle developmental level for trunk and humeral actions. In addition, nearly all trials were categorized at the third and fourth developmental levels for backswing and foot action components. Only the forearm action was not at all advanced, with most trials classified as level-1 actions.

In general, movement patterns used by older adults in this study were characterized by a limited range of motion, particularly at the hip and shoulder. The step length exhibited by many of the throwers was characterized by limited hip and accompanying pelvic rotation. Most subjects were categorized as having a relatively advanced, contralateral step (level 3). This step was short and accompanied by a limited amount of trunk rotation.

The backswing patterns observed suggested that subjects might be limited in shoulder range of motion. Often a thrower started into a circular, downward swing in the directional plane of the throw. However, they cut the downward motion short, bringing the arm to the wind-up position in an oblique plane. This sort of action could result from limited lateral rotation of the humerus like that reported by Murray et al. (1985).

The forearm actions demonstrated by these throwers also suggested limitations in shoulder range of motion. Although called "forearm action," the movements described in this component result from the lateral rotation of the humerus (see Table 1). To be categorized as demonstrating a level 2 or 3 forearm action, a performer must exhibit increasing amounts of lateral humeral rotation. None of the trials performed by these older adults was placed at level 3 of the forearm action, and fewer than 40% were categorized as level 2 actions. Most of the trials (64.3%) fell into level 1, where little or no outward rotation occurs.

Tenets of dynamical systems theory can be used to hypothesize why these older throwers used certain movement patterns. In particular, the data reported in this investigation suggest that changing physical constraints may limit the type of action performed by these older throwers (Yates, 1988). One constraint, range of motion, appeared to affect results of this investigation. That is, functional ranges of motion at the shoulder and hip seemed to dictate which patterns these adults used to perform the throwing action. There is evidence (for a review, see Adrian, 1981) that changes in connective tissues, like increased collagen fiber stability, may result in increased rigidity and, consequently, decreased joint extensibility in older adults.

It is not possible to know from this investigation whether these adults once performed using developmentally more advanced patterns, only to "regress" to less advanced patterns characterized by decreased ranges of motion. The data hint, however, that more practice with the overarm throw may be related to higher levels of flexibility. That is, subjects in this study who had more experience with the overarm throw tended to demonstrate more advanced patterns, requiring greater flexibility. Because all of the subjects had their throwing experience at much younger ages, it is impossible to say whether experienced throwers *attained* more advanced patterns than less experienced performers, or merely *retained* the pattern that they had for a longer period. Repeated testing across the life-span would be required to answer that question.

Of course, general level of current activity cannot be entirely dismissed as potentially contributing to the range of motion available to some subjects. It is possible that activities in which "more experienced" subjects are involved somehow help to maintain levels of flexibility. This argument is weakened somewhat by a further examination of data gathered from these subjects. All of them were actively involved in a variety of exercise programs at the time of data collection. Nineteen of the participants said that they were in a program that included flexibility exercises for the arm, shoulder, and trunk. Fourteen indicated that they participated only once or twice a week. This finding suggests that the nature or amount of flexibility exercise performed was insufficient to maintain the range of motion needed to perform a forceful overarm throw.

In summary, the older throwers observed in this study generally exhibited moderately advanced developmental levels in their throwing performances. Those levels seen infrequently, or not at all, are associated with maximal force production in younger subjects. There is some suggestion that the limitation on performance is associated with limited flexibility, since many throwers reported an extensive background with overarm throw patterns, but at young ages (under 40 years). Future investigations need to focus on the measurement of control parameters like range of motion or balance.

REFERENCES

Adrian, M. L. (1981). Flexibility in the aging adult. In E. L. Smith & R. C. Serfass (Eds.), *Exercise and aging* (pp. 45–58). Hillside, NJ: Enslow Publisher.

Clark, J. E., & Phillips, S. J. (1985). A developmental sequence of the standing long jump. In J. E. Clark & J. H. Humphrey (Eds.), *Motor development: Current selected research: Vol. 1* (pp. 73–86). Princeton, NJ: Princeton Book Co.

Clark, J. E., Whitall, J., & Phillips, S. J. (1988). Human interlimb coordination: The first six months of independent walking. *Developmental Psychobiology, 21,* 445–456.

Cunningham, D. A., Montoye, H. J., Metzner, H. L., & Keller, J. B. (1968). Active leisure time activities as related to age among males in a total population. *Journal of Gerontology, 23,* 551–556.

Gabell, A., & Nayak, U. S. L. (1984). The effect of age on variability in gait. *Journal of Gerontology, 39,* 662–666.

Getchell, N., & Roberton, M. A. (1989). Whole body stiffness as a function of developmental level in children's hopping. *Developmental Psychology, 25,* 1020–1028.

Halverson, L. E., Roberton M. A. & Langendorfer, S. (1982). Development of the overarm throw: Movement and ball velocity changes by seventh grade. *Research Quarterly for Exercise and Sport, 53,* 198–205.

Isaacs, B. (1982). Disorders of balance in old age. In F. Laird (Ed.), *Neurological disorders of the elderly* (pp. 135–145). Bristol, England: J. Wright and Sons.

Langendorfer, S. J. (1980). *Longitudinal evidence for developmental changes in the preparatory phase of the overarm throw for force.* Paper presented at the Annual Convention, American Alliance for Health, Physical Education, Recreation, and Dance. Detroit, MI.

McGraw, M. (1969). *The neuromuscular maturation of the human infant.* New York: Hafner. (Original work published 1945).

Murray, M. P., Drought, A. B., & Kory, R. C. (1964). Walking patterns of normal men. *Journal of Bone and Joint Surgery, 46-A,* 335–360.

Murray, M. P., Gore, D. R., Gardner, B. S., & Mollinger, L. A. (1985). Shoulder motion and muscle strength of normal men and women in two age groups. *Clinical Orthopaedics and Related Research, 192,* 268–273.

Murray, M. P., Kory, R. C., & Clarkson, B. H. (1969). Walking patterns of healthy old men. *Journal of Gerontology, 24,* 169–178.

Murray, M. P., Kory, R. C., & Clarkson, B. H., & Sepic, S. B. (1966). Comparison of free and fast speed walking patterns of normal men. *American Journal of Physical Medicine, 45,* 8–24.

Roberton, M. A. (1977). Stability of stage categorizations across trials: Implications for "stage theory" of overarm throw development. *Journal of Human Movement Studies, 3,* 49–59.

Roberton, M. A. (1978). Longitudinal evidence for developmental stages in the forceful overarm throw. *Journal of Human Movement Studies, 4,* 161–175.

Roberton, M. A., & DiRocco, P. (1981). Validating a motor skill sequence for mentally retarded children. *American Corrective Therapy Journal, 35,* 148–154.

Roberton, M. A., & Halverson, L. E. (1984). *Developing children—Their changing movement.* Philadelphia: Lea & Febiger.

Roberton, M. A. & Halverson, L. E. (1988). The development of locomotor coordination: Longitudinal change and invariance. *Journal of Motor Behavior, 20,* 197–241.

Roberton, M. A., Halverson, L. E., Langendorfer, S., & Williams, K. (1979). Longitudinal changes in children's overarm throw ball velocities. *Research Quarterly, 50,* 256–264.

Roberton, M. A., & Langendorfer, S. (1980). Testing motor development sequences across 9–14 years. In C. Nadeau, W. Halliwell, K. Newell, & G. Roberts (Eds.), *Psychology of motor behavior and sport—1979* (pp. 269–279). Champaign, IL: Human Kinetics.

Roberton, M. A., Williams, K., & Langendorfer, S. (1980). Prelongitudinal screening of motor development sequences. *Research Quarterly for Exercise and Sport, 51,* 724–731.

Schöner, G., & Kelso, J. A. S. (1988). Dynamic pattern generation in behavioral and neural systems. *Science, 239,* 1513–1520.

Schroots, J. J. F. (1988). On growing, formative change, and aging. In J. E. Birren & V. L. Bengtson (Eds.), *Emergent theories of aging* (pp. 299–332). New York: Springer Publishing Co.

Seefeldt, V., Reuschlein, S., & Vogel, P. (1972). *Sequencing motor skills within the physical education curriculum.* Paper presented at the Annual Convention of the American Association for Health, Physical Education, Recreation, and Dance. Houston, TX.

Shephard, R. J. (1978). *Physical activity and aging.* Chicago: Year Book Medical Publishers, Inc.

Spirduso, W. W. (1980). Reaction and movement time as a function of age and physical activity level. *Journal of Gerontology, 30,* 435–440.

Spirduso, W. W. (1982). Physical fitness in relation to motor aging. In J. A. Mortimer, F. J. Pirozzolo, & G. J. Maletta (Eds.), *The aging motor system* (pp. 121–151). New York: Praeger.

Stones, M. J., & Kozma, A. (1981). Adults age trends in athletic performances. *Experimental Aging Research, 7,* 269–280.

Thelen, E. (1988). Dynamical approaches to the development of behavior. In J. A. S. Kelso, A. J. Mandell, & M. F. Shlesinger (Eds.), *Dynamic patterns in complex systems* (pp. 348–369). Singapore: World Scientific Publishers.

Thelen, E., Kelso, J. A. S., & Fogel, A. (1987). Self-organizing systems in infant motor development. *Developmental Review, 7,* 39–65.

Welford, A. T. (1982). Motor skills and aging. In J. A. Mortimer, F. J. Pirozzolo, & G. J. Maletta (Eds.), *The aging motor system* (pp. 152–187). New York: Praeger.

Woollacott, M. H., Shumway-Cook, A., & Nashner, L. (1982). Postural reflexes and aging. In J. A. Mortimer, F. J. Pirozzolo, & G. J. Maletta (Eds.), *The aging motor system* (pp. 98–119). New York: Praeger.

Woollacott, M. H., Shumway-Cook, A., & Nashner, L. (1986). Aging and posture control: Changes in sensory organization and muscular coordination. *International Journal of Aging and Human Development, 23,* 97–114.

Yates, F. E. (1988). The dynamics of aging and time: How physical action implies social action. In J. E. Birren & V. L. Bengtson (Eds.), *Emergent theories of aging* (pp. 90–117). New York: Springer Publishing Co.

AUTHOR NOTE:

The help of Joy Kiger in testing subjects is gratefully acknowledged. The authors also wish to thank Jane Clark and an anonymous reviewer for their thoughtful comments in the review of this manuscript. Portions of this investigation were presented at the Motor Development Research Consortium, Champaign, IL, October 1988.

4

PSYCHOMOTOR AND BEHAVIORAL CHARACTERISTICS OF YOUNG BLACK AND WHITE CHILDREN

Gabie E. Church
Geoffrey D. Broadhead

ABSTRACT

DIAL, Developmental Indicators for the Assessment of Learning (Mardell & Goldenberg, 1975), which measures gross motor, fine motor, concept, and communication skills of 3- to 5-year-olds, is a popular evaluation test used to measure preschool development. This study examined the separate contributions of the 4 DIAL components among 3-, 4-, and 5-year-old black and white boys and girls (N = 610). To establish discriminatory power, 9 separate stepwise multivariate discriminant analyses of the vector of 28 variables were completed for the whole sample and for subsamples identified by all breakdowns of gender and race. In each analysis both discriminant functions were statistically significant ($p < .02$). With one exception, more than half of the items included in the analyses were psychomotor. The tendency was for both gross and fine motor tasks to be overrepresented, for concept skills to be appropriately represented, and for communication skills to be underrepresented. These results occurred regardless of gender and race. Thus, in the overall evaluation of the development of preschool children, psychomotor tasks appear to be at least as important as behavioral characteristics.

Although there are a number of reasons why more and more children are enrolled in some type of formal education during their preschool years, one of the most significant is that the years that precede elementary school influence each child's resultant behavior and performance greatly (Allen & Goetz, 1982; Barnes, 1982; Spodek, 1982; Travers & Light, 1982). It is not surprising, therefore, that the literature on the topic of preschool education is voluminous; much of it describes, evaluates, and/or develops the ideas and practices of Head Start programs and related events of the early 1960s (eg., Chazan, 1973; Stanley, 1972; Westinghouse Learning Corporation & Ohio University, 1979; Zigler & Valentine, 1979). Educators, administrators, parents, politicians and others have confidence in and high expectations for preschool education. However, the results of many studies have been subject to widely differing interpretations, and in general do not support such high expectations (Payne, Mercer, Payne, & Davison, 1973; Spodek, 1982; Stanley, 1972; Travers & Light, 1982).

Typically, Head Start began as a summer program, but later developed into full year and multiyear programs, even extending into the elementary grades (see Weikart, Bond, & McNeil, 1978). The curriculum of preschool programs for the most part has stressed socialization, language development, and cognitive enrichment with the specific emphasis being determined by individual needs (Bloom, Davis, & Hess, 1965; Lorton & Walley, 1979; Spodek, 1982; Weikart, 1982; Weikart et al., 1978). However, the relative importance of different instructional approaches and content areas in preschool programs still has to be determined (Payne et al., 1973; Travers & Light, 1982). Answers may be provided by a better understanding of those factors important to behavior during the preschool years.

Preschool strives to help each child become ready for the requirements of more formal elementary schooling. Yet preschool programs usually omit specific instruction in the types of fundamental motor patterns and skills of early childhood. The development of voluntary movement, of manipulative skills, and of the perceptual-motor system, as well as an emphasis upon awareness of body parts, laterality, and directionality in space, are all important elements of a preschool physical education program.

The importance of movement in the preschool years is emphasized by some of those who have constructed tests and test batteries (Bayley, 1969; Bluma, Shearer, Frohman, & Hilliard, 1976a, 1976b; Frankenburg & Dodds, 1967; LeMay, Griffin, & Sanford, 1977; Mardell & Goldenberg, 1975; Sanford, 1970). But the question to be asked is "How important is movement, compared with other aspects of behavior?"

Thus the purpose of this study was to examine the relative contributions of psychomotor and nonmovement behaviors in young children. The DIAL test, Developmental Indicators for the Asssessment of Learning (Mardell & Goldenberg, 1975), was used because it evaluates gross and fine psychomotor development, and concept and communication behaviors. Information gained extends that reported previously for white children (Broadhead & Church, 1988) by including black children.

METHODS

Sample

The subjects were 610 black and white boys and girls, ages 2 years 6 months to 5 years 5 months, resident in a large mostly metropolitan school district in south Louisiana. Approximately 21% of the sample was black, and 79% white (see Table 1). Test administrators recorded race by skin color—black or white. Participants were volunteered for a district-wide screening program as mandated by state regulations (Louisiana State Department of Education, 1978), organized to determine existence of educationally handicapping conditions. Less than 3% of the sample was eventually provided with special education services, and the sample is considered nonhandicapped.

Evaluation of Subjects

The 28 items of DIAL (see Table 2) were individually administered to every subject, following guidelines set forth in the test materials (Mardell & Goldenberg, 1975).

Like several other tests used to measure the behaviors of young children, the construction and development of DIAL used ideas and data from other researchers such as Bayley (1969) and Gesell (1940). DIAL is made up of 4 elements of 7 items each, and incorporates norms for boys and girls at 3-month intervals from 2 years 6 months to 5 years 5 months. At every stage and for every element of the battery, girls are expected to perform at a higher level than boys of the same age peer group. Although those performance characteristics were confirmed by

Table 1
Descriptive Statistics for Chronological Age Groups by Race and Gender

CA (yrs)	Boys		Girls	
	Black	White	Black	White
3 *M* mos	35.53	34.81	35.71	34.86
SD	3.32	5.45	5.57	3.90
n	17	67	14	76
4 *M*	47.24	47.71	46.15	47.72
SD	4.13	3.38	3.27	3.71
n	21	97	26	55
5 *M*	60.36	59.85	60.82	60.38
SD	4.45	4.40	4.51	4.74
n	28	111	22	76

Table 2
Test Items for Evaluation of Psychomotor and Behavioral Development

Psychomotor		Behavioral	
Gross Motor	Fine Motor	Concept Skills	Communication Skills
Balancing	Building	Counting	Articulating
Catching	Clapping Hands	Following Directions	Classifying Foods
Hopping	Copying Letters	Identifying Concepts	Coping
Jumping	Copying Shapes	Identifying Body Parts	Naming Nouns/Verbs
Skipping	Cutting	Naming Colors	Naming Self/Age/Gender
Standing Still	Matching	Positioning	Remembering
Throwing	Touching Fingers	Sorting Blocks	Telling a Story

Docherty (1983), Broadhead and Church (1985) reported movement performance differences by gender, favoring girls, for yearly age groups but not for 3-month age groupings. In addition, while no performance differences by race were reported by Mardell and Goldenberg (1975), Broadhead and Church (1985) provided data indicating significant differences, some of which favored the movement performance of black subjects, and others of white subjects. While the DIAL test is believed to be widely used, reports of acceptable reliability and validity characteristics are limited to those of associates of the test authors (see Mardell & Goldenberg, 1975).

Analysis of Data

For the purposes of this study, data from the 12 3-month age groupings were collapsed into 3 separate-year groups, with subjects 4 years 6 months to 5 years 5 months being considered as 5-year-olds, etc. Discrimination among 3-, 4-, and 5-year olds was examined through separate discriminant analyses of the vector of 28 DIAL variables for the whole sample and for subsamples identified by all breakdowns of gender and race (male, female, white, black, white male, white female, black male, and black female children). These discriminant analyses, with stepwise selection of variables based on Mahalanobis distance criterion, were executed through the discriminant procedure of SPSS^x (SPSS, Inc., 1983). How well the functions discriminated among the three age groupings was assessed through appropriate estimates of the percent of correct classification of subjects based on the discriminant functions. For those analyses with more than 200 subjects, the split-sample holdout validation technique (Thorndike, 1978) was used with the correct classifications for the two independently classified samples averaged to obtain the estimate. The remaining analyses employed the jackknife estimation technique (Church & Broadhead, 1986; Dixon & Brown, 1979).

RESULTS

To determine the contribution of variables from the 4 components of DIAL, 9 separate stepwise discriminant analyses were performed on the whole sample (*N* = 610) and 8 subsamples of 341 male, 269 female, 482 white, 128 black, 275 white male, 207 white female, 66 black male, and 62 black female children. In each analysis two discriminant functions were obtained, both statistically significant ($p < 0.02$), with the first function accounting for between 74% and 93% of the explained variation. The measure of total discriminatory power, $\hat{\omega}^2$ (Tatsuoka, 1970), ranged from 0.69 to 0.92. Complete statistics for the functions are found in Table 3.

Table 3
Statistics for Nine Separate Analyses

Sample	Function	% Explained Variation	Canonical Correlation	X^2	DF	p	ω^2
All	1	92.72	.81	712.64	38	.00	.69
Subjects	2	7.28	.36	81.92	18	.00	
All	1	92.67	.81	397.33	38	.00	.70
Male Ss	2	7.33	.36	46.22	18	.00	
All	1	90.24	.84	368.75	30	.00	.76
Female Ss	2	9.76	.45	57.97	14	.00	
All	1	90.70	.82	611.42	44	.00	.73
White Ss	2	9.30	.42	89.32	21	.00	
All	1	89.29	.84	170.23	32	.00	.76
Black Ss	2	10.71	.47	28.94	15	.02	
White	1	90.85	.81	335.12	36	.00	.72
Male Ss	2	9.15	.41	47.80	17	.00	
White	1	88.94	.87	339.62	36	.00	.82
Female Ss	2	11.06	.53	63.75	17	.00	
Black	1	74.48	.90	142.37	34	.00	.92
Male Ss	2	25.52	.77	50.16	16	.00	
Black	1	80.76	.85	95.35	24	.00	.82
Female Ss	2	19.24	.62	26.15	11	.01	

Estimates of the percentage of correct classification for each analysis were obtained through validation techniques appropriate to the sample size, split-sample holdout or jackknife. As shown in Table 4, overall correct classification ranged from 63.6% for all male subjects to 75.8% for black male subjects; correct classifications that would be expected from chance alone were at most 42% for maximum chance criterion (C_{max}) and 35% for proportional chance criterion (C_{pro}) (Morrison, 1969). Therefore the proportional reduction in error from classification based on chance alone, tau (Klecka, 1980), was a minimum of 0.53. As would be expected, correct classification for 3- and 5-year-olds was superior to that for 4-year-olds in all analyses, with the exception black female subjects.

The composition of the functions for each analysis is outlined in Tables 5 and

Table 4

Percentage of Group Classifications, Maximum ($_{CMAX}$) and Proportional ($_{CPRO}$) Chance Criteria, and Reduction in Probable Error (Tau) for Nine Separate Discriminant Analyses

Sample	Actual Age Group	Predicted Age Group 3	4	5	Overall	C_{MAX}	C_{PRO}	Tau
All	3	71.3	27.6	1.2				
Subjects	4	16.7	51.8	31.6				
	5	2.1	16.9	81.0	68.7	39	34	.59
All	3	64.4	33.4	2.4				
Male Ss	4	15.3	48.3	36.5				
	5	1.5	22.3	76.3	63.6	41	35	.53
All	3	74.5	20.0	5.6				
Female Ss	4	21.1	41.9	37.1				
	5	2.1	12.3	85.7	68.8	36	34	.59
All	3	72.0	25.2	2.8				
White Ss	4	15.2	52.7	32.2				
	5	2.2	15.5	82.4	69.9	39	34	.60
All	3	58.1	41.9	0.0				
Black Ss	4	25.5	46.8	27.7				
	5	2.0	6.0	92.0	67.2	39	35	.57

Table 4
Continued

Sample	Actual Age Group	Predicted Age Group 3	4	5	Overall	C_{MAX}	C_{PRO}	Tau
White	3	<u>67.1</u>	31.5	1.5				
Male Ss	4	16.5	<u>48.5</u>	35.1				
	5	1.8	22.5	<u>75.7</u>	<u>64.0</u>	40	35	.54
White	3	<u>73.7</u>	23.7	2.6				
Female Ss	4	14.6	<u>52.6</u>	32.7				
	5	2.7	17.1	<u>80.3</u>	<u>70.6</u>	37	34	.62
Black	3	<u>70.6</u>	29.4	0.0				
Male Ss	4	14.3	<u>66.7</u>	19.0				
	5	3.6	10.7	<u>85.7</u>	<u>75.8</u>	42	35	.67
Black	3	<u>57.1</u>	35.7	7.1				
Female Ss	4	23.1	<u>61.5</u>	15.4				
	5	4.5	0.0	<u>95.6</u>	<u>72.6</u>	42	35	.63

6. All four components of DIAL, gross motor, fine motor, concept, and communication, were represented in each analysis with a consistent distribution in all but one case. With the exception of black girls, psychomotor tasks provided at least 53% of the variables (average 60%) selected in the functions for each analysis. The overrepresentation of these psychomotor tasks was offset by an underrepresentation of communication tasks (average 18%).

DISCUSSION

Of the nine analyses, the race by gender breakdowns (white male, white female, black male, black female subjects) were examined first. Based on norms reported by gender (Mardell & Goldenberg, 1975) and reports of differences by gender and race for movement items (Broadhead & Church, 1985), these samples were thought to be most homogeneous and thus would provide the most precise discrimination among the three age groups. Highest total discriminatory power and proportional reduction in error from classification based on chance

Table 5
Dial Items Included in Nine Separate Discriminant Analyses

Item	All Subjects	M	F	W	B	WM	WF	BM	BF	Freq.
Gross Motor										
Balance	X	X	X	X	X	X	X			7
Stand		X	X			X	X	X	X	6
Skip	X	X	X	X	X	X	X	X	X	9
Hop	X	X	X	X	X	X	X	X	X	9
Jump	X		X	X			X	X		5
Catch	X			X			X	X		4
Throw				X	X	X		X		4
Fine Motor										
Clap				X	X			X		3
Finger	X	X	X	X			X	X		6
Letter	X	X	X	X		X	X	X		7
Shapes	X	X		X	X	X		X	X	7
Cut	X	X	X	X	X	X	X	X		8
Build	X	X	X	X	X	X	X	X		8
Match	X	X		X	X	X	X	X	X	8
Concepts										
Body	X	X	X	X	X	X	X		X	8
Concepts	X	X	X	X	X	X			X	7
Directions				X	X		X		X	4
Position	X	X		X			X		X	5
Count				X	X				X	3
Colors		X					X	X		3
Blocks	X	X	X	X	X			X	X	7
Communications										
Story	X		X	X			X		X	5
Foods	X	X		X		X				4
Self		X			X			X	X	4
Coping		X			X	X	X			4
Nouns	X	X		X		X				4
Remember	X		X	X			X			4
Articulate			X				X	X		3
Number of Variables	19	19	15	22	16	18	18	17	12	

Table 6
Frequency and Percent of Items from Four Dial Components Included in Nine Separate Discriminant Analyses

	Gross Motor		Fine Motor		Concepts		Communications	
	f	%	f	%	f	%	f	%
All Subjects	5	26	6	32	4	21	4	21
All Male Ss	4	21	6	32	5	26	4	21
All Female Ss	5	33	4	27	3	20	3	20
All White Ss	6	27	6	27	6	27	4	18
All Black Ss	4	25	5	31	5	31	2	13
White Male Ss	5	28	6	33	4	22	3	17
White Female Ss	6	33	5	28	3	17	4	22
Black Male Ss	6	35	7	41	2	12	2	12
Black Female Ss	3	25	2	17	5	42	2	17

alone (Tables 3 and 4) for three of these four analyses provided further support for this decision.

Two issues are to be noted from these analyses. First, skills selected in the discriminant functions among these four subsamples appear to be related to the nature of the component, psychomotor or behavioral. Four skills, all psychomotor, were selected in all four analyses: standing still, skipping, hopping (gross motor) and matching (fine motor). Of the behavioral skills only one concept skill (identifying body parts) was selected in as many as three analyses, while no communication skills were selected for more than two of the four analyses (Table 5).

Second, the items selected in the discriminant functions for black male subjects coincide with trends reported previously for white male and white female subjects (Broadhead & Church, 1988). While each of the four components of DIAL was represented, psychomotor tasks contributed more than behavioral tasks. The underrepresentation of communication tasks was consistent across all analyses (see Table 6). Thus there was no support for an emphasis by Mardell and Goldenberg (1975) on communication skills (Broadhead & Church, 1988). The four subsamples were combined into larger but more heterogeneous categories by gender, by race, and the entire sample. As expected, lower but acceptable levels of discriminatory power and correct classifications were found for these combination samples. Skills selected for inclusion in the discriminant functions were comparable, however, and provide further evidence of the overrepresentation of psychomotor skills, the underrepresentation of communication skills, and the appropriate representation of concept skills in discriminating among 3-, 4-, and 5-year-olds.

The sole exception to the overrepresentation of psychomotor tasks noted in other samples occurred for the sample of black female subjects, for which underrepresentation was noted. Thus there appears to be a trend of overrepresentation of psychomotor skills for black males, and an underrepresentation for black females. Results such as these have not been reported elsewhere in the motor development literature and, therefore, are important. It is noted from Table 1 that the samples of black subjects were not as large as for white subjects. Therefore, possible implications for differential development and programming may only be in order if studies using larger samples confirm these results.

In summary, it is apparent that the separate elements that comprise both psychomotor and nonmovement behaviors of preschoolers are important. The emphasis in the literature and in practice, on the nonmovement behaviors of young children, is not questioned. However, the exclusion of psychomotor behaviors is not supported by the results of this study. There is definite need for a more balanced approach to both preschool test construction and preschool programming, with specific inclusion of activities stressing gross and fine motor skills.

REFERENCES

Allen, E. K., & Goetz, E. M. (1982). *Early childhood education*. Rockville, MD: Aspen Systems Corp.

Barnes, K. E. (1982). *Preschool screening: The measurement and prediction of children at-risk*. Springfield, IL: Charles C. Thomas.

Bayley, N. A. (1969). *Manual for Bayley Scales of Infant Development*. New York: Psychological Corporation.

Bloom, B. S., Davis, A., & Hess, R. (1965). *Compensatory education in cultural deprivation*. New York: Holt, Rinehart & Winston.

Bluma, S. M., Shearer, M. S., Frohman, A. H., & Hilliard, J. M. (1976a). *Portage Guide to Early Education: Manual*. Portage, WI: Cooperative Educational Service Agency 12.

Bluma, S. M., Shearer, M. S., Frohman, A. H., & Hilliard, J. M. (1976b). *Portage Guide to Early Education: Checklist*. Portage, WI: Cooperative Educational Service Agency 12.

Broadhead, G. D., & Church, G. E. (1985). Movement characteristics of preschoolers. *Research Quarterly for Exercise and Sport, 56*, 208–214.

Broadhead, G. D., & Church, G. E. (1988). Contributions of motor, concept, and communication skills to preschool learning. In J. E. Clark & J. H. Humphrey (Eds.), *Advances in motor development research: Vol. 2* (pp. 115–126). New York: AMS Press.

Chazan, M. (Ed.). (1973). *Compensatory educatiaon*. London: Butterworths.

Church, G. E., & Broadhead, G. D. (1986). Small sample validation of discriminant analysis of motor proficiency. *Perceptual and Motor Skills, 62*, 903–909.

Dixon, W. J., & Brown, M. B. (Eds.). (1979). *BMDP-79 Biomedical computer programs. P series*. Berkeley, CA: University of California Press.

Docherty, E. M. (1983). The DIAL: Preschool screening for learning problems. *The Journal of Special Education, 17,* 195–202.

Frankenburg, W. K., & Dodds, J. B. (1967). The Denver Developmental Screening Test. *Journal of Pediatrics, 71,* 181–191.

Gesell, A. (1940). *The first five years of life: A guide to the study of the preschool child.* New York: Harper.

Klecka, W. R. (1980). *Discriminant analysis.* Sage University Paper series Quantitative Applications in Social Sciences (series no. 07-019). Beverly Hills, CA: Sage Publications.

LeMay, D. W., Griffin, P. M., & Sanford, A. R. (1977). *Learning Accomplishment Profile examiner's manual (Diagnostic ed).* Winston-Salem, NC: Kaplan Press.

Lorton, J. W., & Walley, B. L. (1979). *Introduction to early childhood education.* New York: Van Nostrand.

Louisiana State Department of Education (1978). *Education of All Exceptional Children, Act 754 Regulations.*

Mardell, C. K., & Goldenberg, D. S. (1975). *Manual for the Developmental Indicators for the Assessment of Learning.* Elmer, NJ: Childcraft Education Corporation.

Morrison, D. G. (1969). On the interpretation of discriminant analysis. *Journal of Marketing Research, 6,* 156–163.

Payne, J. S., Mercer, C. D., Payne, R. A., & Davison, R. G. (1973). *Head Start: A tragicomedy with epilogue.* New York: Behavioral Publications.

Sanford, A. R. (1970). *The Learning Accomplishment Profile.* Winston-Salem, NC: Kaplan Press.

SPSS, Inc. (1983). *SPSS^X user's guide.* Chicago: Author.

Spodek, B. (Ed.). (1982). *Handbook of research in early childhood education.* New York: Free Press.

Stanley, J. E. (Ed.). (1972). *Preschool programs for the disadvantaged: Five experimental approaches to early childhood education.* Baltimore, MD: The Johns Hopkins University Press.

Tatsouka, M. M. (1970). *Discriminant analysis: The study of group differences.* Champaign, IL: Institute for Personality & Ability Testing.

Thorndike, R. M. (1978). *Correlational procedures in research.* New York: Gardner Press.

Travers, J. R., & Light, R. J. (Eds.). (1982). *Learning from experience: Evaluating early childhood demonstration programs.* Washington, D.C.: National Academy Press.

Westinghouse Learning Corporation and Ohio University. (1979). *The impact of Head Start: An evaluation of the effect of Head Start on children's cognitive and affective development. Executive summary.* Washington, D.C.: Clearinghouse for Federal Scientific & Technical Information. Report to the U.S. Office of Economic Opportunity (EDO 36321).

Weikart, D. P. (1982). Preschool education for disadvantaged children. In J. R. Travers & R. J. Light (Eds.), *Learning from experience: Evaluating early childhood demonstration programs* (pp. 187–202). Washington, D.C.: National Academy Press.

Weikart, D. P., Bond, J. T., & McNeil, J. (1978). *Ypsilanti Perry Preschool Project: Preschool years and longitudinal results through fourth grade. Monograph No. 3.* Ypsilanti, MI: High/Scope Educational Research Foundation.

Zigler, E., & Valentine, J. (Eds.). (1979). *Project Head Start: A legacy of the War on Poverty.* New York: The Free Press.

AGE, KNOWLEDGE OF RESULTS, STIMULUS SPEED, AND DIRECTION AS DETERMINANTS OF PERFORMANCE IN A COINCIDENCE-ANTICIPATION TASK

Marie Gagnon
Chantal Bard
Michelle Fleury

ABSTRACT

The aim of this article was to investigate the effect of spatial or temporal knowledge of result (KR) on performance and learning of a coincidence-timing task in children aged 6, 8, and 10 years. Three experimental groups were formed at each age level, and children were randomly assigned to one of the three groups. During practice sessions, one group received spatial KR, one group temporal KR, the third group no KR. During acquisition trials with KR, the spatial KR group improved spatially and temporally, whereas the temporal KR group decreased in spatial performance, without improving its overall temporal performance. Overall, 6-year-olds were less efficient than 10-year-olds in their performance in a coincidence-anticipation task. Stimulus speed and direction had spatial and temporal bias effects, but speed only modified global temporal accuracy in terms of absolute temporal errors. Moreover, neither speed nor direction had an effect on absolute—that is, global spatial—accuracy.

The ability to initiate and complete a motor pattern to coincide with the arrival of a moving object at a previously set interception point is called coincidence-anticipation (CA) (Belisle, 1963). *Coincidence* refers to the ability of subjects to predict stimulus duration; it has been described in terms of "anticipation of receptors" (Poulton, 1957; Schmidt, 1968). *Anticipation* refers to the ability of subjects to estimate their reaction time and to program their response to coincide with stimulus arrival; it has been associated with the "anticipation of effectors" (Poulton, 1957).

Most CA studies have investigated how different factors modify dependent variables related to timing accuracy (absolute, constant, variable temporal errors), and time parameters related to motor response (e.g., movement time). However, the analysis of sport or play activities, where a projectile is thrown, often involves *both* temporal and spatial accuracy. That is, the CA paradigm requires precise judgments on the location (spatial aspect) and on the moment of interception (temporal aspect) of a moving stimulus. It is therefore interesting to compare the ontogeny of receptor anticipation on the one hand, and effector anticipation and degree of precision of the throw (effector-related parameters) on the other hand.

A review of developmental studies of coincidence-anticipation tasks involving spatial accuracy (i.e., precision throw), temporal accuracy (i.e. simple CA task), and spatio-temporal accuracy (precision throw + timing accuracy) revealed that the abilities required for a successful response in such tasks do not achieve full maturation until adolescence (Bard et al., 1981; Dorfman, 1977; Dunham, 1977; Gagnon, 1986; Gagnon et al., 1988a, 1988b; Haywood, 1980; Shea, Krampitz, & Northam, 1982; Thomas, Gallagher & Purvis, 1981).

In an experiment where subjects performed a button-press and a throwing task (overarm throw), Fleury and Bard (1985) examined performance over a wide age range (9–11, 11–14, 14–18, 30–41, 41–52 years). The analysis of temporal biases showed that the disappearance of bias, that is, an almost perfect performance, occurred in the 30- to 41-year-old age group for the throwing task, and in the 41- to 52-year-old group for the simple button-press task. These results suggest that synchronization reaches full development only after years of practice. For spatial accuracy in throwing, without the presence of an apparent movement, the authors observed an optimal performance in the 14–18 year-old age group. In the task where subjects had to make a response to an apparent moving stimulus, Bard et al. (1981) observed that all subjects improved spatial accuracy between 6 and 10 years of age.

It can therefore be assumed that, while performing a CA task with temporal and spatial accuracy demands, children between 6 and 10 years will probably be forced into using strategies liable to trade-off. Different though not mutually exclusive strategies may be involved: focusing on either the spatial or the temporal dimension of the task, or attending both aspects in parallel (Martin, 1984; Ramella, 1982; see also Piaget, 1946/1972, pp. 1–84, for a discussion of the nested and sequential relationship that characterize moving objects).

To optimize learning in a CA task presenting both spatial and temporal demands, the child may be provided with different types of supplementary information or knowledge of results (KR): KR on either spatial or temporal accuracy (i.e., coincidence). From a purely cognitive point of view, a logical assumption would be that, in younger children, the informational content conveyed in spatial KR will be more efficiently used than the information contained in the temporal KR, since spatial concepts are mastered well before temporal concepts (Acredolo & Schmidt, 1981; Piaget, 1946/1972; Siegler & Richards, 1979).

KR may trigger the use of a specific learning strategy such as focusing on specific pieces of information contained within the KR. Will this result in the acquisition of additional information on a specific task component, e.g., timing? Will it bring some incidental learning effects on another task component, e.g., spatial accuracy? Finally, will this intentional learning produce a beneficial effect on overall spatio-temporal performance and learning within each age group?

Lieberman & Ray (1987), in a study where two experimental groups were assigned to either distance or time learning, demonstrated that subjects do learn the time it takes to produce a movement incidentally, while practicing on movement extent. This is not the case, however, for the incidental learning of distance when the focus was on time.

Whatever the type of information conveyed, KR has traditionally been considered crucial in skill acquisition in adults (Bilodeau & Bilodeau, 1961). In CA studies in adults, Haywood (1975), Magill and Chamberlin (1988), and Green et al. (1988) suggested that the task itself may provide enough information for fairly accurate performance, making KR redundant. On the other hand, only a few experiments investigated the role of KR in children performing a CA task. Ramella (1984) observed a beneficial effect of KR on temporal performance of first and third graders. These results suggest that KR is more beneficial for children than for adults. It may be that children are not using the available visual information that is sufficient for adequate performance in adults, and that KR orients children's attention toward important aspects of the task. Nevertheless, no transfer design was included in Ramella's study, therefore leaving the learning aspect unanswered.

Practice alone (without KR) has been found to affect CA performance; children show clear improvement with repetition (Dorfman, 1977; Hoffman, Imwold, & Koller, 1983; Stadulis, 1971). These studies, however, did not investigate practice effects on learning, since retention trials were not included (Salmoni, Schmidt, & Walter, 1984; see Schmidt, 1988, pp. 345–363, for a detailed discussion of the importance of a retention test in experimental design where learning is an investigated factor). Therefore the comparative effects of KR and practice alone on learning a CA task are still to be determined in children.

Coincidence-anticipation tasks with spatio-temporal demands involving a projectile displacement in space are not of common use in coincidence-anticipation studies. Traditionally, most coincidence-anticipation experiments have used a very simple "press- or release-button" type of response (Belisle, 1963; Bruker, Pauwels, & Meugens, 1988; Dunham, 1977; Dunham & Reid, 1987; Gagnon, 1986; Haywood, 1977, 1980; Haywood, Greenwald, & Lewis, 1981; Isaacs, 1983; Slater-Hammel, 1960; Stadulis, 1971; Thomas, Gallagher, & Purvis, 1981; Wrisberg & Ragsdale, 1979). This type of movement requires a very small segmental displacement. Moreover, the number of degrees of freedom used to produce the response is minimal during these experiments; as a result, motor synchronization (effector computation) is expected to be easily performed, creating a situation wherein emphasis is mainly on anticipation of subjects' receptors. These studies, therefore, have put more emphasis on the input information by minimizing the output processes.

More complex motor tasks have also been used (Ball & Glencross, 1985; Dorfman, 1977; Shea et al., 1981, 1982; Williams, 1985; Wrisberg & Mead, 1981, 1983). For the coincidence portion of the task, subjects had to produce an arm displacement parallel to the displacement of the apparent motion. Such a task required the effectors to engage in a more complex temporal calculation than a mere button-press response. Yet, both movements may be considered as very simple compared to most CA responses required in daily life.

Nevertheless, a few experimental studies have used more ecological movements to study coincidence-anticipation behavior. These studies used different types of throwing tasks: overarm throw (Bard et al., 1981; Fleury & Bard, 1985; Hoffmann, Imwold, & Koller, 1983) and sliding throw (Gagnon et al., 1988a, 1988b). For such tasks, coincidence occurred when the projectile (disk or ball) hit the target. This type of task, in addition to adequate receptors and effector computation, requires taking into consideration duration of spatial displacement of the projectile. This latter type of response is definitely more complex and closer to every-day life coincidence-anticipation activities than the former tasks.

As shown by von Hofsten (1979, 1980) and von Hofsten and Lindhagen (1979) in infants, the limiting factors to adequate performance are more tightly linked to effector than to respector anticipation. Thus for older children it would seem appropriate to use complex motor tasks in attempting to specify children's levels of CA development.

The presence of a moving stimulus is an intrinsic characteristic of all coincidence-anticipation tasks. It is therefore interesting to examine how the output process of a complex throwing CA task is related to changes in the input information (speed and direction). A few developmental CA studies have demonstrated that speed influences performance differently according to age (Ball & Glencross, 1985; Bard et al., 1981; Gagnon et al., 1988b; Haywood, 1977, 1980; Shea et al., 1982; Wade, 1980; Williams, 1985). Moreover, this speed-age interaction is always present in temporal bias (constant error). Bard et al. (in press), in a review of CA studies, observed that the "bias effect" reflected in constant temporal errors is more pronounced in younger children who seem to be more context-dependent.

Direction—that is, the origin of the stimulus (right, left)—is another potential factor linked to stimulus characteristics. Opposite to speed, which influences the overall performance in CA, direction seems to merely modify constant error. Direction effect is also less marked than the speed effect on all CA accuracy measurements (Bard et al., 1981; Fleury & Bard, 1985; Moujane, 1984).

In a developmental study using different input information and an unusual complex response wherein a projectile displacement must be taken into consideration to produce coincidence (complex output demands), we will compare the efficiency of KR and practice on spatio-temporal performance and learning of CA tasks.

Consequently, the purposes of the present investigation are: (1) to determine the effect of temporal and spatial KR on performance and learning of a CA task compared to the effect of practice alone; (2) to investigate the liability of spatial and temporal KR to induce the production of different response strategies in children; (3) to determine the liability of temporal and spatial KR to produce incidental learning as well as intentional learning; (4) to determine if the temporal concept conveyed in temporal KR is as well understood by younger as by older children; (5) to determine the effects of contextual factors (speed and direction) on the performance of a complex CA task when the duration of projectile displacement has to be integrated to produce coincidence; and (7) to specify the interactions between various selected variables.

METHOD

Subjects

Ninety randomly selected children, with no apparent motor problems (nine groups of 5 boys and 5 girls), participated in this study. Three groups of 6-year-olds ($M = 6.3$ years, $SD = 6$ months), three groups of 8-year-olds ($M = 8.3$ years, $SD = 8$ months), and three groups of 10-year-olds ($M = 10.2$ years, $SD = 7$ months) were formed.

Task and Apparatus

During testing, children were standing facing a table 210 cm long and 102 cm high (see Figure 1). They stood on blocks (adapted to their height) so that the table was just above hip level. Before stimulus presentation, subjects placed their hand on a 9-cm plastic disk, resting on a red circle drawn on the table. This starting position (#8 in Figure 1) was 195 cm from the central target.

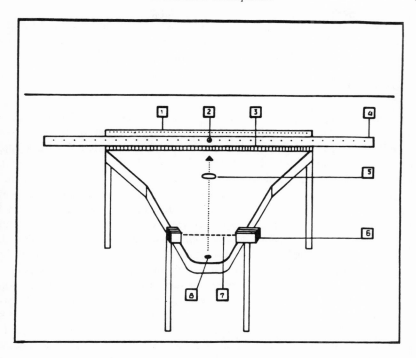

FIG. 1. Experimental setting (1) LEDS used for spatial KR (2) Target (3) Phototransistors (4) Apparent movement (5) Disk (6) Light source (phototransistor) (7) Disk-releasing line (8) Starting position of the disk.

Children with a horizontal extension of the arm, had to make a slide-throw in order to intercept an apparent movement (4) on a central target (2). The apparent movement was produced by a series of 87 light-emitting diodes, 5 cm apart, that could be lit successively. The diodes extended to a total width of 4.40 m. The target was a red central diode surrounded by a white circle. A light source (6) was situated at a distance of 30 cm from the disk starting position. The subject crossed it while releasing the disk from his hand. Twenty nine phototransistors (3) situated at the end of the table extended to a width of 160 cm. They were responsible for the recording of disk's time to impact and horizontal disk impact point.

Spatial KR was provided via a series of 28 green diodes (1), 5 cm apart, located directly above the apparent movement. Temporal KR was provided by a microcomputer. The sound provided by the computer (50 ms auditory bips) was transmitted by means of two amplifiers located on both sides of the apparatus.

All dependent measures:—temporal error, spatial error, and disk traveling time—were visible on the screen following each trial. If the child did not pay attention, that is, if the child showed an important delay in triggering his or her action (TR > 900 ms), the trial was discarded and retaken.

Experimental Procedures

Each child completed seven sessions: a pretest, four practice sessions (acquisition period with KR provided for experimental groups), a posttest (transfer test to a no-KR situation), and a retention test without KR, administered a week later. Each session included 20 trials: 5 trials at fast speed (150 cm/s), with stimulus coming from the right, 5 trials at fast speed, with stimulus coming from the left; the same combination was used at slow speed (110 cm/s), all trials being randomly presented. Sessions took place every half-day (pretest, morning, day 1; practice session # 1, afternoon, day 1; practice session # 2, morning, day 2; and so on), except for the retention test, which was administered a week after the posttest. For all trials and sessions, subjects performed the same sliding task. For the experimental groups, KR was provided after each trial during practice sessions (4 practice sessions × 20 trials per session = 80 KR). During temporal KR, the experimenter gave the child a verbal KR indicating if the subject was late or early. He or she then received an auditory KR composed of a certain number of bips. Each bip indicated a 25 ms error (e.g., 4 bips corresponded to a 100-ms error). If the child was less than 25 ms early or late, he or she received positive reinforcement, a little tune of 16-s duration. The temporal KR was provided under an auditory form in order to avoid the use of spatial cues to formalize the abstract notion of time. Moreover, for spatial KR, the experimenter provided the child with a verbal KR indicating if the subject threw the disk on the right or on the left side of the target. Spatial KR was provided by the lighting of a green diode over the impact end point of the disk trajectory. Whenever the subject was directly on target, the diode started blinking, thus giving the child a positive spatial reinforcement of 16 ms duration. Verbal KR was provided in order to insure the child's attention. During no-KR trials (practice trials for control group and pretest, postest, and retention test for all groups), no reinforcement and no KR was provided.

During the familiarization period, the experimenter verified that children understood both types of KR. For temporal KR, children had to successfully order three sets of auditory bips of different durations.

The independent variables were: (a) KR conditions (no-KR, spatial KR, and temporal KR), (b) age of subjects (6, 8, 10 years), (c) stimulus speed (110 cm/s, slow speed; 150 cm/s, fast speed), (d) stimulus direction (originating from right or left), (e) sessions (S1 = pretest, S2 = practice #1, S3 = practice #2, S4 = practice #3, S5 = practice #4, S6 = posttest, transfer test, without KR, S7 = retention test without KR).

The dependent measures were: (a) constant temporal error (CTE) and constant spatial error (CSE). They reflect the directional bias of the error. CTE (in ms) is the temporal interval between the arrival of the apparent movement on the central target and the disk arrival. CTE (in cm) indicates if the subject is early (–) or late (+), according to stimulus arrival. CSE represents the difference between the spatial localization of the target and the end point of disk trajectory (impact point). CSE indicates if the subject throws the disk on the right side (+) or on the left side (–) of the target; (b) variable temporal error (VTE) and variable spatial error (VSE), which are indices of the variability around the mean; (c) absolute temporal error (ATE) absolute spatial error (ASE), representing CTE and CSE without algebraic sign respectively; (d) disk traveling time (TT) and variability of disk traveling time (VTE—standard deviation), a measure of disk displacement between the phototransistors located at the end of the subject's movement and the photoelectric cell responsible for the recording of the spatial error. The last two measures are indicative of variations in velocity between different throws, that is, they are estimation of variations in the motor response strategy. Moreover, such parameters must be taken into account for adequate timing, since a posteriori control with subjects of the same age revealed a significant correlation of -0.28 $p < .001$, between movement time and TT.

Statistical Treatment

Three doubly multivariate analysis of variance (MANOVA, BMDP, 4V), 3 (Age) $\times$ 3 (KR) $\times$ 2 (Speed) $\times$ 2 (Direction) $\times$ 7 (session), were applied to three sets of measures: constant errors (CE), variable errors (VE), and absolute errors (AE) (see Table 1 and Bock, 1975, pp. 502–505, for a discussion of the analysis used in this design).

Univariate F tests were used, whenever significant multivariate Fs were obtained to determine which dependent variable contributed most to differentiating the factors. For all analyses, Age, KR, Speed, Direction, and Session were considered as independent variables. Speed, Direction, and Session were used as repeated measures for each subject (within-subject factors). Age and KR were considered as between-subject factors.

In the absence of interaction in the univariate analysis, (a) Tukey's post hoc analysis was applied between KR conditions and Age, whenever significant differences were found for main effects; (b) means of adjacent sessions were submitted to comparisons (profile of repeated measures), whenever the dependent variable was significantly affected by this factor. The analysis was done by generating contrasts between adjacent factors.

RESULTS

Table 2 and 3 present F values for main effects and interactions for the MANOVA and ANOVAs.

Table 1
Statistical Model for the Doubly Multivariate Analysis of Variance

Manova on Constant Errors	Manova on Variable Errors	Manova on Absolute Errors
(1) Disk travelling time (TT)	(1) Variability of Disk travelling time (VTT)	(1) Disk travelling time (TT)
(2) Constant temporal error (CTE)	(2) Variable temporal error (VTE)	(2) Absolute temporal error (ATE)
(3) Constant spatial error (CSE)	(2) Variable spatial error (VSE)	(2) Absolute spatial error (ASE)

Table 2

F Values for Constant, Variable, and Absolute Errors for Main Effects

Factor	Constant Errors	Variable Errors	Absolute Errors
Age	Mult F = N/S	Mult F(6,158) = 7.58** VTT F N/S VTE F(2,81) = 15.51** VSE F(2,81) = 12.60**	Mult F(6,158) = 10.27** TT F N/S ATE F(2,81) = 9.38** ASE F(2,81) = 26.17**
KR	Mult F(6,158) = 3.41* TT F N/S CTE F(2,81) = 5.98 CSE F N/S	Mult F(6,158) = 3.90** VTT F N/S VTE F(2,81) = 7.90** VSE F(2,81) = 4.84**	Mult F(6,158) = 3.16* TT F N/S ATE F N/S ASE F(2,81) = 5.94*
Session	Mult F(18,64) = 7.95** TT F(6,76) = 8.23** CTE F N/S CSE F(6,76) = 3.25*	Mult F(18,64) = 10.24** VTT F(6,76) = 5.02** VTE F(6,76) = 25.62** VSE F N/S	Mult F(18,64) = 10.79** TT F(6,76) = 8.23** ATE F(6,76) = 29.71** ASE F N/S
Speed	Mult F(3,79) = 47.11** TT F(1,81) = 35.97** CTE F(1,81) = 105.20** CSE F(1,81) = 4.99**	Mult F(3,74) = 31.30** VTT F N/S VTE F(1,81) = 9.38** VSE F N/S	Mult F(3,79) = 16.37** TT F(1,81) = 35.97** ATE F(1,81) = 10.71** ASE F N/S
Direction	Mult F(3,79) = 13.01** TT F N/S CTE F N/S CSE F(1,81) = 27.59**	Mult F N/S	Mult F N/S

*p < .01
**p < .001

Table 3

F Values for Constant, Variable, and Absolute Errors for Interactions

Factor	Constant Errors	Variable Errors	Absolute Errors
KR X Speed	Mult F N/S	Mult F N/S	Mult F(36,128) = 3.67** TT F N/S ATE F(2,81) = 5.67** ASE F N/S
KR X Session	Mult F(36,128) = 1.88*** TT F N/S CTE F N/S	Mult F N/S	Mult F(36,128) = 2.71* TT F N/S ATE F N/S ASE F(12,486) = 2.65**
Session X Speed	Mult F(18,64) = 6.04** TT F N/S CTE F(6,486) = 24.71	Mult F N/S	Mult F(18,64) = 2.77** TT F N/S ATE F(6,486) = 6.28** ASE F N/S
Session X Direction	Mult F(18,64) = 2.26* TT F N/S CTE F(6,486) = 3.20 CSE F(6,486) = 7.34*	Mult F N/S	Mult F N/S
Speed X Direction	Mult F(3,79) = 2.71* TT F N/S CTE F(1,81) = 9.96* CSE F N/S	Mult F N/S	Mult F(3,79) = 3.67** TT F N/S ATE F(1,81) = 5.67 ASE F N/S

Constant Errors (CE)

Age had no effect on constant errors (Table 2, Table 4). However, KR had a significant effect on CE. The univariate analysis was significant for CTE only. The post hoc analysis demonstrated that the temporal KR group was different from all other groups, showing a slight anticipation whereas the control and spatial KR groups were late in their response. There was a significant interaction between Session and KR for constant error (Table 3). Follow-up univariate analysis revealed that, only CSE was significant. In this case, the Temporal KR group demonstrated very erratic behavior over sessions. The children shift from a stong bias to the left to a strong bias to the right across sessions, showing greater instability. Session also had an effect on constant errors, although only CSE showed significant differences in the univariate analyses. There was a significant interaction between Session and Speed for constant error. Only CTE was significantly different in the univariate analysis (Figure 2). During the pretest, subjects responded differently to stimulus velocity. They anticipated at slow speed and delayed there response at the fast speed; the speed effect decreased over sessions. For the last session (S7), CTE was similar regardless of the stimulus velocity used. The Session by Direction interaction also was significant for constant error. The univariate analysis showed a significant effect for CTE, demonstrating that the effect of direction on CTE did not hold with practice. Moreover, CSE also was significant in the univariate analysis. CSE results demonstrated that, at the beginning of practice, subjects responded to the right of target when the stimulus came from the left and to the left when stimulus came from the right. With practice, as with CTE, stimulus direction did not affect the location of constant spatial errors, and subjects responded more accurately.

Speed also affected constant errors (Table 2). The univariate analysis demonstrated a significant effect on CTE. CSE also was significant in the univariate analyses. Subjects were less biased at fast speed than at slow speed. They threw to the right of target with both speeds; however, their bias was less pronounced at the slow speed. Direction had a significant effect on constant errors. CSE only showed significant differences in the univariate tests, revealing that subjects threw the disk to the left side of target when the stimulus came from the right and to the right side of the target when the stimulus came from the left. There was a significant Speed by Direction interaction for constant errors (Table 3). When analyzed in a univariate procedure, this interaction was significant only for CTE. At the fast speed, there was no effect of stimulus direction. Conversely, at the slow speed, subjects showed no bias whenever the stimulus came from the left, and they anticipated when the apparent movement came from the right.

Variable Error

Age had a significant effect on variable errors (Table 2). Both VTE (Figure 3) and VSE (Figure 4), when analysed in a univariate analysis, revealed significant

Table 4
Means and Standard Deviations for Constant Errors According to Knowledge of Results, Speed, and Direction

Session					CTE								
	S1		S2		S3		S4		S5		S6		S7
Factor	M	SD	M	SD	M	SD	M	SD	M	SD	M	SD	M	SD
KR													
KR	13.5	106.2	15.4	56.7	27.9	57.6	9.6	48.3	24.3	48.9	32.8	48.8	69.4	50.0
TKR	−29.5	70.2	−25.9	46.9	−8.7	54.0	−16.6	60.5	−3.9	47.2	26.7	39.8	57.2	53.9
SKR	−5.1	50.1	25.1	58.3	29.9	59.9	17.3	56.7	30.6	52.7	46.2	46.0	62.7	43.8
Speed													
Slow	−61.4	107.3	−35.0	76.7	−21.2	84.7	−23.1	71.7	−2.7	61.5	17.5	53.5	60.2	58.7
Fast	47.2	81.9	44.8	64.5	53.9	66.4	30.0	69.0	36.7	64.5	53.0	56.9	66.1	58.2
Direction													
Left	3.4	87.7	13.3	77.1	20.8	69.5	12.6	67.9	24.4	59.9	38.1	54.3	57.1	62.7
Right	−17.6	88.7	3.5	63.3	12.0	69.8	5.7	66.1	9.6	60.2	32.4	52.1	69.1	54.2

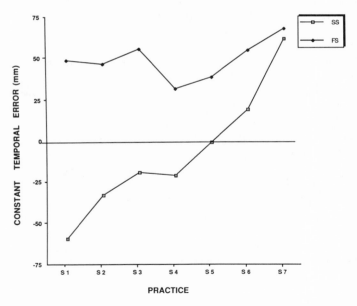

FIG. 2. Constant temporal error according to session and speed. SS = slow speed; FS = fast speed.

						CSE							
S1		**S2**		**S3**		**S4**		**S5**		**S6**		**S7**	
M	**SD**	**M**	**SD**	**M**	**SD**	**M**	**SD**	**M**	**SD**	**M**	**SD**	**M**	**SD**
0.21	2.6	1.5	6.3	1.2	2.7	0.98	4.1	0.7	3.5	0.9	3.3	−0.1	3.7
−0.6	4.5	0.6	2.9	−0.3	4.7	1.6	4.6	4.6	9.1	1.0	2.7	−0.1	3.8
0.1	3.4	0.3	1.8	−0.6	2.9	0.2	2.8	0.5	3.9	0.4	2.3	−0.0	3.1
−1.1	4.8	0.3	7.1	−0.01	4.9	0.7	4.7	1.5	8.0	0.4	3.8	−0.5	4.4
0.8	4.5	1.2	3.9	−1.0	4.8	1.1	4.7	2.4	7.3	1.1	3.9	0.3	3.8
1.1	5.5	2.9	7.3	1.2	4.9	1.4	5.6	2.4	9.0	0.9	4.0	0.6	4.8
−1.4	4.3	−1.4	3.8	−0.1	4.7	0.5	4.7	1.4	7.1	0.5	3.7	−0.6	4.6

differences according to age. Post hoc analyses on VSE and VTE showed differences between all age groups. KR also had an effect on variable error (Table 2). VTE was significant when analysed univariately. The post hoc analysis showed that VTE was larger in the control than in experimental groups (Table 5). VSE also showed significant differences in the univariate analyses. The post hoc analysis revealed that subjects from the Spatial KR group were less variable than Temporal KR and no-KR subjects.

Session had an effect on variable errors. Univariate analysis demonstrated a significant difference for VTT and VTE. Comparison of means between adjacent sessions showed significant differences between sessions 1 and 2, and sessions 4 and 5 for VTT and VTE. With practice, subjects became temporally less variable. Speed had an effect on variable error also. Univariate analysis revealed that VSE was not affected by stimulus speed. However, subjects demonstrated more variability in temporal error (VTE) at the slower speed.

None of the interactions for variable error were significant (Table 3).

Absolute Error

Age had a significant effect on absolute error. Univariate analysis revealed significant difference for both ATE and ASE. Post hoc analysis for ATE and ASE showed that 6-year-olds were more accurate than 10-year-olds (Table 6).

Table 5

Means and Standard Deviations for Variable Error According to Age, Knowledge of Results, Session, Speed, and Direction

		Age			KR			Speed		Direction		Session						
		6	8	10	KR	TKR	SKR	F	S	L	R	1	2	3	4	5	6	7
VTE	M	120.0	106.9	95.3	117.2	105.0	100.1	98.7	116.2	107.7	107.2	138.4	115.4	105.0	103.5	97.4	96.7	95.8
	SD	17.7	19.9	17.3	20.4	22.6	15.4	19.1	25.1	22.5	21.5	39.9	32.6	34.4	27.4	24.7	26.2	23.5
VSE	M	14.0	11.6	10.2	12.2	13.0	10.6	11.9	11.9	11.8	12.1	11.5	13.0	11.4	11.6	13.7	11.3	11.1
	SD	2.5	3.8	2.8	3.9	3.6	2.3	3.5	4.0	3.6	4.1	3.5	7.9	3.6	3.5	10.0	3.3	3.2
VTT	M	48.5	37.5	41.3	47.1	40.6	39.7	41.5	43.5	41.6	43.4	47.3	43.2	41.7	46.0	37.2	37.1	44.8
	SD	19.6	13.0	24.7	17.6	24.8	16.4	29.3	18.6	22.1	19.5	24.7	21.0	23.0	37.6	16.4	20.0	66.9

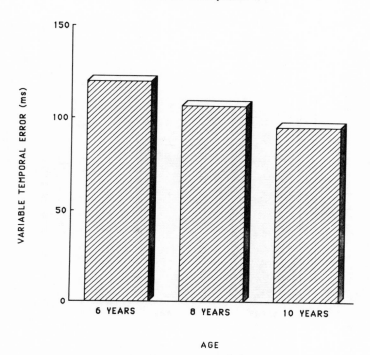

FIG. 3. Variable temporal error according to age.

Multivariate analysis revealed that KR had an effect on absolute error. However, only ASE was significant when analyzed univariately. There was a Session effect on absolute error. Univariate analysis showed a significant effect for TT. Comparisons between adjacent sessions revealed significant differences between sessions 1 and 2, where a decrease in TT was noticed. There was also a significant difference in the univariate analyses for ATE. A significant interaction between Session and KR also was observed for absolute error. The univariate analysis on the interaction revealed a significant effect on ASE. Subjects in the spatial KR group reduced their ASE during sessions where KR was provided, whereas the control and Temporal KR groups showed no improvements during practice. However, for the retention test, Spatial KR subjects no longer differed from the control group. A significant interaction, Session by Speed, was present for absolute errors. ATE only showed a significant difference univariately. Subjects had greater ATE at slower speeds for all sessions, except for the posttest. Moreover, there was a significant interaction, KR by Speed, for absolute errors (Table 5). In the univariate analyses, there was a significant

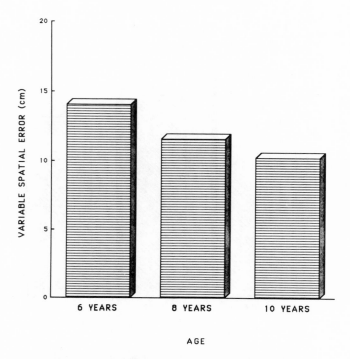

FIG. 4. Variable spatial error according to age.

difference for ATE (Figure 5). Subjects receiving spatial KR had a similar ATE at slow and fast speeds. This was not the case for the temporal KR and no-KR groups. Speed had a significant effect on absolute error. Univariate analysis revealed a significant effect on TT. Subjects had faster TT at the fast speed than at the slow speed. ATE also was significant in the univariate analyses. Subjects were more accurate at the fast than at the slow speed. Direction had no effect on absolute errors.

DISCUSSION

Age

The present results on ATE and ASE confirm that CA performance improves between 6 and 10 years of age (Bard et al., 1981; Dorfman, 1977; Hoffman et al., 1983; Moujane, 1984; Shea & et al., 1982). Six-year-olds exhibit larger absolute errors (temporal and spatial) than ten-year-olds, whereas both types of variable error differed for all three age groups as children become less variable with age.

Table 6
Means and Standard Deviations for Absolute Errors According to Age, Speed X KR Interaction, and Speed X Session Interaction

Factor	ATE		ASE		TT	
Speed X KR	M	SD	M	SD	M	SD
–KR - SS	126.2	28.6	10.5	3.7	436.1	80.7
–KR - FS	114.8	29.4	10.2	3.3	411.0	75.3
–TKR - SS	120.8	37.1	11.2	3.3	377.8	72.8
–TKR - FS	99.6	22.3	11.2	3.1	370.6	69.8
–SKR - SS	107.3	17.9	9.1	1.9	411.4	83.2
–SKR - FS	106.3	29.0	9.5	2.2	394.9	76.6
Speed X Session	M	SD	M	SD	m	SD
SS - S1	156.5	68.9	10.2	3.8	430.6	95.6
SS - S2	127.3	39.4	10.9	7.2	415.1	91.5
SS - S3	116.3	50.2	9.8	3.8	412.6	96.8
SS - S4	115.3	41.1	10.4	3.6	403.8	84.5
SS - S5	100.3	37.0	11.0	7.6	401.9	91.2
SS - S6	96.4	30.8	9.7	3.4	398.5	91.0
SS - S7	114.3	35.2	9.8	3.2	396.7	84.1
FS - S1	128.7	51.2	10.2	3.8	412.1	92.7
FS - S2	107.8	35.3	10.8	4.4	403.2	85.1
FS - S3	109.5	39.3	10.4	3.8	393.1	87.4
FS - S4	101.2	35.2	10.0	3.6	398.9	78.2
FS - S5	97.0	34.5	11.6	6.8	378.6	77.9
FS - S6	99.9	35.4	9.6	3.2	381.3	84.4
FS - S7	104.3	38.7	10.0	3.6	387.1	88.6
Age	M	SD				
6 years	125.2	54.1				
8 years	112.8	51.0				
10 years	99.3	46.8				

Knowledge of Results

Knowledge of results has a significant effect on the parameters directly linked to the information it conveys. Thus, temporal KR significantly reduces constant temporal error, whereas spatial KR improves spatial accuracy (absolute and variable spatial errors) and diminished temporal variability. Nevertheless, it is

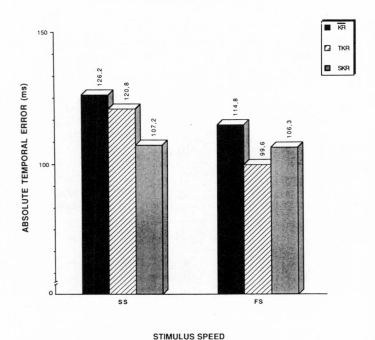

FIG. 5. Absolute temporal error according to speed and knowledge of results.

interesting to note that certain factors, specially stimulus speed, interact with KR and modify its effect.

The significant interaction of KR by Speed shows that under temporal KR, subjects present the greatest modification in their temporal timing according to stimulus speed. These subjects perform efficiently when fast stimuli are presented; conversely, whenever slow speed is used, their temporal performance is erratic compared to spatial KR subjects' performance. This suggests that under temporal KR, subjects are greatly influenced by the speed context. At fast speed, when no-KR and temporal KR subjects' results are compared, temporal KR appears to be more efficient for adequate temporal performance than no KR. It is therefore possible that temporal KR is useful mainly for fast speed presentations (150 cm/sec or above). This hypothesis requires further investigation such as providing temporal KR in an experimental setting where two faster speeds are used. Results obtained at fast speed are in agreement with Ramella's findings (1984). Using a single stimulus speed (223.5 cm/s), which is faster than the one used in the present study, Ramella showed that children (6 and 9 years old) receiving verbal temporal KR had lower ATE and VTE than control subjects. In the present study, children faced two different stimulus speeds, and temporal KR did not improve overall temporal performance. These partly divergent results suggest that temporal KR effects on timing performance are linked to stimulus-related and contextual factors, and perhaps to the motor response; they are thus closely associated with the experimental setting.

Conversely, subjects in the spatial KR group show similar ATE at slow and fast speed, indicating that those children are not disturbed by changes in stimulus speed. Moreover, the spatial KR group showed a decrease in temporal variability (VTE) compared to the no-KR group, and a decrease in spatial variability (VSE) compared to no-KR and temporal KR groups. Since decreased variability characterizes learning, it can be stated that spatial KR allows intentional spatial learning and incidental temporal learning.

Those three findings emphasize that spatial KR subjects pay less attention to the properties of the moving stimulus, that is, they focus their attention on the motor response. Children are becoming less context-dependent. This orientation of attention on motor response results in a decreased temporal variability performance, probably via better integration of movement duration (TM + TT), that is, better anticipation of the effectors. Consequently, a child should be provided with added information (e.g., verbal KR, kinematic, kinetic) linked to the motor rather than to the visual-perceptual component of a CA task.

Practice

The fact that practice results in a more accurate and less variable performance is a common finding (see Dorfman, 1977; Hoffman et al., 1983; Stadulis, 1971; Wrisberg & Mead, 1983). Our results go further in demonstrating a monotonic reduction in VTE and a nonmonotonic reduction in VSE.

The pretest and posttest learning curves, according to the interaction of Session X Speed (ATE, CTE) and Session X Direction (CSE, CTE), demonstrate that subjects progressively assume a similar response pattern for both speeds and both directions. The interactions, Speed X Session and Direction X Practice, for CTE demonstrates that, with practice, subjects delay their response. The "too early behavior" at the slow speed when a stimulus comes from the right transforms into a "too late behavior" across practice sessions. Differences according to stimulus characteristics fade and give way to a progressively more delayed and unique response. Moreover, subjects decrease their TT at the fast speed as well as at the slow speed. These results indicate that subjects use a strategy whereby they prolong the time interval when they are actively controlling the perceptual and motor components of the task. Such a stragegy allows a reduction in the global temporal error across sessions.

Stimulus Speed

Our results failed to show that speed is differentially influencing timing performance according to age. The overall performance for ATE is always better at fast (150 cm/s) than at slow speed (100 cm/s). Temporal variability of response is also reduced at fast speed. A better response, therefore, is linked to "preferential stimulus speed" rather than to stimulus-exposure duration, prolonged duration at slow speed revealing a less accurate performance. Williams (1985) indeed observed that stimulus speed at which subjects perform better is highly matched to the use of a preferential speed. The favored movement speed is defined as the execution speed spontaneously and freely adopted, without specific duration or speed constraints and without temporal requirements associated to stimulus speed. Three different stimulus speeds were manipulated in other studies using a similar CA task. Fleury and Bard (1985), having subjects perform at 75, 150, 300 cm/s, found the lowest ATE at the 150 cm/s velocity. Gagnon et al. (1988b), using two different speeds (167 and 222 cm/s), with subjects performing the same task as in the present study, found that subjects have the lowest ATE while performing at the 167 cm/s stimulus velocity. Such results indicate that for a complex task, where a projectile is thrown at a fixed target, the "preferential stimulus speed," in terms of absolute error, rests around 150 cm/s.

Speed has very little effect on spatial errors. When fast stimulus presentation is used, subjects throw to the right side of the target. This systematic bias toward the right as fast speeds is probably due to the fact that most of our subjects, being right handed, have a biomechanical bias toward the right side.

Bard et al. (1981), Fleury and Bard (1985), and Gagnon (1988a, 1988b) did not find any effect of speed on spatial accuracy, suggesting that spatial performance is little influenced by the perceptual component of the CA task.

Direction

In the present experiment, direction modifies only directional bias of spatial and temporal errors, without any effect on global performance (absolute error). This difference, however, disappears across practice sessions.

The significant interaction of Speed by Direction for CTE indicates that a direction-related difference is present only at slow speeds. Thus, the bias introduced by the origin of the stimulus is no longer found whenever the stimulus comes from the left at slow speed, as this condition allows a smooth visual pursuit of the stimulus and enables subjects to get spatiotemporal information about the mobile stimulus. This finding might be explained by the fact that subjects are well acquainted with reading from left to right and seem to benefit from slow pursuit in such a familiar situation. In CA tasks, stimulus direction may therefore be used to decrease the predictive probabilities of stimulus characteristics without critically modifying spatiotemporal accuracy.

In summary, whatever their age, children process information similarly. Overall, 6-year-olds are less efficient than 10-year-olds in their performance of a CA task. Spatial KR information results in an improved spatial performance and a decreased variability in temporal performance, whereas temporal KR information yields a decreased overall temporal variability and absolute error at fast speed. Conversely, it bears no effect on temporal performance when both speeds are considered. Moreover, temporal KR provided during acquisition trials deteriorates spatial accuracy. Stimulus speed and direction have a spatial and temporal bias effect, but speed only affects global temporal accuracy in terms of ATE. Moreover, neither speed nor direction has an effect on absolute, that is, overall spatial accuracy.

REFERENCES

Acredolo, C., & Schmidt, J. (1981). The understanding of relative speeds, distances and durations of movements. *Developmental Psychology, 17,* 490–493.

Ball, C., & Glencross, D. (1985). Developmental differences in a coincident timing task under speed and time constraints. *Human Movement Sciences, 4,* 1–15.

Bard, C., Fleury, M., Carrière, L., & Bellec, J. (1981). Component of the coincidence-anticipation behavior of children aged from 6 to 11 years. *Perceptual and Motor Skills, 52,* 547–556.

Bard, C., Fleury, M., & Gagnon M. (1990). Coincidence anticipation timing: An age-related perspective. In C. Bard, M. Fleury, & L. Hay (Eds.), *Development of Eye-Hand Coordination across Life Span.* (pp. 283–305). Columbia, SC: University of South Carolina Press.

Belisle, J. J. (1963). Accuracy, reliability and refractoriness in a coincidence-anticipation task. *Research Quarterly, 34,* 271–281.

Bilodeau, E. D., & Bilodeau, I. (1961). Motor skills learning. *Annual Review of Psychology, 12,* 243–280.

Bock, R. D. (1975). *Multivariate statistical methods in behavioral research.* New York: Mc Graw-Hill.

Bruker, M., Pauwels, J., & Meugens P. (1988). Temporal and spatial anticipation in twelve-year-old boys and girls. In A. M. Colley & J. R. Beech (Eds.), *Cognition and Action in Skilled Behaviour* (pp. 283–292). New York: North Holland.

Dorfman, P. W. (1977). Timing and anticipation: A developmental pespective. *Journal of Motor Behavior, 3,* 281–287.

Dunham, P. (1977). Age, sex, speed and practice in coincidence-anticipation performance of children. *Perceptual and Motor Skills, 45* 187–193.

Dunham, P., & Reid, D. (1987). Information processing: Effect of stimulus speed variations on coincidence-anticipation of children. *Journal of Human Movement Studies, 13,* 151–156.

Fleury, M., & Bard, C. (1985). Age, stimulus velocity and task complexity as determiners of coincident timing behavior. *Journal of Human Movement Studies, 11,* 305–317.

Gagnon, M. (1986). *Connaissance des résultats et évolution du contrôle temporel et spatial dans une tâche d'anticipation-coïcidence.* Unpublished master's thesis, Université Laval, Québec, Canada.

Gagnon, M., Fleury, M., & Bard, C. (1988a). Connaissance des résultats et contrôle spatiotemporel dans une tâche d'anticipation-coïcidence chez des enfants de 6 à 10 ans. *Canadian Journal of Psychology, 42,* 347–363.

Gagnon, M., Bard, C., Fleury, M., & Michaud, D. (1988b, June). *Age and stimulus velocity as determinants of time-sharing between information processing and motor response in a coincidence anticipation task.* A paper presented at the annual meeting of the North American Society for the Psychology of Sports and Physical Activity, Knoxville, TN.

Green, K. J., Chamberlin, C. J., & Magill, R. A. (1988, June). *Verbal KR and novel transfer for an anticipation timing task: A case for information redundancy.* A paper presented at the annual meeting of the North American Society for the Psychology of Sports and Physical Activity, Knoxville, TN.

Haywood, K. M. (1975). Relative effects of three knowledge of results treatments on coincidence-anticipation performance. *Journal of Motor Behavior. 7*, 271–274.

Haywood, K. M. (1977). Eye movements during coincidence-anticipation performance. *Journal of Motor Behavior, 9*, 313–318.

Haywood, K. M. (1980). Coincidence anticipation accuracy across the life span. *Experimental Aging Research, 6*, 451–462.

Haywood, K. M., Greenwald, G., & Lewis, C. (1981). Contextual factors and age group differences in coincidence-anticipation performance. *Research Quarterly for Exercise and Sport, 52*, 458–464.

Hoffman, J. S., Imwold, C. H., & Koller, J. A. (1983). Accuracy and prediction in throwing: A taxonomic analysis of children's performance. *Research Quarterly for Exercise and Sport, 54*, 33–40.

Hofsten, C. von. (1979). Development of visually directed reachings: The approach phase. *Journal of Human Movements Studies, 5*, 160–178.

Hofsten, C. von. (1980). Predictive reaching to moving objects by human infants. *Journal of Experimental Child Psychology, 28*, 369–382.

Hofsten, C. von., & Lindhagen, K. (1979). Observations on the development of reaching for moving objects. *Journal of Experimental Child Psychology, 28*, 158–173.

Issacs, L. D. (1983). Coincidence anticipation in simple catching. *Journal of Human Movement Studies, 9*, 195–201.

Lieberman, P., & Ray, T. (1987, October). *On intentional and incidental learning and estimation of temporal and spatial information*. A paper presented at the 20th annual meeting of the Canadian Society for Psychomotor Learning and Sport Psychology, Banff, Alberta.

Magill, R. A., & Chamberlin, C. J. (1988, June). *Verbal KR can be redundant information in motor skill learning*. A paper presented at the 20th annual meeting of the North American Society for the Psychology of Sports and Physical Activity, Knoxville, TN.

Martin, J. H. (1984). Coincidence anticipation and the space-time concept in mentally retarded and non-retarded individuals (Doctoral dissertation, University of Tennessee, 1982). *University Microfilms International*, 8303706.

Moujane, M. (1984). *Etude ontogénétique des mécanismes perceptuels, moteurs et de contrôle sous-tendant la coordination visuo-manuelle d'interception d'un stimulus en mouvement*. Unpublished master's thesis, Laval University, Québec, Canada.

Piaget, J. (1946/1972). *Les notions de mouvement et de vitesse chez l'enfant*. Paris: Presses Universitaires de France.

Poulton, E. C. (1957). On prediction of skilled movements. *Psychological Bulletin, 54*, 467–468.

Ramella, J. R. (1982). Learning a motor skill with spatial and temporal parameters. *Perceptual and Motor Skills, 55*, 519–525.

Ramella, J. R. (1984). Effects of knowledge of results on anticipation timing by young children. *Perceptual and Motor Skills, 55*, 519–525.

Salmoni, A. W., Schmidt, R. A., & Walter, C. B. (1984). Knowledge of results and motor learning: A review and critical reappraisal. *Psychological Bulletin, 95*, 355–386.

Schmidt, R. A. (1968). Anticipation and timing in human motor performance. *Psychological Bulletin, 70*, 631–646.

Schmidt, R. A. (1988). *Motor control and learning* (2nd ed.). Champaign, IL: Human Kinetics.

Shea, C. H., Krampitz, J. B., & Northam, C. C. (1982). Information processing in coincident timing tasks: A developmental perspective. *Journal of Human Movement Studies, 8*, 73–83.

Shea, C. H., Krampitz, J. B., Tolson, H., Ashby, A. A., Howard, R. M., & Husak, W. S. (1981). Stimulus velocity, duration and uncertainty as determiners of response structure and timing accuracy. *Research Quarterly for Exercise and Sport, 52*, 86–99.

Siegler, R. S., & Richards, D. D. (1979). The development of time, speed and distance concept. *Developmental Psychology, 15*, 289–298.

Slater-Hammel, A. T. (1960). Reliability, accuracy and refractoriness of transit reaction. *Research Quarterly, 31,* 217–228.

Stadulis, R. I. (1971). *Coincidence-anticipation behavior of children.* Unpublished doctoral dissertation, Columbia University, New York.

Thomas, J. R., Gallagher, J. D., & Purvis, C. J. (1981). Reaction time and anticipation time effects of development. *Research Quarterly for Exercise and Sport, 52,* 359–367.

Wade, M. G. (1980). Coincidence-anticipation of young normal and handicapped children. *Journal of Motor Behavior, 12,* 103–112.

Williams, K. (1985). Age differences on a coincident anticipation task: Influences of stereotypic or "preferred" movement speed. *Journal of Motor Behavior, 17,* 389–410.

Wrisberg, C. A., & Mead, B. J. (1981). Anticipation of coincidence in children: A test of schema theory. *Perceptual and Motor Skills, 52,* 599–606.

Wrisberg, C. A., & Mead, B. J. (1983). Developing coincident timing skill in children: A comparison of training methods. *Research Quarterly for Exercise and Sport, 54,* 67–74.

Wrisberg, C. A., & Ragsdale, M. R. (1979). Further tests of Schmidt's schema theory: Development of a schema rule for coincident timing task. *Journal of Motor Behavior, 11,* 159–166.

6

EFFECTS OF OCCLUDING A BALL'S TRAJECTORY ON THE INTERCEPTION PERFORMANCE OF ADULTS AND CHILDREN

Carol France Haller
Jane E. Clark

ABSTRACT

Previous research on the role of trajectory information in explaining age-related differences in catching has focused on the amount of time that trajectory information is available. The present study focused on the possibility that seeing selected portions of the trajectory is more important than time per se. To test this hypothesis, 7- and 9-year-old children and adults were videotaped catching one-handed under four conditions of trajectory view: full view, and occlusion of first, middle, and last segments of the trajectory. Analysis of the effects of trajectory occlusion on hand positioning and grasp revealed the importance of viewing the last segment of the ball's trajectory for 7-year-olds. Trajectory occlusion did not affect the adults or 9-year-olds' hand positioning or grasping.

For adults, catching a ball appears to be an easy task. For the young child, however, catching a moving object often is a difficult, if not impossible, task. Indeed children as old as 5 and 6 years of age still have difficulty catching balls tossed 5 meters (Du Randt, 1985). What is it about catching a thrown ball that is so difficult? One possible answer to this question may be found in the way young children use trajectory information. The speed, direction, height, and angle of the object's trajectory are all important sources of information for the performer. But for children the unpredictability of this information may overwhelm their ability to process the information in the time before the ball arrives

Previous research has shown that the longer a performer has to view a moving object the greater the chance for successfully catching the object (Sharp &

Whiting, 1974; Whiting, Gill, & Stephenson, 1970; Whiting & Sharp, 1974). It seems logical to assume that a longer viewing time would be to the perceiver's advantage, since it would provide more time to gather information about the object to be intercepted. Kay (1957), however, has suggested that it may not be necessary to watch the entire flight of a ball to initiate an accurate catch. In fact, Bahill & LaRitz (1984) found that performers are unable to track a ball throughout the entire flight due to visual limitations. They argue that even the best athletes are unable to track a fast ball closer than 5 ft from themselves.

If performers do not need to view the entire ball's flight, is there a specific window of time that affords a better opportunity for judging a ball's trajectory? And is this window the same for children and adults? Research on the importance of specific time windows for receiving trajectory information on adult performance has yielded contradictory results. Carlton (1981), for example, found that vision is used only during the last half of the movement when the striking object is near the target location. Bahill and McDonald (1982), on the other hand, report that adult batters extract very little information from the middle segment of the trajectory and that first *and* last segments provide the critical information for an accurate swing. An examination of skilled batters, however, would suggest that the necessary interception information may be obtained from *any* segment of the flight (DeLucia & Cochran, 1985). Indeed the results of Fischman and Schneider's study (1985) indicate that the performer's experience determines the importance of a particular segment of flight information. For the inexperienced adult catcher, losing sight of the ball immediately prior to ball-hand contact adversely affected their hand positioning. Experienced catchers were not similarly affected. Apparently the experienced catcher could more accurately determine flight characteristics from earlier views of the ball's trajectory and subsequently use that information to predict more precisely the correct interception point.

Similar research on children's viewing time of trajectory information is limited. In one of the earliest studies of the issue, Williams (1968) had children ages six through twelve perform a task in which they could see only the initial portion of a ball's flight before it disappeared and they were to move to the site where they would predict the ball was to land. The youngest children, 6, 7, and 8 years of age, responded quickly but overshot the target point by 22 ft. The 9- and 10-year-olds were more accurate but slow to respond, arriving at the landing point too late to have intercepted the ball. By 12 years of age, children were both quick and accurate in their responses. Williams (1968) concluded that younger children do not know when to use visual information. If it comes early in flight, the young children use it immediately. Later, Williams (1973) would suggest that younger children need more time to view an object than older children who can gather the necessary information more quickly or can get by with less. A study by Wade (1980) offers support for this position. In this study, children ages

7 to 14 years pushed an aluminum doughnut down a steel rod to intercept a moving target. When one-third of the trackway was occluded from view, smaller errors were made than if two-thirds of the trackway was blocked. Similar results were found in a study of 6- to 19-year-olds who were required to intercept a moving target dot on a screen by moving a slide to control the movements of the dot (Dorfman, 1977). On one-third of the trials, the target dot was blocked after 90 ms, giving the subjects only a brief initial view of the dot's speed and direction. The subjects then had to intercept the target without further visual reference. Again the younger children had a relatively greater increase in absolute error.

To date, the extant research would seem to suggest that children have difficulty when trajectory information is occluded for part of the time. But as Fischman and Schneider (1985) suggested, for inexperienced catchers occluding the last third of the trajectory can be the most detrimental. Since trajectory segments were not systematically varied in the developmental studies, it is not clear whether it is the time of occlusion or the specific segment occluded that is important developmentally. Indeed, for the most part, these studies have occluded the last segments of the flight trajectory. Perhaps it is the middle or earlier segments that are most important to the child's performance. It was the purpose of this study, therefore, to examine the effect of occluding specific segments of trajectory information on catching performance.

In addition, we sought a better understanding of the nature of trajectory information on catching. To do this, we adopted an analysis strategy first developed by Alderson and his colleagues (Alderson, 1974; Alderson, Sully, & Sully, 1974). In their work, one-handed catching was described as having an orientation and a flexion phase that are controlled by information from different segments of the ball's trajectory. In the orientation or *positioning* phase, the arm and hand are first moved grossly into position based on early flight information. A finer orientation occurs as the hand rotates, the wrist extends, and fingers differentiate. These finer orientations are based on later flight information. The flexion or *grasp* phase of the catch begins as the fingers close for the grasp. Alderson et al. determined that the grasp phase takes about 40 ms, whereas the grip takes about 25–30 ms.

Using this analysis scheme, Alderson (1974) described the one-handed catching performance of children 7, 10, and 11 years of age. Alderson found that it was the grasp that was the most difficult for the younger children. They made relatively few orientation errors. These younger children achieved 77% success in contacting the ball with the hand, 61% of the time contacting the ball within 1 in. of the optimum contact area. In comparison, the actual percentage of balls caught for this age group was only 7%. Clearly the children were moving their hand to contact the ball (77% contact), but as the 7% success rate catches would indicate, they were unable to make the necessary grasp to secure the ball. This may be related to the late initiation of flexion, for while the 7-year-olds had a flexion time similar to that of the older children, they initiated this phase 10 to 15 ms later than the older children. The younger children appeared to have difficulty getting flexion to coincide with the motion of the ball.

While Alderson was able to demonstrate the part of the catching action that was the most problematic for the young child, the work did not include a study of the effect of trajectory information on these phases of the catch. In the present study, then, we examined not only the effect of occluding selected portions of the trajectory on catching in children, but we specifically examined the effect of this occlusion on the grasp and positioning phases of one-hand catching.

METHODS

Subjects

Two groups of 15 right-handed males aged 7 ($M = 7.3$ years; SD in years = 0.25) and 9 years ($M = 9.3$ years; $SD = 0.26$) participated in this experiment. These two age groups were selected for study based on previous research in the literature and our pilot work. Both suggested to us that these two age groups were representative of: (1) a group that had just begun to be successful in one-handed catching (the 7-year-olds), and (2) a group that was improving its performance such that it was successful in catching the ball over half the time (9-year-olds). A third group of 15 right-handed male adults ($M = 22.2$ years; $SD = 1.92$) also took part and represented a group that presumably had mastered one-handed catching.

Children were recruited from a parochial school in the College Park community of Maryland; the adults were students at the University of Maryland, College Park. Two 7-year-old subjects were dropped and replaced due to their inability to make hand contact with the ball in 8 of 10 baseline trials.

Apparatus

A catapult was constructed to throw the balls to subjects. The catapult was constructed from PVC pipe and mounted on a wooden platform. Its dimensions were 22 in. in height, 21 in. in length, and 9 in. in width. A release handle, 26-½ in. in length, insured that ball projection was consistent over time and distance throughout all trials. A rubber band (no. 107) provided the tension on the handle and when released permitted the throwing arm to pivot freely over an arc of 50 degrees. Action of the catapult's arm was stopped by striking a rubber band that was positioned across its path. The rubber band was secured in place on hooks 4 in. from the back of the catapult.

In order to maintain the same arc for adults as for children, the ball thrower was placed on a table 24 in. in height. Total flight time of the ball was determined to be 0.96 sec. Initial horizontal velocity was 48.3 ft/sec, initial vertical velocity was 24.0 ft/sec. The screening device to occlude segments of ball flight consisted of a wooden frame 92 in. in height and 40 in. in width and an adjustable cloth screen measuring 40 in. long and 36 in. wide. The cloth screen was dark blue canvas with blackout cloth attached to the other side for an opaque effect. The subject viewed the blue side of the cloth. Wooden rods were fitted into both the top and bottom edges of the screen in order to suspend it from the hooks in the framework. The location of the screen could be adjusted on the wooden frame according to the segment occluded, first (O_1), middle (O_2), or last (O_3), as well as to the subject's height. Screen position for occlusion of ball flight was calculated by a computer program that used the ball's flight trajectory and the subject's eye height. Sponge balls with a hard rubber center under the commercial name of "Dwight Gooden Baseball" were utilized for all testing. A video camera mounted on a tripod was positioned facing the subject so that subject's hand movements could be recorded.

Task and Procedure

Subjects were randomly selected from their daily physical education classes. Handedness was verified at the start of testing by tossing a ball to the subject. Date of birth, height, and ball experience also were obtained prior to testing. To identify from the videotape where the ball contacted the hand, a large black dot was placed on the thenar and hypothenar eminence and at the base of the second and fifth digit.

Subjects were told that they would be videotaped catching balls with one hand in a standing position. Before the trials began, each subject was given the opportunity to handle the ball. Pilot work had indicated that the opportunity to handle the ball alleviated the child's anxiety about catching the projected object. All subjects received 3 practice trials without the screen to familiarize them with the task. Since the task was of high interest, incentive to participate was not necessary. Verbal reinforcement ("very good, name") was given by the experimenter after every five (5) trials, regardless of success on that trial.

The video camera was operated by an assistant who was instructed not to interact with subjects. After every five trials a break was taken to change the position of the screen. After the three practice trials, five baseline trials were conducted with no screen in position. After an interval 35 s, five more baseline trials were administered. Baseline trials served to eliminate those subjects unable to make hand contact on a minimum of eight balls. For subsequent trials the screen device was positioned to occlude the first (O_1), middle (O_2), or last (O_3) segment of ball flight. Screen position was randomly ordered for each set of five trials (total of ten per position).

Data Analysis

The dependent measures for this study were the mean scores for position and grasp performance in each condition (baseline—B, O_1, O_2, O_3). These performance scores were obtained from analysis of the videotape. A rating system was established in which hand position performance was scored as 1, 2, or 3. A score of 1 was given if the subject totally failed to make ball contact. If a ball contacted the peripheral area of the hand and it was deflected rather than reversed, it was scored as a 2. Relevant parts of the hand for this error were above distal phalangeal joints, base of palm below thumb, and extreme sides of hand. Contacts with metacarpophalangeal pads of palm area were scored as a 3. The second performance score was derived for grasp action. Again these errors were categorized into three groups. No grasping action was scored as a 1; movement of fingers with a failure to grip was as scored as a 2. A ball securely held was scored as a 3 (i.e., a successful catch).

All videotapes were reviewed and scored by two independent raters. These raters were given instructions on scoring and practiced until they understood the scoring system. The inter-rater reliability calculated between the independent scoring of the trials was 0.987.

Statistical Design

The mean hand position and grasp scores were analyzed separately using a multivariate approach to the analysis of variance. The design was an age (3) x condition (4) with repeated measures on the second factor. Post hoc analyses were carried out using the Newman-Keul's procedures. Alpha level was set at .05.

RESULTS

Table 1 summarizes the results in terms of the percentage of contacted balls, either all contacts or optimal contacts (in parentheses) and the percentage of grasped balls (i.e., a caught ball). As shown in Table 1, 7-year-olds caught only 22% of the balls under the baseline condition, while the 9-year-olds caught 55% and the adults caught all the balls. The percentage of contacted balls when *any* contact was considered was quite high for all groups under all conditions (ranging from 89% to 100%). However when the contacts were examined for their optimality (i.e., in the palm area), the percentage dropped markedly for the 7-year-olds (e.g., in the baseline fom 91% to 56%), but only slightly (11%) for the 9-year-olds.

Mean scores for the two performance scores for all conditions and groups are displayed in Figures 1 and 2.

Table 1
Percent Contact, Optimal Contact (in parentheses), and Caught by Age Group and Occluded Trajectory Segment

Age	Baseline	O_1	O_2	O_3
	Contact			
7 years	91 (56)	91 (69)	96 (70)	89 (52)
9 years	97 (86)	99 (96)	98 (87)	98 (87)
Adults	100	100	100	100
	Caught			
7 years	22	29	27	16
9 years	55	60	56	64
Adults	100	100	100	100

Hand Positioning

The results of the multivariate approach to the analysis of variance with repeated measures for the mean hand position scores revealed main effects for age [$F (2,42) = 23.1, p < .0001$], condition [Hotelling's $T^2 = 16.2, F (3,40) = 5.1, p < .0043$], and the age by condition interaction [Wilk's Lambda $= .704, F (6,80) = 2.56, p < .0254$]. Results of the Newman-Keul's post hoc analysis indicated that adults and 9-year-olds were significantly better than 7-year-olds (in each condition) but not from each other in any condition (see Figure 1). For 7-year-olds, conditions O_1 and O_2 in which the first and middle segments of the balls trajectory were occluded did not differ from each other in hand positioning

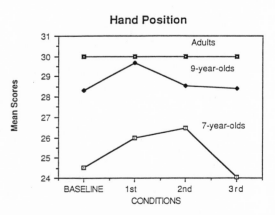

FIG. 1. Mean performance scores for hand positioning of the three age groups in the baseline and three occlusion conditions.

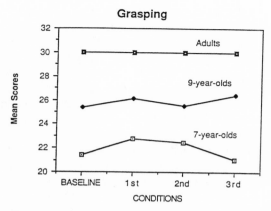

FIG. 2. Mean performance scores for grasp phase of the three age groups in the baseline and three occlusion conditions.

however, they were significantly better than the baseline and O_3 condition. The baseline and O_3 did not differ from each other.

Grasp

The multivariate approach to the analysis of variance with repeated measures of the mean grasp scores revealed a significant main effect for age [F (2,42) = 62.79, $p > .0001$] and an age by condition interaction [Wilk's Lambda = .669, F (6,80) = 3.01, $p > .0106$). The results of the post hoc analysis indicated that adults were significantly better than both 7- and 9-year-olds in all conditions. Furthermore, 9-year-olds were significantly better than the 7-year-olds in all conditions. The effect of occluding vision had no effect on the performance of the 9-year-olds or adults. However, the 7-year-olds had poorer grasp performance when the last segment (O_3) of the ball flight was occluded than under O_1 and O_2. However, occluding the last segment (O_3) did not differ from the baseline.

DISCUSSION

Previous research on object interception skills has consistently found young children to be less proficient than older children and adults. It was not surprising then to find in the present experiment that 7-year-olds could catch one-handed only 22% of the balls while the 9-year-olds caught 55% and the adults all of the balls. While previous speculation had focused on the amount of time available to see the projected object, the present experiment sought to answer the question of whether visually occluding portions of the ball's trajectory affected children and adults' hand positioning and grasping in one-handed catching differentially.

Examining the effects on hand positioning first, it is clear that occlusion did have an effect on the youngest children's performance. However, this effect was limited to the last segment of the ball's trajectory. Indeed, occluding the last segment (O_3) nearest ball contact was more detrimental to the 7-year-olds than occluding the first or middle segments, suggesting that this group was still using trajectory information close to ball contact to position the hand. A similar trend was not seen in either the adults or 9-year-olds.

Surprisingly, the baseline and O_3 did not differ. The finding that under full view of the ball flight (i.e., baseline) hand positioning was affected adversely in the 7-year-old group may have been due to one of at least two causes, neither of which can be excluded in the present design. The first cause could be attributed to a practice effect. All baseline trials were given before the occluding trials. Although three practice trials were administered before the start of the baseline trials, it is possible that the 7-year-olds required more practice. The other possible cause for the baseline performance may be attentional differences. Two possibilities exist here. First, the baseline trials may not have been as attention demanding as the occlusion trials. The 7-year-olds then may not have been attending as much under the full-view condition. However, when part of the trajectory was occluded, they were forced to attend more. The other possibility is that the openness of the full-view condition was distracting.

Further study, of course, is necessary to clarify the baseline differences found. However, while the 7-year-olds' performance on the baseline was not anticipated, it should not be overlooked that hand-position performance under O_3 was significantly different from O_1 and O_2—a trend that was not observed in either the adults or 9-year-olds.

Results for the grasp phase also revealed a similar trend for the 7-year-olds. Here again the grasp phase was affected adversely by the occlusion of the segment closest to ball contact (O_3), and again the baseline performance was as poor as the performance under O_3. The finding that the O_3 was again detrimental to the 7-year-olds was not altogether surprising. If one does not get the hand in the proper position for the catch, then the grasp phase can hardly be effective. The finding here again that the baseline performance was poorer than performance under the O_1 and O_2 probably reflects the poor performance on hand positioning. As discussed earlier, however, the causes of the baseline performance remain unclear.

Results for the grasp phase differed from those found for the position phase for the 9-year-olds. While no differences had been observed between the positioning scores of the 9-year-olds and adults, in the grasp phase there was a difference across all conditions (Fig. 2). This might have been expected, since the 9-year-olds were only successful in catching the ball on 55% of the trials compared to 100% for the adults. Since there were no differences between the 9-year-olds and adults for hand positioning, the differences in catching success would seem to be attributable to the grasp phase. Developmentally, these results might suggest that the proximal control system is emerging first and that the distal control system appears later (Brinkman & Kuypers, 1972).

In conclusion, we have shown that it may not be time per se that is an important determinant of developmental differences in catching. Rather, it seems that the last segment of an object's trajectory is particularly important to the young child of 7 years. Like the novices in Fischman and Schneider's study (1985), occluding the last segment of the ball's flight adversely affects catching performance. For our 7-year-olds, this was evident in both the positioning and grasping phases of this age group's one-handed catch. Why this segment of the ball's flight is critical to this age group is not clear from this experiment. Work on adults, however, would suggest that it is in this latter phase that the final hand adjustments are made both spatially and temporally (Schneider & Fischman, 1985). The less experienced catcher is unable to use early flight information to predict final hand position and proper timing of the grasp. From the percent of contact data (see Table 1), it is clear that the early flight information can be used by the 7-year-old to get the hand in the "contact" region. Using this information for optimal contact and grasping, however, seems poorly developed in the young child. While this experiment has not provided an answer as to why 7-year-olds need to see the last third of the ball's trajectory, this experiment has identified this segment of the flight as an important source of developmental differences. Our future research, then, should be directed to understanding the developmental changes in the use of this later trajectory information in catching.

REFERENCES

Alderson, G. J. K. (1974). *The development of motion prediction ability in the context of sports skills.* Unpublished dissertation, University of Leeds, England.

Alderson, G. J. K., Sully, D. J., & Sully, H. G. (1974). An operational analysis of a one-handed catching task using high speed photography. *Journal of Motor Behavior, 6,* 217–226.

Bahill, A. T., & McDonald, J. D. (1982). Zero-latency tracking of baseballs and other targets. *Investigative Ophthalmology and Visual Science, 22* (Supplement of abstracts), 265.

Bahill, A. T., & LaRitz, T. (1984). Why can't batters keep their eyes on the ball? *American Scientist, 72,* 249–253.

Brinkman, J., & Kuypers, H. G. J. M. (1972). Splitbrain monkeys: Cerebral control of ipsilateral and contralateral arm, hand, and finger movements. *Science, 176,* 536–538.

Carlton, L. G. (1981). Processing visual feedback information for movement control. *Journal of Experimental Psychology: Human Perception and Performance, 7,* 1019–1030.

DeLucia, P. R., & Cochran, E. L. (1985). Perceptual information for batting can be extracted throughout a ball's trajectory. *Perceptual and Motor Skills, 61,* 143–150.

Dorfman, P. W. (1977). Timing and anticipation: A developmental perspective. *Journal of Motor Behavior, 9,* 67–79.

Du Randt, R. (1985). Ball-catching proficiency among 4-, 6-, and 8-year-old girls. In J. E. Clark and J. H. Humphrey (Eds.), *Motor development: Current selected research: Vol. 1* (pp. 35–43). Princeton, NJ: Princeton Books.

Fischman, M. G., & Schneider, T. (1985). Skill level, vision, and proprioception in simple one-hand catching. *Journal of Motor Behavior, 17,* 219–229.

Kay, H. (1957). Information theory in the understanding of skills. *Occupational Psychology, 31,* 218–224.

Sharp, R. H., & Whiting, H. T. A. (1974). Exposure and occluded duration effects in a ball-catching skill. *Journal of Motor Behavior, 6,* 139–147.

Wade, M. G. (1980). Coincidence anticipation of young normal and handicapped children. *Journal of Motor Behavior, 12,* 103–112.

Whiting, H. T. A., Gill, E. B., & Stephenson, J. M. (1970). Critical time intervals for taking in flight information in a ball-catching task. *Ergonomics, 13,* 265–272.

Whiting, H. T. A., & Sharp, R. H. (1974). Visual occlusion factors in a discrete ball-catching task. *Journal of Motor Behavior, 6,* 11–16.

Williams, H. (1968). *Effects of the systematic variation of speed and direction of object flight and of age and skill classifications on visuo-perceptual judgments of moving objects in three-dimensional space.* Unpublished doctoral dissertation, Unversity of Wisconsin, Madison.

Williams, H. (1973). Perceptual-motor development in children. In C. Corbin (Ed.), *A textbook of motor development* (pp. 111–150). Dubuque, IA: William C. Brown.

AUTHOR NOTE:

This work was conducted in partial fulfillment of the requirements for the masters degree of the first author under the supervision of the second author. We are grateful to our subjects, who all gave willingly of their time. Special thanks to Michael O'Connor, Tom France, John Winkam, and Drs. Haller and Shaffer for their assistance in the design and construction of the ball-throwing apparatus. Also, special appreciation is extended to Jill Whitall and Ann Lanphear for their thoughtful comments and helpful criticisms at all stages of this research.

Computer time for this research was supported in full through the facilities of the Computer Science Center of the University of Maryland, College Park.

Reprints may be obtained from J. E. Clark, Department of Physical Education, University of Maryland, College Park, MD 20742.

7

THE SIGNIFICANCE AND DEVELOPMENT OF CRAWLING IN HUMAN INFANCY

Janette B. Benson

ABSTRACT

The emergence of self-produced locomotor-skills (i.e., creeping and crawling) is examined in light of its proposed significance as a mediator of spatial, cognitive and perceptual development in human infancy. A selective review of the early literature on motor development in infancy is presented, followed by a discussion of why previously proposed relations between motor and intellectual development in infancy were not supported. Recent advances in developmental psychology and the movement sciences have rekindled interest in these issues. As a consequence, researchers are now in a better position to develop new research strategies to document the link between motor and intellectual development. Some new research strategies are presented, and a research program is described that seeks to better understand both the processes underlying the acquisition of self-produced locomotion and the relations between locomotor and intellectual development in infancy.

During the course of the first year of life, the human infant acquires a remarkable number of motor skills. These include, but are not limited to, controlling the head, grasping, reaching, sitting, crawling, standing, and walking. These developmental motor milestones are fundamental to development during the first year of life, yet we know very little about how these skills are acquired and the role that these skills may play in mediating intellectual and social development. Early researchers of motor development attempted to study these skills, but usually with one of the following aims in mind: (1) to chart developmental motor milestones to indicate the normative ages at which each motor milestone was achieved (Ames, 1937; Bayley, 1935; Gesell, 1928; Trettien, 1900); (2) to propose biological and neural processes underlying motor development in infancy (Gesell, 1939; 1945; McGraw, 1935, 1943); (3) to conduct detailed empirical observations of the emergence of motor skills in infancy (Ames, 1937; Burnside, 1927); (4) to examine the influences of maturation and experience on locomotor development (Gesell & Thompson, 1929, 1941; McGraw, 1935); or (5) to link rates of motor development directly to rates of intellectual development (Bayley, 1935, 1949). Recently there is renewed interest in several of these issues, and new attention is being paid to the processes that underlie the acquisition and mastery of motor skills in infancy (Benson, 1987b; Thelen, 1985; Thelen & Fogel, in press; Thelen, Kelso, & Fogel, 1987) and how the onset of such skills may be related to intellectual as well as social development (Benson, 1987a; Bertenthal, Campos, & Barrett, 1984).

Movement is so fundamental to all living beings that it pervades almost every aspect of functioning. As mobile adults, it is sometimes difficult to imagine what it would be like not to possess mature locomotor skills, or to retrace how a young infant evolves from nonmobility into a creature adept at scaling furniture and staircases. To appreciate the importance of the acquisition of independent, self-produced locomotion, consider what the world might be like for the pre-locomotor infant. Imagine that your infant's only experience with moving around in the world is literally in the hands of someone else. In the early months, infants are either carried or pushed in a stroller from place to place. The prelocomotor infant has virtually no control over where it may be moved at any given time. At one moment the infant may be on the floor with its favorite toy, and the next moment it may be whisked away with no idea of where it will end up next. And, when an infant is moved by someone, there is almost no way it can relate the changes that it sees during movement with its own immediate actions. The kicking of the legs as the baby is wheeled in a stroller has little or no correspondence to changes in the optic flow pattern during movement through the environment.

On the brighter side, young infants are not completely helpless. At about 6 or 7 months of age infants typically gain skill at rolling over and sitting up, and can easily grasp and explore interesting objects—that is, just as long as the desired object is within reach! However, there is still no direct way the baby can physically act on the world that exists beyond the length of its arms.

Soon, all this will change. When an infant first begins to position the knee under the hip and reach ahead with outstretched arms, grasping at a toy or perhaps the floor to pull forward, an achievement begins that has long-lasting and profound consequences. With the acquisition of self-produced locomotion, infants soon learn how to more through space; to correlate changes in their movements with corresponding changes in the visual environment; to use new means to plan and carry out goal-directed actions; and to gain increasing autonomy.

Learning how to crawl is a complex skill that is attained in a dynamic context and is acquired by most human infants throughout the world. The acquisition of independent locomotion has profound social and intellectual consequences; it is an event eagerly awaited by parents, who reward each halting movement. These milestones also are used by parents and pediatricians as signals by which new levels of maturity may be recognized in the developing child. In turn, parents often use the achievement of motor milestones to guide their expectations about the changing capacities of their infant. In addition, the acquisition of gross locomotor skills is often used as an index of normal neurophysiological growth and development, and, as we will see in this chapter, may very well serve to mediate important intellectual and social developmental achievements.

Crawling and creeping are often used interchangeably to describe different types of self-produced locomotion in infancy. To make matters more confusing, the lay usage of creeping and crawling contradicts with the way these terms were defined and used by some of the early motor development researchers. I will follow the convention used by most of the early motor development researchers that will be discussed in this chapter. *Crawling* refers to prone locomotion in which the infant propels itself forward with the movements of its arms and legs while its belly remains in contact with the supporting surface. In contrast, *creeping* will be used to describe the form of prone locomotion in which the infant contacts the supporting surface with its hands and knees and propels itself forward with alternating movements of the hands and knees.

In this paper I will argue that the onset of self-produced locomotor skills (i.e., crawling, walking) plays a significant role in human infancy. The onset of self-produced locomotor skills appears at times of rapid behavioral reorganization, and the onset of these locomotor skills plausibly serves to mediate or promote the unfolding of spatial cognitive and perceptual development. In addition, the processes by which infants acquire these locomotor skills are worthy of study in their own right. An understanding of these processes may teach us much about the general processes of development and may also provide insight into the age-old question of how new forms of behavior emerge and become organized.

I will begin by providing a selective review of the early theoretical and empirical research in motor-skill development in infancy, including the work of those who initially searched for, but did not find, relations between motor development and intellectual development. I will discuss why these relations were not found, and then I will offer a rationale for why these relations between locomotor and intellectual development should exist and the research strategies that are being used today to document these relations. In the process I will speculate about which mechanisms may underlie the importance of crawling and how these mechanisms serve to mediate intellectual development. To conclude, I will describe the research program that I am pursuing in order to better understand both the processes underlying the acquisition of self-produced locomotor skills, and the relation between locomotor and intellectual development.

PRAGMATIC AND THEORETICAL IMPLICATIONS OF SELF-PRODUCED LOCOMOTION

Several rearchers and theorists have implicated the onset of crawling as an important mediator or facilitator of a wide range of psychological functions—as diverse as ego development to spatial cognitive development. Mahler and her colleagues (Mahler, Pine, & Bergman, 1975) proposed that crawling plays an important role in ego development in the separation-individuation process as the young infant uses locomotion to become increasingly more autonomous and independent. Self-produced locomotion is also seen as an important regulator of the emotional relationship betwen the infant and the caregiver (Fraiberg, 1959; Spitz, 1965). This regulatory function is most evident in the attachment of the infant to the caregiver as the infant uses new capacities to explore the environment when secure and to seek the caregiver's proximity when distressed (Ainsworth, Blehar, Waters, & Wall, 1978; Bowlby, 1973). Moreover, the onset of self-produced locomotion appears to be an important regulator of emotional communication with respect to both social referencing (Klinnert, Campos, Sorce, Emde, & Svejda, 1982) and the onset of wariness of heights on the visual cliff (Bertenthal & Campos, 1984; Rader, Bausano, & Richards, 1980).

In addition to its importance for social and emotional development, locomotor experience also has been implicated as an important mediator of intellectual development and perceptual functioning. Active movement experience plays a central role in Piaget's (1952; 1954) theory of the infant's objectification of space, time, and causality. With the same spirit, the early researchers of motor development equated the acquisition of locomotor skills with general intellectual development (Bayley, 1935; Gesell, 1928; McGraw, 1935; Shirley, 1931). Moreover, locomotor experience is a prominent factor in theories of perception as an important element in the detection of information in the visual environment (Gibson, 1979), and for the calibration of distance required for normal depth and distance perception (Kaufman, 1979).

Despite this rich array of proposed relations between self-produced locomotion and behavioral functioning, surprisingly little empirical work has been directed at examining these relations. One exception has been the systematic empirical efforts by Campos and his colleagues (Bertenthal & Campos, 1984; Bertenthal, Campos, & Barrett, 1984; Campos, Hiatt, Ramsey, Henderson, & Svejda, 1978; Campos, Svejda, Campos, & Bertenthal, 1982) and Richards and his colleagues (Richards & Rader, 1981, 1983; Rader, Bausano, & Richards,

1980), who have investigated relations among the onset of self-produced locomotion, the duration and type of self-produced locomotion experience, and wariness of heights and avoidance on the visual cliff.

To put current research in perspective, I will shift to a consideration of the early work on motor development.

EARLY EMPIRICAL INVESTIGATIONS OF LOCOMOTOR DEVELOPMENT

In the developmental psychology literature, most of what is known about the acquisition of infant locomotor skills and relations between these skills and intellectual functioning comes from early empirical investigations conducted between 1920 and 1940. In the follwing section I will highlight some of the studies that exemplify the major research orientations during this period. By necessity, this review will be limited to the research on motor development that was conducted by developmental psychologists who specifically focused on the period of infancy. The important contributions from other related fields, such as pediatrics, physical therapy, neurology, and physical education, and research on the relations between motor development and perceptual and intellectual development in older children and adults will not be discussed as they are beyond the current scope of this chapter.

Catalogues of Developmental Motor Milestones

The first goal of early motor development researchers was to conduct normative studies in order to compile lists of the age norms at which most infants acquired various motor skills. The best-known of these efforts were conducted by Gesell (1928; Gesell & Thompson, 1934) and Bayley (1935). These lists, or to use Gesell's (1928) term "developmental schedules" or McGraw's (1935) term "inventory," were used to chart the timetable of normal motor development. Although these schedules are often still used today by parents, pediatricians, and students of motor development, it is important to remember that these norms were frequently gathered from highly select samples by a wide range of methods.

Gesell (1928) made use of the growing technology of cinematography to produce objective records of the complexities of infant motor behavior. Gesell used these objective recordings to develop descriptive accounts of normal motor development. These descriptive accounts were often highly subjective interpretations, as few techniques existed to objectively measure or quantify the movement sequences that were captured on film. Also, it is not clear whether the norms reported in Gesell's schedules were confirmed by longitudinal observation. In several of Gesell's papers (e.g., Gesell & Thompson, 1934) it is difficult to determine whether cross-sectional and/or longitudinal observations were used to generate the norms for the different motor sequences that were reported. For example, in 1919, Gesell and his associates studied 50 children at each of the following ages: 0, 4, 6, 9, 12, and 18 months and 2, 3, 4, and 5 years (Gesell & Thompson, 1934). In 1927, Gesell and his associates studied

> . . . 15 age levels from 4 weeks through 56 weeks. . . . All told, 107 different infants were studied; 58 girls and 49 boys. Many of these were seen repeatedly; 7 were examined at lunar-age intervals from 4 through 56 weeks. The total number of examinations was 524. An extended cinema record was made of one-third of these examinations; for 82 per cent a partial cinema record was made. . . . (1934, pp. 5–6)

The results from these large studies, generally cross-sectional in nature, were compiled to form the basis of Gesell's developmental schedules. Apparently, cross-sectional data were combined with a small number of longitudinal observations to suggest the existence of intransitive stages of motor development. Nonetheless, Gesell created one of the most popular infant tests by which the development of any individual infant could be compared to a presumably normal schedule of developmemt. Contrary to most reviews of the early motor development literature, these schedules were *not* the first attempts to catalogue motor-skill acquisition.

The first known normative study of locomotor development is credited to Feldman (1833, as cited in Rosenblith & Sims-Knight, 1985), who reported the average ages of walking in a sample of infants. Trettien (1900), in collaboration with G. Stanley Hall at Clark University, compiled data from medical journals, hospital reports, and the return of 182 questionnaires completed by local professionals working with infants who reported their observations in a "topical syllabus" titled "Straightness and Uprightness of Body." Trettien reported the normal range of anthropometric measures (e.g., length of the arms and legs, relative proportion of the parts of the body, circumference of the limbs), as well as descriptions of the various motor skills (e.g., sitting, creeping, rolling, going up and down stairs, standing, walking) and the range of ages when these skills were acquired. Trettien's report was unusual in at least two respects. First, in addition to listing the ages at which motor skills were normally acquired, Trettien was among the first to also discuss anomalies in motor skill development. In a section titled "Reversions," Trettien (1900) wrote, in the typical prose of the day,

> . . . According to the famous riddle of the Sphinx, man shall again surrender his upright posture and turn his face toward the earth from whence he came. We have thus traced his rise, now let us observe some of the causes of his reversion. . . . after children have learned to walk and run, they frequently revert to their early stage of creeping due to some physical or psychic disturbance. . . . (p. 47)

Trettien proceeded to report scattered observations of infants who, after learning to walk took a bad fall or became ill, reverted to creeping until a month or so passed until they once again attempted to walk. Second, Trettien was among the first to speculate about relations between motor activity and intellectual processes by reporting differences in the rates of motor development between normal children and "idiots and imbeciles." Trettien (1900) concluded his report with the following:

> . . . the state of intelligence depends upon mobility in animals in general, whose limbs are used entirely for locomotion, what an advantage is given to man over other creatures. . . . human intelligence, as such, has arisen in direct consequence of man's assuming the upright position, so close is the relation existing between the mental life and muscular movements. . . . (p. 56)

More than two decades would pass before these proposed relations between motor functions and intellectual functions would be more closely scrutinized (Bayley, 1935; Gesell, 1928; McGraw, 1935).

Some early motor development researchers believed they had provided adequate descriptions of the development of locomotor skills with the cataloging of developmental motor milestones. However, the developmental schedules or the inventory approach is often criticized because it only offered descriptions of the onset of discrete, gross motor skills, and gave no insight into the actual processes underlying motor development. This viewpoint was captured by John Dewey in his introductory remarks to Myrtle McGraw's (1935) book, *Growth: A Study of Johnny and Jimmy,* when he wrote,

> . . . The inventory method supplies us with a detailed scheme of cross-sectional achievements. It does not show how the transitions from one stage to another are effected. It marks out mile-stones but does not show the road. . . . (p. x)

In response to this type of criticism, motor development researchers began to move away from the developmental schedules or inventory approach, and to look for underlying mechanisms and processes that guided the acquisition of various motor skills. These efforts followed four parallel paths. One focus was upon the theoretical issues concerned with the sequence of stages of motor development as influenced by neurological and maturational factors (Gesell, 1939; McGraw, 1943). Another focus consisted of the pursuit of empirical evidence to shed light on how motor skills were actually acquired (Ames, 1937; Burnside, 1927; Shinn, 1900; Watson, 1919). At the same time attention was focused to unravel the relative contributions of maturational and hereditary factors from environmental and experiential factors in the emergence of sequential stages of motor development (Dennis & Dennis, 1940; Gesell & Thompson, 1929; McGraw, 1935). And yet another direction was to examine correspondences between motor development and mental development (Bayley, 1935).

Proposed Mechanisms Underlying Motor Development

Along the more theoretical path, both McGraw (1941, 1943) and Gesell (1928, 1954) viewed infant ontogeny in a similar light to the evolution and embryology of the human species. With different emphasis, each proposed that motor skills in infancy emerged during sequential stages that were guided by biological factors. McGraw believed that overt changes in "neuro-motor behavior" (i.e., changes in prone progression or crawling) reflected changes in underlying "neuro-muscular mechanisms" (i.e., increasing differentiation of the cerebral cortex). When McGraw was describing the sequential changes in the patterning of prone and erect locomotion, she also believed that she was gaining insight into the vital nervous-system changes that were occurring as a function of maturation. McGraw's developmental approach was maturational in the sense that her thinking was influenced by the growing field of embryology, and the elegant studies of the day that revealed variation in biological determinism. That is, she believed that there were guiding principles that dictated that the increasing differentiation of neuromuscular mechanisms in early infancy prescribed or determined changes in overt neuromotor behavior. Some of these principles included the inhibiting and facilitating effects of higher and lower cortical centers on motor behavior during infant development.

There is a different sense of maturational determinism in Gesell's writings. Gesell pursued a biological orientation that emphasized the continuous reorganization of existing behavioral forms out of which emerged, in a spiral fashion, more distinct yet complex behavioral forms. Whereas McGraw argued for increasing differentiation in both neuromuscular and neuromotor development, it appears that Gesell argued in favor of increasing integration and reorganization of previously existing structures and functions into new, more advanced motor behaviors. Thelen (1987) has recently made the point that Gesell's framework appears as a precursor of modern dynamical systems approaches to motor development, whereas McGraw's approach is characterized by a reductionist belief that biological organization is under the guidance of "a central directing agency."

Gesell belived that motor development was endogenous to biology and thus was not entirely contingent upon exogenous influences or experiences. The emergence of intransitive, sequential stages of motor behavior is a logical consequence of both McGraw's and Gesell's maturational emphasis. For example, building upon Sherrington's (1906) notion of reciprocal innervation to describe functional relations in patterns of muscle excitation, Gesell (1939, 1954) suggested the term "reciprocal interweaving," and offered it as one of several processes underlying motor development. For Gesell (1954), the observable changes in the patterning of motor behavior had to be closely linked with structural changes in physical growth and maturation; he wrote,

> . . . In as much as behavior patterning and structural growth are intimately correlated, we shall describe this developmental principle as a reciprocal interweaving process. . . . Neurologically, this process implies an intricate cross-stitching or involuted interlacing which organizes opposing muscle systems into reciprocal and increasingly mature relationships. Functionally, such a

process results in a progressive spiral kind of reincorporation of sequential forms of behavior. . . . (p. 342)

Gesell used this principle to suggest that motor development proceeds along a series of invariant, sequential stages. In the case of locomotor development, Gesell and Ames (1940) identified "twenty-three" separate stages in the "patterning of prone progression" (or self-produced locomotion) from one week of age until 60 weeks, when walking was acquired. Gesell (1954) described these stages in the following manner.

. . . None of these stages or patterns can be dismissed as being merely recapitulatory or vestigial. Each stage, however transient, appears to be a necessary feature of developmental mechanics, because of the numerous motor relationships which must be coordinated, that is reciprocally interwoven. . . . (pp. 432–345)

Although Gesell cautioned that many of these stages were transient, he often relied mostly upon cross-sectional data to support his intransitive-stage conception. As we will see next, those motor development researchers who conducted longitudinal investigations of the process of locomotor development actually found that there was considerable variability in the acquisition of Gesell's or similar intransitive-stage theories of motor development (Burnside, 1927; McGraw, 1935). Despite these findings, some researchers persisted in their belief of universal, intransitive stages of motor development (e.g., Ames, 1937). In contrast to Gesell, Shirley's (1931) research showed that there could be both intransivity and variability in the sequencing of motor skills. Shirley outlined major stages of motor development that were sequential and intransitive, but within these major stages of development there were substages within which the sequence of motor skills could vary from child to child. However, neither Shirley's alternative conception nor a growing number of studies that highlighted irregularities in motor development would deter the leading motor development researchers from the conviction that motor development proceeded in a universal, intransitive, and sequential fashion.

Empirical Studies of the Emergence of Locomotor Processes

In contrast to the goal of conducting normative studies to compile catelogues of *when* discrete stages of motor development appeared, some researchers sought to describe *how* various motor skills are acquired by detailed analysis of behavioral sequences. Most of these efforts consisted of painstaking descriptions of the various limb and torso movements made by infants as they acquired locomotion. For example, Shinn (1900), one of the best-known baby-biographers of the day, included very detailed entries that describe the sequence of how her niece acquired creeping and crawling skills. The leading learning theorist of the day, John B. Watson (1919), made observations on how four infants learned to move their limbs so as to creep or crawl. Watson and his associates (Jones, 1926; Watson & Watson, 1921) even attempted to apply principles from the growing field of behaviorism to train or teach various motor skills to infants. Given what we have subsequently learned about relations between maturation and learning, it is not surprising that Watson's attempts were unsuccessful.

In sharp contrast, Burnside (1927) attempted a longitudinal study of the same infants throughout their acquisition of prone locomotion by using both qualitative, subjective descriptions and quantitative, objective measures. Burnside, armed with a Bell & Howell Filmo Automatic Cine camera, attempted to film the locomotor development of the same nine infants over the course of a year. The qualitative descriptions were made by only one observer and are interpretive of how the observer thought each baby was controlling its limbs during movement. The more objective and quantitative measures were derived from tracings made from the cinema records. Burnside (1927) succinctly describes a common dilemma of the developmental researcher that has withstood the test of time:

> . . . an effort was made to have each child for re-photographing at successive intervals of not more than a month. This proved to be impossible. . . . Anyone who has worked with babies knows the difficulties to be encountered in such a situation. . . . (p. 297)

Nevertheless, Burnside was able to photograph a few repeated attempts at locomotion made by a small number of infants. Incidently, Burnside also filmed the quadrupedal movements of an English bulldog, a mongrel cat, an adult, and an adolescent to serve as a basis of comparison for the infant movement patterns. Burnside is also credited (by Ames, 1937) as the first one to clearly distinguish between crawling—"progression in which the abdomen is in contact with the supporting surface while the body is pulled along by the arms only, with the legs dragging"—and creeping—"progression in which the trunk is carried free above the floor" (1937, p. 338). Although this distinction is counter intuitive to the lay usage of these terms, it was typically used in the early motor development literature (for an exception see McGraw, 1941), and it is the convention followed in this chapter.

Burnside was inventive in her methods of analysis. She viewed her films repeatedly, at various speeds, so that a detailed narrative description of each infant's particular pattern of limb movements could be made. Then each frame of film was projected so that outlines of the changes in the infants' bodily forms could be drawn by hand so as to illustrate changes in limb positioning during forward locomotion. Moreover, attempts were made to record quantitative measures such as the speed and sequencing of the limbs as the infants moved.

Despite these attempts to collect quantitative measures of infant locomotion, Burnside's analysis rested heavily upon the qualitative descriptions that accompanied the drawn outlines of the changes in interlimb position during locomotion. From these data, a wide range of variability among individuals in the acquisition of locomotion was reported. Burnside concluded that there was little evidence to suggest that infants progress through a series of intransitive stages of motor development. She wrote, "The variations on locomotion are so great that an exact idea of them can scarcely be given except by describing the mode of progression adopted by each . . ." (1927, pp. 300–301).

In contrast, Ames (1937), one of Gesell's students at Yale, reported longitudinal data that she interpreted as support for the existence of 14 intransitive stages of prone progression. This interpretation will be challenged below. Using photographic techniques that were similar to those described by Burnside, Ames photographed the locomotor attempts made by 5 babies at monthly intervals. Data from 15 supplemental subjects were also analyzed, but 11 of these infants were observed biweekly and were not photographed. Ames charted each stage of prone progression by the age at which the behavior typifying each particular stage was first observed for each infant. Although behavior from several sequential but different stages was reported to have been observed during the same monthly observation, Ames did not comment on how one could know whether these behaviors appeared sequentially, nonsequentially, or simultaneously. Assuming that these stagelike behaviors did occur sequentially, only 8 of the 20 infants in her sample showed all 14 sequential stages of prone progression. Of the remaining 12 infants, 11 skipped one or two stages, and one infant skipped more than two stages. These findings do not offer clear support for the intransitive motor stage hypothesis. Nevertheless, Ames concluded that these data show ". . . a nearly complete and universal form from child to child and from one environment to another . . ." (1937, p. 456). In passing, Ames suggested that the skipped stages reflect incomplete data rather than the absence of an intransitive sequence. It is ironic that data from Gesell's very own lab did not offer clear support for the intransitive motor-stage hypothesis.

On an interesting methodological note, Ames, compared with Burnside, more closely examined timing relations among limb movements and even compared limb movement durations over repeated longitudinal observations. Ames reported that the timing relations among the duration of the movement of each limb varied little from the first observation when compared with each sequential observation. Echoing the strong maturational bias that was held by many motor development researchers, Ames concluded,

> . . . the basic patterns of progression are the result of internal maturational factors rather than the products of practice. When a new and complex pattern appears for the first time in a form so complete that several weeks, possibly several months, of exercise of that pattern do not appreciably change its form or its speed, we must conclude that it occurs because of internal mechanisms rather than as the result of practice (or the chaining of independent reflex abilities). . . . (1937, p. 445)

At this point in motor development research, there existed several descriptive studies, catalogues of motor milestones, and a prevalent maturational point of view that suggested several biological principles that might underlie motor processes. Given the prevalence of maturation as the model of intransitive motor development processes, but inconsistent or at best weak supporting data, a group of motor development researchers were also interested in the nature-nurture controversy, and sought to examine the relative contributions from internal (maturational) and external (environmental) influences. The co-twin control method seemed to be the ideal context for these researchers to test the assertion that maturational factors were more influential in guiding development than were experiential factors.

Maturational and Experiential Influences on Motor Development

As another focus, early motor development researchers studied maturational and experiential factors (e.g., Dennis & Dennis, 1940; Gesell & Thompson, 1929; McGraw, 1935). With a strong bias toward the maturational viewpoint, several of the early motor development researchers jumped feet first into the torrid nature-nurture debate by conducting co-twin control studies. This method, presumably permitted developmentalists to test the influence of maturation and experience on behavior by training one identical twin and then comparing the performance of the trained twin with that of a control twin who received no such training. The logic of this approach is to vary specific training experience while biological maturation is held constant.

Gesell and Thompson (1929) conducted one of the first co-twin control studies with the observation of just one twin pair. First, using the physical criteria of the day to determine zygosity, Gesell and Thompson reported a wide range of comparisons of anthropometric and behavioral data to indicate that the twin pair under study was identical. This was a necessary first step to insure the twins were identical since biological tests of zygosity were not available at this time. In addition to describing physcial identity, it was also necessary to insure that the environmental conditions of each twin were similar. To this end, the environmental conditions of the twins was carefully described. The twins were orphaned and lived together in a "Nursery Home." It is carefully noted that two weeks before the training began, each twin contracted an intestinal infection that resulted in hospital isolation. The twins were isolated from each other for two weeks, after which the designated "training" twin began the six-week training period. The control twin, however, remained isolated with the infection for an additional five weeks. Although the protracted isolation of the control twin introduced various methodological confounds, Gesell and Thompson argued that this isolation tended to more heavily weight the training experience in the training twin's favor.

When the twins were 46 weeks of age, one was trained daily for a 20-min session for a period of 6 weeks. Ten minutes of this training session were devoted exclusively to the "stimulation and guidance" of the following locomotor activities: (1) stair climbing; (2) creeping for a desired object; (3) pulling to stand; (4) walking while holding on to a chair or the crib; and (5) walking while holding the experimenter's hand. During these training sessions the twin's behavior was recorded on film, and Gesell, acting as the sole observer, dictated aloud to a stenographer, in great detail, everything that the twin was observed to be doing. At the end of the 6-week training period, Gesell and Thompson decided to expose the control twin to the daily training sessions, but only for a 2-week training period, in order to determine the "trainability" (at an advanced age) of the control twin.

All observational records—in pretraining, during training, and in posttraining—for each infant were tallied and compared. Although both twins were reported to be comparable in the development of postural and locomotor behavior from birth to the time of the beginning of the training at about 46 weeks of age, the control twin was superior to the training twin in the *acquisition* of stair climbing skills. That is, when the training sessions began at about 46 weeks of age for the training twin, she was not able to climb the stairs until the fourth session, and did not show "peak performance" on the stair-climbing task until the 25th session, or when she was 52 weeks of age and had 6 weeks of practice. The control twin was able to climb the stairs successfully during the first session at the age of 52 weeks without previous stair-climbing experience, and showed "peak performance" during her 9th training session, at about 55 weeks of age. Therefore, the two weeks of practice given to the control twin brought her to a level of skill at 55 weeks of age that was far superior to the training twin at 52 weeks of age after six weeks of practice. Gesell and Thompson (1929) concluded that an advantage of just three weeks in maturity of age was the factor that could account for the control twin's superior skill. The training twin, however, did begin independent walking two weeks prior to the control twin. From various comparisons of the onset, duration of training, and rate of stair-climbing skill acquisition and ability, Gesell and Thompson concluded that "Training does not transcend maturation . . ." (1929, p. 75).

A close reading of Gesell and Thompson's (1929) report yields some contradictions concerning the degree of similarity between the twins. Given the logic of the co-twin control method, these contradictions pose problems in interpreting Gesell and Thompson's findings. For example,

> In addition to her slight advantage in weight, T appeared also to be more active soon after birth than C. (1929, p. 8)
> The general distribution of ratings, however, supports the clinical judgment that Twin T showed a slight though inconstant superiority over C. . . . (1929, p. 31)

Nonetheless, Gesell and Thompson insisted that the twins were truly identical and the logic of the co-twin control method was valid:

In summary, the evidences of physical correspondence are thoroughgoing. Although one cannot draw exact inferences relating to the development of behavior from such correspondence, this physical similarity suggests, at least, that there was no underlying anatomic, orthopedic, or biological advantage to favor the development of locomotor or prehensory abilities in either twin. . . . (1929, p. 26)

However, in a later report that summarized the twins from infancy to adolescence, Gesell and Thompson (1941) appear to contradict themselves.

Both in the execution of patterned movement and in general motor demeanor there is a consistent difference mostly in favor of Twin T. This difference is detectable by acute observation and by minute time-space measurements. T has been posturally more alert since infancy. . . . (1941, p. 40)

Despite these critical differences, Gesell and Thompson (1941) continued to argue for the validity of the co-twin control method, and to promote their general conclusions regarding the dominance of maturational processes in motor development. They reconciled differences in the twins by resorting to discussions of "ontogenetic timing" and "physiological tempo," while claiming that it is these organismic factors, and not environmental influences per se, that direct development as well as individual variation. Again, the extent to which some early motor development researchers held to the maturational point of view in the face of nonconvergent evidence is striking.

McGraw's co-twin control study differed from Gesell's in several ways. McGraw (1935) undertook her well-known co-twin control study of Johnny and Jimmy with two clear goals: (a) to conduct a longitudinal study of the growth of particular behavior-patterns, i.e., creeping or walking; and (b) to evaluate the influence of external factors, i.e., exercise, on the modifiability of the growth of a particular behavior-pattern. McGraw not only compared the trained twin to the control as did Gesell, but also compared the trained twin to a sample of 68 different infants. Unlike Gesell's hard-line stance on the dominant influence of maturation, McGraw suggested a precursor of the critical-period hypothesis that would receive attention several years later—that there were early periods in development when the influence of external factors would be greatest, but after these periods, external influences would have little effect on development.

When faced with the initial problems of determining the zygosity of the her twin subjects, McGraw keenly observed that Jimmy appeared better developed at birth than Johnny. Although she had other criteria to suggest that the twins were identical, McGraw wisely selected Johnny to be the twin that would receive special exercise and training. It is not widely known that several years later McGraw confirmed her growing suspicion that the twins were not identical. Indeed, as the twins grew, she learned that Johnny and Jimmy were not identical twins, but instead were fraternal twins (*Scientific American, 1987*)!

In her co-twin control study, McGraw (1935) wisely distinguished between what she called "phylogenetic activities," those which function in the development of the species and are indispensible to development, and "ontogenetic activities," those activities which an individual may or may not acquire. Unlike Gesell, who did not make this distinction, McGraw studied the different effects exercise would have on these two types of motor activities. As for the effects of exercise on the phylogenetic activities of crawling and creeping, McGraw concludes,

> The comparative development of these infants in relation to each other and to the larger group indicates that in general the somatic aspect of the behavior-patterns discussed . . . was not materially influenced by exercise of the performance during postnatal development. However, even from the earliest, more extensive experience appeared to develop a more acquiescent attitude. In some instances the attitude determined the persistence or duration of a particular somatic pattern though it did not alter the essential sequential phases observed in the growth of a behavior-pattern. (1935, p. 118)

McGraw also suggested that the effects of external influences on development would be susceptible to the duration of the gap in which phylogenetic activities, first seen as rudimentary activities (e.g., the stepping reflex) that are controlled by infracortical centers, are later replaced by performance activities (e.g., walking) that are controlled by higher cortical centers. McGraw also reported that "Ontogenetic behavior-patterns are subject to far greater modifiability by repetition of the performance than are activities of phylogenetic origin" (1935, p. 191).

Many of McGraw's findings have been glossed over and equated with those of Gesell. Even today, it is widely believed that both Gesell and McGraw found similar evidence to suggest that the control twin acquired various motor skills before or at the same as the training twin. Moreover, both Gesell's and McGraw's co-twin studies are often cited as evidence in support of the view that motor development in infancy is mainly guided by processes of biological maturation, and that experiential factors, such as training or environmental differences, exert little if no direct influence. The overwhelming emphasis placed on maturational factors that is typically attributed to McGraw and Gesell is generally accurate, although there are clear instances in their later writings in which both discuss the effects of external influences (see Gesell, 1954, and McGraw, 1946). However, the widely believed conclusions about maturational influences on motor development were challenged in the 1970s when cross-cultural studies (e.g. Super, 1976) and training studies (e.g., Zelazo, Zelazo, & Kolb, 1972) demonstrated that various experiential factors could exert strong influences on the rate of motor-skill acquisition.

Motor Development and the Growth of Mind

For some of the early motor development researchers, the results of the co-twin control studies provided further support for a strong maturational orientation to conceptualizations about motor development. At this point, the compiled developmental schedules and inventories of motor development norms were used for tests by which the rate of development for individual infants could be assessed. This practice, and Gesell's (1928, 1929) influential writings, led some motor development researchers to equate infant motor development to the growth of mind and intelligence. As Kopp (1979) put it, some early motor development researchers were guided by a growing conceptual theme that was founded on the proposition that "without activity there could be no infant intellect . . ." (p. 10). Thus, the next logical step for some early motor development researchers was to look at the rates of motor development, to compare how these rates varied from child to child, and then to link the rates of motor development to rates of intellectual development. Another research goal then emerged—to discover whether correspondences existed between rates of motor development and rates of mental development (e.g., Bayley, 1933, 1935, 1949; Gesell, 1928, 1929; Shirley, 1931, 1933; Wellman, 1931).

In order to check the correspondences between rates of motor development and rates of intellectual development, researchers typically conducted correlational analyses between the age at which an infant walked and some measure of intelligence or intellectual functioning in school. The findings were generally mixed and tended to be controversial. For example, Wellman's (1931) review of this literature cited numerous studies that found moderate to strong correlations between age of onset of walking with grades in school or with various measures of intelligence. Other investigations, however, suggested that the relation was strong only in extreme cases. For example, in his *Genetic Studies of Genius,* Terman (1925) reported that gifted children walked only about a month earlier than children of average intelligence, but that there was a difference of about 12 months in walking age when children of average intelligence were compared with "feebleminded" children. Bayley (1935) reported moderate correlations between age of first walking and mean mental score of 0.46 at 18 months of age, and first prewalking progression and mean mental scores of 0.20 at 18 months of age. Shirley (1931) found a similar correlation of 0.28 between age of walking and the Minnesota preschool test at 18 months of age. Bayley (1949) subsequently reported longitudinal data that followed up on her initial sample (Bayley, 1935). In this later report, Bayley (1949) focused on the patterns of the growth of intelligence from measures taken at 38 different time points from one month to 18 years of age. The flavor of earlier expected correspondences between motor and mental scores remained as Bayley suggested, that variability in intelligence measures were linked to variability in physical growth changes in both infancy and adolescence. However, Bayley also concluded that a variety of sensory-motor measures taken during infancy did not predict later intelligence scores.

The conviction that relations exist between rates of motor and mental development is still strong despite weak and mixed empirical results. This conviction has had wide implications that have persisted over the years. For example, parents and various professionals look cautiously at the development of motor milestones to the extent that almost any sign of atypical or delayed motor development may signal protracted intellectual development, or otherwise less than average intellectual functioning. Another example is the theoretical importance that is placed on sensorimotor actions in the infant's acquisition of knowledge (e.g., Piaget, 1952, 1954). Given the belief that relations do exist between motor and mental development, an interesting paradox results: How can it be the case that there is a strong belief that motor actions play an important role in the infant's acquisition of knowledge, yet the empirical evidence strongly suggests that no relation exists between early motor competence and later intelligence? This paradox will be discussed in greater detail below.

The research just described represents the creative efforts of a very dedicated group of researchers; the efforts of these researchers formed a generative base from which several lines of investigation followed. However, we know now that this work was dependent upon the conceptual and methodological trends of the day. Today, over 60 years of growth has been enjoyed by the field of developmental psychology (and other related disciplines). Also, the benefit of 20-20 hindsight permits us to see that the early motor development researchers accomplished much despite what we see today as conceptual and methodological limitations. In the next section, I will discuss these limitations within the context of current thinking.

PROBLEMS IN EARLY MOTOR DEVELOPMENT RESEARCH: THE DECLINE IN INTEREST IN MOTOR DEVELOPMENT FROM THE LATE 1940s TO THE MID-1960s

The discrepancy between the conceptual claims and the empirical evidence led to a period of relative inactivity in motor development research by developmental psychologists that spanned the late 1940s to the mid-1960s. In this section, I present an analysis of the various factors that led to this loss of interest. Moreover, I also discuss the conceptual and methodological advances that ended this period of inactivity and renewed interest in the study of motor development (Benson, 1987a; Bertenthal, Campos, & Barrett, 1982; Kopp, 1979; Thelen, 1984; Zelazo, 1983).

Methodology

While careful, the early investigations of developmental motor milestones and the emergence of locomotor skills were imprecise. Researchers were interested in the onset and changes of gross, global behaviors, and often looked for these changes in relatively small, cross-sectional samples, or even smaller longitudinal samples. Even though photographic records were kept and quantitative analyses were attempted, most frequently investigators were satisfied with cataloging gross motor behaviors that were only described subjectively. The attempts at quantitative analysis seemed half-hearted, perhaps because of an underlying belief that these more objective and quantitative methods were not entirely adequate when compared to direct observation. This sentiment was expressed by Gesell and Thompson when they wrote,

> Attention should be called to the fact that the comparative method of behavior observation, in spite of its absolute shortcomings, is effectual and highly discriminating in actual application. Behavior patterns in their detail and in their integrated complexity, as embodied in a living child, become for the time objective, critical norms, which yield delicate shadings and diversities of comparison at present utterly beyond the scope of any available psychotechnology. . . . (1929, p. 31)

Accompanying these sentiments was the simple fact that technology was of limited help without tools to represent and analyze the complexities of human movement data. Researchers made use of photographic techniques to record behavior, but then they were often left with the problem of how to convert this analogue information to a form that would lend itself to objective representation and quantitative analysis. The high-speed photographic, video, and computer technology simply did not exist, as it does today, to permit the fine-grained microanalyses of specific, quantitative aspects of complex motor behavior. Moreover, early researchers did not have access to today's techniques from the movement sciences that make it possible (but certainly not always easy!) to conduct precise, automated three-dimensional tracking and digitizing of photographed or videotaped movement data, and to represent and analyze these movement data with three-dimensional kinematics or biomechanical methods. Modern researchers have many advantages, but today's technology has not solved all the problems; there is still a tension between capturing the physical aspects of motor-skill acquisition and/or performance and describing the more expriential aspects of motor skill learning and competence.

Maturational Bias and Persistent Conviction in Unfounded Beliefs

Many of the early motor development researchers had particularized conceptualizations of development in general, and motor development in particular, although this partly was a function of the "youth" of developmental psychology as a discipline. Even though early motor development researchers were often mischaracterized in the strength of their beliefs and findings, this early period has generally been viewed as promoting a strong maturational bias and a general tendency to view development in terms of absolute, all or none principles. In some cases these principles proved to be satisfactory. For example, it was possible to apply general principles to patterns of physical growth and motor development, such as the trend toward both cephalocaudal and proximodistal motor progression. However, some proposed principles were too specific and unyielding, such as the 23 separate, intransitive and sequential stages in prone progression proposed by Gesell & Ames (1940).

The strong maturational point of view engendered an intransitive-stage theory of motor skill acquisition that could not explain sources of variability in either the lack of appearance of some of the proposed units of behavior or in the rates of their acquisition. The maturational emphasis was so strong that looking to external factors as potential sources of variability was out of the question. When researchers specifically looked for individual difference factors, they focused on genetic factors (i.e., race, sex, intelligence, size, illness) and found no clear answers. When this search failed, some researchers resorted to factors such as "talent" to explain individual differences in motor skill acquisition (Shirley, 1931). Simply put by Shirley, the sentiment of the day was,

> The unfolding of motor skills proceeds in accordance with biological laws. . . . we may conclude that such an important function as the baby's muscular control is not left to the exigencies of chance, training, or incidental practice. Instead, functional development is predetermined and controlled by the same growth gradients that predetermine and control the development of body structure. . . . (1931, p. 254)

There is the sense that a narrow maturational focus and conception of development was steadfastly held even when the empirical findings did not match the theoretical prediction. The belief in maturational processes was not supported by various research efforts (e.g., Ames, 1937; Bayley, 1935; Burnside, 1927; McGraw, 1935), yet this hypothesis persisted with little attempt to reconceptualize the issue (perhaps with the exception of Shirley). A similar state of affairs was evident with the search to find correspondences between motor and mental development; when the data failed to confirm the expectation that these correspondences existed, there was a general sense to hold onto these beliefs when the data did not support their conceptualizations. When hypotheses and convictons are held in the face of contradictory empirical results, advances in theory tend not to occur (Kuhn, 1962). The lack of such advances more than likely led to a decline in interest in motor development, but also led to very particularized conceptualizations of motor development and its relation to other areas of functioning.

Overgeneralization of Relations Between Motor and Intellectual Development

The proposed relation between motor development and intellectual development seemed logical but was overgeneralized. An infant that was precocious in the acquisition of walking was expected to be precocious intellectually; moreover, it was speculated that athletic or bright adults were most likely precocious in motor development during their babyhood (Shirley, 1931). Investigators expected that relations between motor skill and intellectual ability were direct and persistent throughout the life-span. Gross motor measures, such as age of onset of walking, were thought to predict gross measures of mental functioning, such as school grades or I.Q. measures. The underlying belief was that motor behavior was simply an early reflection of mental capacity, and contrawise, intelligent individuals were thought to possess advanced motor abilities. One can reasonably ask, however, why motor ability and intelligence should be related to one another. The expectation was that a single developmental pathway connected motor function to intellectual function.

In line with prevailing expectations, there was no recognition that, rather than reflecting intelligence, the acquisition of motor skills provided a *means* for infants to acquire knowledge about the world (e.g., through active exploration of the environment). Instead, investigators focused just on differences in the rate of locomotor acquisition as a direct index of differences in intellectual functioning. By focusing just on differential rates of motor-skill acquisition, is it possible to miss real relations that may exist between motor and intellectual functioning? For example, if relative motor skill does influence intellectual development, rate of acquisition may not be the important variable because it may make no difference at all precisely when a motor competence is acquired; what is important is that a higher level of motor competence has been achieved.

Moreover, there was a lack of appreciation that not all intellectual processes are necessarily linked to motoric ability. There were few attempts, if any, to look for specific relations between motor development and areas of functioning that would either be logically or theoretically influenced by crawling or walking, such as spatial cognitive and perceptual development, or the use of self-produced locomotion to regulate the attachment relation. This tendency to overgeneralize the relations between motor and intellectual functioning both over time and across intellectual processes naturally led researchers to expect that the rate of motor development would be related to the general rate of intellectual development over the lifespan.

Several factors impeded the early motor development researchers in their attempts to find support for relations between motor and mental development. Typically, investigators believed that a motor predictor variable, such as the age of onset of walking that occurred in infancy, would be related to an outcome variable, such as I.Q. or school performance, which was measured in later childhood or early adolescence. There were often huge time gaps, on the order of several years, between the measurement of a motor predictor variable and an outcome variable, such as I.Q. One problem was that during the time gap from infancy to later childhood or early adolescence a wide range of factors could intervene to mask the expected relation. For example, if tested in infancy, an infant who was late to walk might perform at a *different* intellectual level from a same-aged infant who acquired walking within the normative range. Yet, both children might perform at the *same* intellectual level when tested several years later. The time gap between the measurement of the motor predictor variable and the outcome variable would mask the accelerated rate in intellectual development that may have occurred once walking was achieved. A direct relation might well exist between onset of walking and intellectual performance, but the relation may be most clearly evident at the time of walking acquisition, and not several years later.

It did not occur to the early motor development researchers that motor skills were not equivalent to intelligence, or that motor activity might mediate rather than reflect the acquistion of knowledge. Consequently, there was no recognition that relations between the acquisition of motor skills and intellectual development would be most clearly evident during periods of rapid behavioral reorganization in early infancy. Many years later several different groups of infant researchers (Emde, Gaenesbauer, & Harmon, 1976; Fischer, 1980; McCall, Eichorn, & Hogarty, 1977; Uzgiris, 1976) would independently point to two periods of rapid behavioral reorganization in infancy—one at 6 to 9 months and the other at 11 to 14 months, ages that correspond remarkably well with, first, the onset of crawling and creeping, and second, with the onset of walking.

Historical Changes—The Dominance of Operationalism and Stimulus-Response Theory

In addition to the factors listed above, a number of historical trends contributed to a loss of interest in motor development both as a process and as a factor related to intellectual development. First, between 1940 and 1970, psychology as a field was dominated by operationalism (Cairns, 1983); phenomena that were not subject to direct experimental manipulation and subject to ready quantitification were often thought to be unscientific. The difficulty of objectively representing the complexities of movement data remained, along with less than satisfactory ways to quantify changes in locomotor development. In addition, with the exception of training studies, there were no clear experimental methods to independently manipulate locomotor experience. As a result, during the height of operationalism the study of motor development was often neglected.

Moreover, the popular stimulus-response theories of the day tended to neglect the contribution of the organism to its own psychological development. Experience was often equated with the passive registration of experimenter-manipulated stimulation. The failure of early motor development researchers to predict later intelligence from the rate of motor development further fueled the conviction that the study of locomotor contributions to psychological development was fruitless (Kopp, 1979). As a result, there was no longer an impetus to

examine how the acquisition of one skill, such as crawling or walking, might
serve to mediate the development of other skills. Thus the development of
appropriate research strategies and the posing of specific research question
about the relation between motor and intellectual and emotional development
were impeded.

Many of these historical trends and conceptualizations were dramatically
reversed in the mid-1960s with the rediscovery by American psychologists of
Piaget's (1952, 1954) theory of development. Piaget's view of development
helped to revitalize motor development research in the mid-1960s in spite of the
theory's strong maturational thrust. Not only did Piaget's theory emphasize the
link between sensorimotor activity and intellectual function, but it argued that
action is the *basis* of knowledge. At this point, our thinking about the processes
of development became much more sophisticated, as Piaget's constructivist
approach highlighted both organismic and environmental influences on development. Within this theoretical framework, developmentalists could now consider
how both maturational factors and environmental factors contribute to both
stability and variability in development. For example, Piaget's theory motivated
researchers to examine whether or not varied experiences could influence the rate
and sequence of certain types of motor development (e.g., White, Castle, &
Held, 1964), or how severely motorically impaired infants could attain levels of
object permanence through limited interactions with objects (e.g., Decarie
1969). Piaget's theory provided researchers with a foundation from which the
study of developmental processes was almost as important as the study of
developmental products themselves (Kopp, 1979).

The renewed interest in motor development that was prompted by Piaget'
theory has continued today as a function of exciting advances in con
ceptualizations about motor control (e.g., Gallistal, 1980; Kelso & Clark, 1982
Stelmach, 1976; Turvey, 1977). Moreover, recent methodological and tech
nological advances in data collection and analysis techniques have set the stage
for a renewed and continued interest in the study of motor control and motor skill
acquisition. Together these developments have motivated some developmental
psychologists to take a second look at the epistemological question of how
infants acquire knowledge, and what relations may exist between motor development and the acquisition of knowledge.

I have argued that the attempts of the early motor development researchers to
study motor development and correspondences between motor development and
intellectual development were not successful, and I have discussed why. I have
also suggested that contrary to the lack of success of this early research, there are
good reasons to reexamine these issues. We are now better equipped both
methodologically and conceptually to study the possibility that unique relations
exist between motor development and intellectual functioning. More specifically, I will now argue that the onset of crawling serves as an epigenetic event that
may facilitate, mediate, or induce spatial cognitive and perceptual development

This argument grew out of the initial work by Campos and his colleagues, who have made a similar argument that the onset of self-produced locomotion serves to mediate social and emotional development in addition to intellectual development (Bertenthal, Campos, & Barrett, 1984). Along this same line of reasoning, I will now present the theoretical view that infants are active organizers of their own knowledge, and that infants acquire knowledge through their own actions. From this framework I will describe several research strategies aimed at documenting the proposed relations between spatial cognitive and perceptual development.

NEW CONCEPTUALIZATIONS ABOUT RELATIONS BETWEEN MOTOR AND INTELLECTUAL DEVELOPMENT: AN ACTION-BASED VIEW OF KNOWLEDGE ACQUISITION

My approach to the study of motor development and its consequences for the acquisition of certain types of knowledge in infancy is based on three well-known Piagetian concepts. The first concept is that the infant is an active organizer of knowledge, not merely a passive receptacle for sensory experiences. This is another way of saying that the infant is seen as an active contributor to its own psychological development. Second, knowledge is assumed to be constructed or acquired by the infant initially through motor actions, and specifically through sensorimotor interactions with objects and events in the world. And third, it is through these sensorimotor interactions that infants acquire basic knowledge about space, objects, time, and causality. As an extension of these concepts, Bullinger (1987) has suggested that the infant's sensory systems and limbs be thought of as tools for exploration and knowledge acquisition. Before these "bodily" tools can be used by the infant to explore and learn about the world, the infant must first learn to control its tools. Thus the acquisition of the major motor milestones can be viewed within a unique framework. This framework considers developing psychological factors that influence motor-skill acquisition *and* the specific intellectual and social consequences of this acquisition.

Over the last four years, I have used a variety of different research strategies to examine relations between motor development and specific intellectual development. At the outset, I want to be clear that I am *not* suggesting that there is a causal relation, such that the earlier a baby crawls, the smarter or more advanced he or she will be. On the contrary, there is probably a bidirectional relation such that "action guides knowledge" and, in turn, "knowledge guides action." What I am proposing is that there are relations between motor development and intellectual behavior and that the nature of these relations must be clearly spelled out. However, it may not matter whether these relations are experienced relatively early or late in an infant's life.

Gottlieb (1976, 1983) provided a scheme for analyzing how various factors may relate to one another during the course of development. Gottlieb suggested that one factor may relate to another by serving to *facilitate, induce, maintain,* or *correlate* with a particular behavioral outcome. Thus, I will suggest that the onset of crawling may be viewed as an important setting event that functions to either *facilitate, induce,* or *maintain* developmental transitions in spatial cognitive and perceptual development. (I will not discuss here how the onset of crawling may be viewed as a *correlate* with these developmental transitions.) I will describe several different research strategies that are designed to examine these logical relations between locomotor and intellectual development. The rationale behind the claim for each one of these relations is detailed in Table 1. The reader should refer to this table as each of the following research strategies is described. I will describe these research strategies as they occurred in the evolution of my research, and not in the order they are listed in the table. Thus, the first reseach strategy I will describe examined whether or not the onset of self-produced locomotion served to *maintain* certain types of spatial cognitive knowledge.

Table 1
Logical Inferences about the Developmental Role of Self-Produced Locomotion Based upon the Following Possible Empirical Tests

Role Played by Self-Produced Locomotion	Description of the Role and Empirical Outcome that Supports the Inferred Role
INDUCTION	
Locomotor experience is necessary for the emergence of specific psychological skills.	
Empirical test:	Comparison of performance of prelocomotor infants who have artificially-induced locomotor experience with prelocomotor infants.
Conclusion:	Prelocomotor infants must show *no* evidence (beyond chance levels) of the specific psychological skill.
Comment:	Difficult to demonstrate *no* evidence of the specific psychological skill because prelocomotor infants may respond randomly.
FACILITATION	
Locomotor experience permits the emergence of the specific psychological skill *earlier* or *better* than in the absence of locomotor experience.	
Empirical test:	Comparison of performance of prelocomotor infants who have artificially-induced locomotor experience with the performance of prelocomotor infants.
Conclusion:	Prelocomotor infants who have artificially induced locomotor experience perform significantly better on specific psychological skills than prelocomotor infants.
Comment:	Most probable role that will be demonstrated with the age-held-constant approach.

Table 1
Continued

Role Played by Self-Produced Locomotion	Description of the Role and Empirical Outcome that Supports the Inferred Role

CORRELATION

Only endogenously acquired locomotor experience is associated with the emergence of specific psychological skills.

Empirical test:	Comparison of performance of infants who have endogenous locomotor experience with the performance of prelocomotor infants who have artificially induced experience with the performance of prelocomotor infants.
Conclusion:	Infants who have endogenous locomotor experience perform better than prelocomotor infants,

AND

Prelocomotor infants who have artificially induced locomotor experience perform *no* differently than prelocomotor infants.

MAINTENANCE

Locomotor experience is needed *after* the achievement of locomotion in order to keep performance of specific psychological skills at a functional level.

Empirical test:	Comparison of performance on specific psychological skill during *active locomotion condition* with performance during *passive locomotion condition*.
Conclusion:	Performance during *active locomotion condition* is better than during *passive locomotion condition*.
Comment:	Infants who have recently achieved self-produced locomotion require the opportunity to move themselves in order to maintain spatial orientation.

Research Strategy #1: The Maintenance Role of Self-Produced Locomotor Experience

The first research strategy was designed to examine whether or not active self-produced locomotor experience serves to *maintain* certain types of spatial knowledge in already locomoting infants. I assumed that active, self-produced locomotor experience plays an integral role in spatial orientation. Infants were then encouraged to solve a spatial orientation task after experiencing both active and passive locomotor experiences that result in a spatial transformation. The pattern of performance was then compared after each type of locomotor experience. If infants perform better after active locomotor experience than after passive locomotor experience, one can infer that self-produced locomotor activity plays a role in the maintenance of spatial knowledge.

One type of spatial knowledge that should be directly related to the onset of self-produced locomotion, and continued locomotor experience, is the ability to keep track of spatial locations when either an object or an individual is displaced in space. Piaget (1954) proposed that the development of spatial knowledge in infancy develops from a self-centered spatial coding strategy to an increasingly objective, or allocentric, spatial coding strategy. Initially, infants keep track of the location of objects relative to the self. When either the infant or an object moves, this strategy creates problems. For example, if an infant codes the location of a toy as "in front of me," and then the infant moves, it is likely that the object will no longer be located "in front of me." However, if the infant uses an allocentric spatial coding strategy, the location of an object is coded with reference to an external landmark; no matter where the infant may move through the environment the spatial relation between the landmark and the target location remains unchanged. Thus, if the location of a toy is coded as "next to the toy box," then no matter where the infant moves the toy is still located "next to the toy box." The transition in spatial knowledge from the use of a self-centered to a landmark-centered spatial coding system has been well-documented (Acredolo, 1978; Acredolo & Evans, 1980; Bremner & Bryant, 1977). The first study examined whether self-produced locomotion plays a maintenance role during the transition in spatial knowledge from the use of a self-centered to a landmark-centered spatial coding strategy.

Twenty-six already locomoting infants, from 10 to 11 months of age, performed an object search task that required their relocation from one side of a two-position hiding box to the other side, either through active or passive movement (for more details, see Benson & Uzgiris, 1985). Infants first learned to locate a hidden object in one of two locations next to one another. When infants experienced a spatial relocation to the other side of the hiding box, an egocentric spatial reversal occurred of the spatial orientation of the two hiding positions. As a result, on test trials, an object that was initially hidden and found to the infant's right would now be situated to the infant's left. In one condition (the active condition) infants actively crawled around the hiding box after the object was hidden, and in the other condition (the passive condition) infants were carried around the hiding box to the opposite side before search was permitted. In a within-subjects design, infants received four test trials in each movement condition, and the order of the movement conditions as well as the hiding side were counterbalanced. It was expected that infants could maintain the spatial relations between the target location and their own location in the active, or self-initiated movement condition, but that they would not be able to in the passive, or other-initiated movement condition.

Table 2
Number of Infants Showing Correct Search Responses Out of Four Trials for Each of the Two Movement Conditions

Movement condition	Number of Correct Search Responses		
	3–4	2	1–0
Self-initiated	16	1	9
Other-initiated	1	6	19

NOTE. N = 26.

As predicted, infants were better at finding the hidden object when they actively moved themselves around the hiding box. These results are shown in Table 2, where it can be seen that 16 of 26 infants made three or four correct searches out of four trials in the active, or self-initiated, movement condition, whereas only one infant made three or four correct searches out of four trials after passive, or other-initiated, movement. Conversely, 19 of 26 infants made either one or no correct searches out of four trials after passive movement, whereas 9 of 26 infants made one or no correct searches out of four trials after active movement. Table 2 indicates how infants responded when only one movement condition is considered at a time. Remember, each infant received both active and passive movement conditions. Table 3 shows how each infant performed in each movement condition. For example, it can be seen that 13 infants made three or four correct searches in the active, or self-initiated movement condition, *and* these same 13 infants made only one or no correct searches after passive movement. A Wilcoxon test revealed that the search responses made after self-initiated movement were significantly more accurate than search responses made after other-initiated movement ($T = 56$, $p < .01$).

Table 3
Number of Infants Showing Combinations of Correct and Incorrect Search Responses Out of Four Trials For Both Movement Conditions

Number of correct searches in Self-initiated movement condition	Number of correct searches in Other-initiated movement condition		
	3–4	2	1–0
3–4	1	2	13
2	0	0	1
1–0	0	4	5

NOTE. N = 26.

These results suggest that, within this experiemental context, for infants who can locomote, the experience of actively moving through space *maintains* an action-based "knowing by doing"; when the opportunity to control one's movement is taken away, however, "no longer doing, means no longer knowing." These findings are especially powerful when one considers that the only variable that was manipulated was whether or not infants actively moved themselves or were passively carried around the hiding box.

Apparently, when the *same* babies were carried around the hiding box, there were no active means for keeping track of the spatial transformation. This situation is analogous to a common adult experience. Suppose you are a passenger in a car, and you and the driver follow a set of directions to arrive at "location X," a place that you have never been before. A week passes, and now you are the driver and must find your way back to "location X." Even though you have had the experience of having been taken to "location X," now that you must control your actions it is not always easy to find your way.

It might be argued that search performance was poorer after passive movement because infants were simply distracted from the task during the passive movement condition. An analysis of where infants looked during the passive movement condition revealed that many infants simply fixated on the hiding locations during passive movement and did not appear to be distracted by the passive movement. However, distribution of attention may be an important mechanism in this situation for infants during the active movement condition. During active movement, infants often looked back and forth between where they had started from, where the hidden object was located and the next step along the path they were following around the hiding box. From this pattern of visual attention we might speculate that the locomoting infants were "mapping out and updating" the changing spatial relations between the initial and current location of the self and the location of the hidden object. These results appear to be robust, for they have been independently replicated in another laboratory (Acredolo, Adams, & Goodwyn, 1984).

Thus, in an experimental situation where active and passive movement experiences can be manipulated and compared, action served to *maintain* a certain type of spatial knowledge. It can be inferred then that forms of self-produced locomotion such as crawling and creeping act as an important mediator in maintaining spatial knowledge during the transition from subjective to objective spatial development.

The procedure that was used in this study did not permit a direct comparison of spatial knowledge between locomotor and nonlocomotor infants because the experimental task itself required locomotor ability. A comparison between the locomotor and nonlocomotor infants would be necessary for an examination of whether or not the onset of crawling serves to *facilitate* or *induce* transitions in spatial knowledge. The research strategy I discuss next describes how a modified spatial orientation task was used so that a comparison could be made between locomotor and nonlocomotor infants on a similar spatial orientation task.

Research Strategy #2: The Facilitative or Inductive Role of Self-Produced Locomotor Experience

A second research strategy—the age-held constant approach—was designed (by Joe Campos and Bennett Bertenthal) to examine whether or not endogenously acquired self-produced locomotor experience serves to *facilitate* or *induce* certain types of spatial knowledge. The basic logic is to compare same-aged infants who differ in amounts of locomotor experience on a spatial orientation task that does not involve active locomotion. If the performance of these same-aged infants differs, then (with some caveats) logical inferences can be made about how locomotor experience influences spatial knowledge. For example, if locomotor infants perform better than nonlocomotor infants, one might infer that locomotor experience *induces* certain types of spatial cognitive knowledge. If nonendogenous locomotor infants who have had artificially induced locomotor experience (with the aid of infant walkers) perform at levels inferior to endogenous locomotor infants *and* superior to nonlocomotor infants, then some types of locomotor experience may *facilitate* some types of spatial cognitive knowledge. The outcome of empirical comparisons among these three locomotor experience groups would provide information on whether self-produced locomotion induces and/or facilitates spatial cognitive knowledge.

Benson, Bertenthal, and Campos (in preperation) compared infants who were all 8.5 months of age, but who had different types and amounts of locomotor experience. The first locomotor experience group consisted of *locomotor* infants who had been crawling for at least four weeks; the second locomotor experience group consisted of *prelocomotor* infants who had not yet begun to creep or crawl; and the third locomotor experience group consisted of infants who could not yet crawl, but had at least 40 hours of *artificially induced locomotor* experience in infant walker devices that had been provided by their own parents. Thus, we attempted to hold chronological and gestational age constant while amount and type of locomotor experience varied.

A total of 60 infants, 20 in each locomotor experience group, were tested in Acredolo's (1978) spatial orientation procedure, which uses a logic that is similar to the logic of the hiding task that was described in the previous study. Infants were seated in a highchair that was mounted on a mobile platform that could be moved (by a parent) along a predetermined 180° path. This chair was located in the center of an experimental room that was composed of four walls. The four walls were identical except that the two side walls, located to the left and right of the infant, each had a window-flap behind which a puppet could appear. Infants were trained to turn their head to the left or right window, at the sound of a buzzer, to a clearly landmarked window to anticipate the appearance of the puppet. When the training criterion was achieved—four consecutive head turns to the traget window *before* the puppet's appearance—the test phase began. A parent relocated the infant 180° to the opposite side of the test room, the buzzer was sounded, and the baby's response was observed.

As in the previous study, the infant must compensate for the spatial relocation. If the infant was trained to look to the target window by making a right head turn, then after spatial relocation the infant must compensate and make a left head turn to find the target window. All infants received five test trials, after spatial relocation, during which the puppet did not appear after the buzzer was sounded. Since all infants underwent passive relocation in the experimental space, attempts were made to provide landmarks by which the infant could keep track of the target window during the passive spatial relocation. These landmarks consisted of bright vertical stripes along the wall where the target window was located and blinking lights and a bright blue star around the opening of the target window.

In line with previous predictions about relations between locomotor experience and spatial cognitive knowledge, we expected that *locomotor* infants would make the fewest spatial errors, followed by infants in the *artifically induced locomotor* group, and that *prelocomotor* infants would make the most spatial orientation errors. The results, shown in Table 4, confirmed our predictions.

Infants in each locomotor experience group were classified according to the predominance of correct or incorrect head-turn responses made over the five test trials. As shown in Table 4, the majority of *locomotor* infants (14 of 20) showed a predominance of correct head turns to the target window over the five test trials, compared with 10 of the 20 *artificially induced locomotor* infants and only 5 of 20 *prelocomotor* infants. The difference in frequency of infants from each locomotor group across the different response categories was reliable ($p < .05$).

Table 4
Number of Infants Showing Predominance of Search Response over Five Test Trials

Locomotor Group	Type of Response		
	Correct	Correct = Incorrect[a]	Incorrect
Locomotor	14	2	4
Artificial Locomotor	10	1	9
Prelocomotor	5	4	11

Note. $n = 20$ in each locomotor group.
[a] It was possible to show an equal number of correct and incorrect responses over the five test trials when instances of no response were included.

Moreover, an analysis of the proportion of incorrect responses revealed a significant main effect for locomotor experience ($p < .05$), and a planned comparison revealed that the source of the significant effect was the comparison between infants in the locomotor group and the prelocomotor group, such that prelocomotor infants made significantly more incorrect head turns to the target window after spatial relocation than did locomotor infants.

These results converged with the findings from the first study, and the paired comparisons across the three locomotor experience groups suggested that locomotor experience may *induce* and *facilitate* the transition from subjective to objective spatial coding. That is, the finding that infants in the locomotor group made fewer spatial errors than infants in the prelocomotor group suggests that locomotor experience may induce the use of objective spatial coding strategies. In addition, the finding that infants with artificially induced locomotor experience performed at a level about midway between the locomotor and prelocomotor infants suggests that some locomotor experience may facilitate objective spatial coding, although it does not substitute for endogenously acquired locomotion. In sum, endogenously acquired locomotor experience appears to induce spatial cognitive knowledge, and artificially induced locomotor experience appears to facilitate spatial cognitive knowledge. This finding makes sense, since endogenously acquired locomotor experience differs greatly from walker-aided locomotor experience.

Although we did find the patterns of performance that we predicted, these results are also very puzzling. Why did some of the infants from the locomotor-experience group respond as if they had no locomotor experience or could have come from either the prelocomotor or artificially induced locomotor group? Clearly the trends were in the predicted direction, but nonetheless, not *all* infants with locomotor experience made correct responses, and not *all* prelocomotor infants made incorrect responses.

There are at least three possible explanations of the variability that we found. First, we assigned subjects to the three locomotor-experience groups primarily on the basis of parental report, even though we made careful observations in the lab to determine that an infant assigned to the locomotor experience group could indeed locomote. However, we repeated an error made by some of the early motor development researchers by relying upon parental report for information about the duration of locomotor experience. Second, the variability in responding could have come from individual differences in locomotor skill in infants who really did have similar durations of crawling experience, or in prelocomotor infants who were already beginning to show prerequisite interlimb coordination. Thus, if relations truly exist between motor development and specific types of intellectual functioning, then variability in performance might be a function of individual differences in level of motor skill. Third, even though chronological age was held constant, age by itself may not be the best matching variable to use with infants, and might be one more source of variation. For example, most of us would agree that it is rare to find two 8.5-month-old infants who are developmentally similar. To guard against individual variation in maturation, the age-held-constant approach is best used along with some measure of discriminant validity. That is, ideally, one would need to demonstrate that when age is held constant and locomotor experience is varied, infants with locomotor experience perform better than prelocomotor infants on relevant tasks (e.g., spatial and cognitive tasks), but that infants from all locomotor experience groups perform at similar levels on an intellectual task that is not relevant to locomotor experience (e.g., preference for novelty, or recognition memory). Finally, the variability we saw with the age-held-constant approach could have come from a combination of any of these sources. These concerns led to a third research strategy.

Research Strategy #3: The Collection of Locomotor Skill Data and Intellectual Performance Data from the Same Infants

The first two research strategies are promising and will continue to illuminate the relations between locomotor experience and intellectual functioning. However, if one truly wants to understand the relation between motor development and intellectual development, the study of how infants actually acquire locomotor skills cannot be avoided. Thus, the research strategy I will describe next involves an attempt to study how infants acquire locomotion, and how the process of locomotor skill acquisition can be quantitatively measured. Once reliable and objective measures of locomotor-skill acquisition are developed, then I plan to relate these measures of locomotor skill to similar measures of spatial-cognitive and perceptual performance as previously described.

THE DEVELOPMENT OF LOCOMOTOR-SKILL MEASURES

Before I describe these attempts to measure locomotor development, it is important to make clear that I am interested in more than devising new ways to measure the mechanics of infant locomotor behavior. If measuring movement patterns was my only goal, then I would gladly defer to experts in the movement sciences who have devised truly remarkable techniques to handle this difficult task. As a developmental psychologist, I also hope to gain insight into the psychological factors that underlie how an infant gains control and coordination of its limbs, and to understand how an infant comes to use newly acquired motor skills in order to act upon and understand its world. With this in mind, students of the movement sciences may come to appreciate why I have not simple adapted their well-established kinematic techniques.

This work is preliminary and ongoing, as we are still struggling with how to analyze and represent the complexities of the emergence of locomotor behavior in real time. The goal is to create quantitative indices of how babies learn to creep and crawl. These measures will then permit me to find ways to directly relate how crawling skills are related to spatial cognitive and perceptual development. In the process, this work has also uncovered some interesting findings about changes in the interlimb dynamics of infants as they acquire locomotion.

Although psychology often defines itself as the science of behavior, we really do not have very good techniques for the analysis and representation of the flow of complex behavior as it unfolds and emerges in real time. Recent advances in the fields of kinesiology and the movement sciences, however, have provided tools for the collection and representation of the complexities of human movement. Basic biomechanical techniques can work quite well for the description and analysis of movement behavior, especially for highly skilled or routinized movements. Unfortunately, when infants begin to show forward progression, their movements are neither highly skilled nor routinized. However, I have begun to develop and modify aspects of kinematic techniques in order to create objective measures of coordination, and to begin to represent the interlimb dynamics of crawling.

In a preliminary longitudinal study (Benson, Welch, Campos, & Haith, 1985; Benson, 1987b), kinematic analyses were used to examine changes in interlimb coordination for three infants who were followed during the transition from nonlocomotion to self-produced, independent locomotion. Three infants were brought to the lab once every five days, beginning at 6.5 months of age, until each could crawl or creep a distance of 1.5 m along a raised platform. A range of 14 to 25 separate videotaped observations were collected from each infant over a period ranging from 3 months for one infant to 4 months, 3 weeks for another infant.

Infants were placed on a platform that was constructed with a solid base and clear plexiglas side panels so that the infants would move along a predetermined path that also permitted an unobstructed view of their movements. All clothing, except the diaper, was removed, and black makeup was placed over the lateral center of selected body joints (i.e., the wrist, elbow, shoulder, hip, knee, and ankle joints). To insure consistency in identifying the body joints each research assistant marked the same infant for all observations. In addition, the research assistants had frequent discussions about the exact locations they were using to mark the lateral center of the body joints.

A video camera was positioned perpendicularly to the platform so that the movements made by each infant were recorded, as he or she crawled or crept along the platform. The video record produced a side-view of the infant as it moved along the platform. The output of a time/date generator was also recorded on each video frame to produce a constant time record. Each videotape was viewed on a single-frame-advance videocassette recording deck (Panasonic model AG-6300) that was interfaced with a lab computer (DEC 11/23) and an electromechanical scoring system originally designed for the measurement of infant eye movements (for details on this scoring system, see Haith, 1980). A data scorer sits in front of a television monitor and rotates, by hand, two potentiometers that move two white crosshairs over a single frame of a video-recorded image. When the crosshairs intersect the center of a marked joint, the data scorer presses a button that records the coordinate, within a 512 × 512 matrix, where the joint center is located. The coordinate is recorded and stored in a computer file for later analysis. After the coordinates of 15 different locations are recorded (6 joint centers on each side of the body and 3 locations to indicate head position), the data scorer advances to the next video frame. The location of each joint center is sampled at a rate of 30 video frames per second.

During each laboratory visit, at least three separate attempts made by the infant to locomote along the platform were videotaped. Infants were placed on one end of the platform while a parent, located at the opposite end of the platform, manipulated a toy and encouraged the infant to obtain the toy. Two data scorers viewed the videotape record from each laboratory visit and selected the segment in which the subject moved, without stopping, and in which all joints could be clearly scored. When there was more than one scorable segment, or for observations when infants were still nonlocomotor, the segment that depicted the infant's optimal performance was determined by both scorers and was selected for analysis. In most cases there was only one scorable segment for analysis from each laboratory visit. The duration of the scorable segments ranged from 3 to 6 s, or 90 to 180 frames of X,Y coordinate data. An index of reliability between two data scorers was calculated after each scored the same 3-s segment from each of the three subjects in the study. Percent agreement between the two scorers averaged 0.90; there was a range of +/– 1 cm in scoring the position of the X or Y coordinate.

A complete data set for each observation consisted of the X,Y coordinate data, indicating the locations of each marked joint as the infant crawled along the platform, and the continuous time record. From these primary coordinate data the following kinematic parameters were calculated by following the procedures described by Hay (1985): (1) linear displacement of each selected joint center (i.e., wrist, elbow, shoulder, hip, knee, and ankle); and (2) angular displacement of these same body joints. In addition, the following spatiotemporal parameters were derived from the coordinate data and the continuous time record: (1) the onset time of the movement of each limb; (2) the offset time of the movement of each limb; (3) the duration of each limb movement; and (4) the sequence in which each limb was moved.

Limb Sequence Relations

One of the most important components of prone locomotion that the infant must master is the coordination of the knee and the hip joints so that the knee can be positioned under the hip; the knee and the hip joints work together as a linked unit. This component action is critical for the infant to maintain the hands and knees (or four-point) posture when creeping. Once the hands and knees posture is mastered, the body weight can be distributed over the hands and knees, so that balance can be maintained as the hands and knees are moved forward. One measure of limb coordination is the change in the relation between the angular displacement of the hip and the knee. Angular displacement refers to the angles formed around the body joints and how much these angles change—extended or flexed—as the limbs move. As a rough measure of coordination, correlation coefficients were computed for the angular changes of the knee and hip joints from the X,Y coordinate data generated during the laboratory observations. That is, the degree of angular displacement of the knee was correlated with the degree of angular displacement of the hip over each video frame for the duration of the analyzed movement segment from particular observations. The observations included the visit just before the first occurrence of forward movement (defined as a linear displacement of the hip joint center through space of at least 5 cm) and each subsequent observation. The patterns of these correlations, for the hip and the knee joints, for both sides of the body, are shown in Figure 1.

This is a preliminary study, and caution is clearly warranted because of the small sample size. Given this forewarning, changes in the relations among the correlations between the hip and the knee joints over successive observations are provocative. First, notice that the angular displacement of the hip and knee joints appear to become more positively correlated at different times for the two sides of the body, and that this relation can be seen for each subject. This pattern of correlations may suggest that the knee and hip joints on the right and left sides of the body become coordinated at different rates with two infants showing an initial left-side dominance and one infant an initial right-side dominance. In contrast to the movements of experienced actors, or other early movements such as stepping, there does not appear to be an initial bilateral symmetry in the movements of the hip and knee across the right and left sides of the body. Bilateral symmetry, however, does become evident in later stages of locomotor-skill acquisition when the correlations of the angular displacement of the hip and the knee both approach $+1.0$ for the right and left sides of the body. Second, notice what appears to be a characteristic dip in the hip-knee correlation for a previously coordinated side of the body when an increase in correlation occurs for hip-knee joints on the other side of the body. That is, the correlation of the hip-knee joints for the side of the body that was initially strongly positive appears

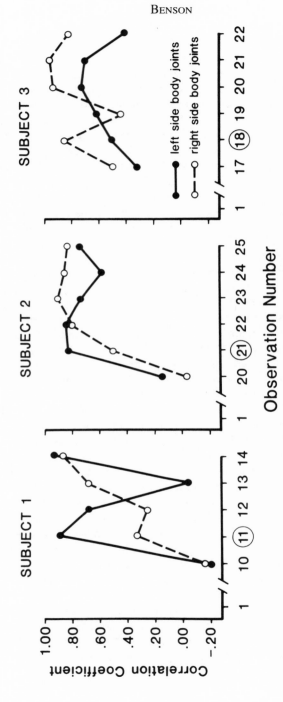

FIG. 1. Changes in the correlation between the angular displacement of the knee and hip joints during the acquisition of prone, self-produced locomotion. (The numbered observation that is circled indicates the first occurrence of forward progression.)

to decline as the correlation for the opposite side hip-knee joints becomes more positively related. Also notice that the sequence of partial correlation and then regression eventuates in highly positively correlated hip-knee movements for both sides of the body as shown at the last observations for each infant. Aspects of this same pattern of coordination can be seen for all three subjects, with a slight deviation for subject #3. Presumably, this pattern reflects changes or reorganizations of interlimb coordination during different phases of skill acquisition. Moreover, this pattern of limb-joint organization, disorganization, and eventual reorganization is reminiscent of Gesell's (1954) concept of reciprocal interweaving, and reflects at least one quantitative instantiation of this concept.

Next, limb sequence and timing relations were analyzed. First, we struggled with how to represent graphically the movements of the hands and knees during forward movement. Figure 2 shows a schematic representation of the sequencing and timing of limb movements, during a 5-s period, across four consecutive observations spanning the acquisition of crawling for one of the three subjects. In this figure, time is represented horizontally from left to right, and the movement of each limb is shown horizontally beginning with the left hand and knee and then the right hand and knee. Each "H" (for hand), "K" (for knee), and "-" represents movement of the limb every 0.05 s. That is, the longer the dashed line between any two "H's" or two "K's," the longer the duration of that particular limb movement. First, note the changes in the organization of the sequence and duration of the limb movements across the four sequential observations. For example, at observation #11, the first observation of forward progression for this infant, the difference between sequential onsets and offsets of limb movements appears longer than for observation #14. This is, the time gap or duration between the onset and offset of sequential movements is shorter at observation #14 than at observation #11. Moreover, notice that the duration of each movement becomes shorter and more regular across the four observations. Likewise, notice that the sequential patterning of the limbs differs across these observations. For example, during observation #12, the left knee is moved several times sequentially, and at around the fourth second of that observation, the left and right knees are moving at the same time, as if the baby was moving forward by hopping. Compare this with a more regular pattern of limb sequencing shown at observation #14. At this observation, a very distinct and regular alternation pattern of the hands and knees can be seen.

Next, each of these descriptive features was quantified and compared across the three subjects. The percent of alternation of the sequential movements of the hands and knees was calculated for each subject across the observations spanning the acquisition of crawling. Percent alternation is calculated by dividing the number of sequential alternating hand and knee movements by the total number of limb movements made in a particular movement segment. For example, the sequence of moving a hand and then a knee is counted as an alternation, whereas

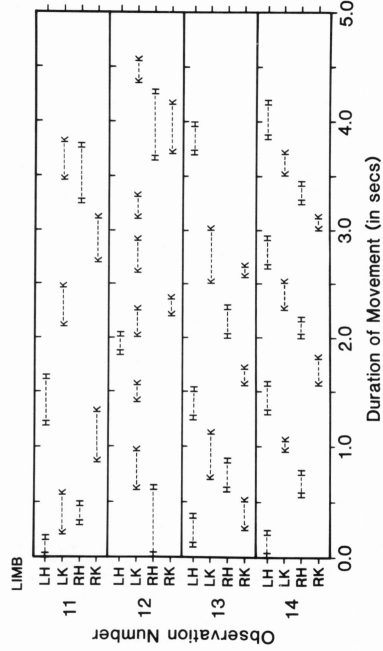

FIG. 2. Successive gait profiles showing changes in interlimb coordination for subject 1 during the acquisition of prone, self-produced locomotion. ("L" and "R" indicate left- and right-side limbs. "H" and "K" indicate hand and knee. Each "H", "K", or "-" indicate movement of a limb every 0.05 s.)

the sequence of moving a hand and then a hand is not counted as an alternation. The pattern of how these alternation percentages changed across observations is shown in Figure 3. Again, there appears to be a general sequence of organization, disorganization and then reorganization for the percentage of alternation of the hands and knees. This pattern is similar to the pattern of changes in the coordination of the hip and knee joints shown in Figure 1, and is not surprising given this previous shift from bilateral asymmetry to symmetry in opposite-side limb dynamics.

Limb Timing Relations

Typically, definitions of skill involve timing relations as well as form. The timing relations for the onset, offset, and duration of limb movements were examined next. The lag, or mean difference, between the onset times of two sequential limb movements, was calculated for each subject across the sequential observations. The onset lag is calculated by taking the difference between the onset times of two sequential limb movements. These mean lags are plotted in Figure 4. A uniform pattern can be seen where there is a steady decrease in the mean lag of limb onset for each subject over observations. There is a slight deviation for subject #2 with an increase in the mean lag of limb onset at the final observation. With the exception of this deviation, this pattern appears to reflect the increasing tendency of infants to begin the successive movement of one limb while the previously moved limb is in motion. Thus, the successive movements of the limbs appear to become chained more closely in time with increasing skill acquisition.

Another timing measure, the total duration of each limb movement, also became more regular across observations. As a measure of regularity, the variance of the duration of limb movements seen during each observation was calculated. These variances showed a steady decrease across the observations for each subject. This steady decrease in the variability of the duration of each limb movement indicates that the duration of each limb movement became more regular with skill acquisition.

These changes in timing relations are contrary to Ames's (1937) report that the duration of limb movements did not change over successive observations for her longitudinal sample. As presented in an earlier section of this chapter, Ames (1937) argued that little or no change in the timing relations of limb movements suggested that internal maturational factors were at work rather than the products of experience or practice. She believed that only maturational factors could be responsible for the appearance of a behavioral "form so complete that several weeks, possibly several months, of exercise of that pattern do not appreciably change its form or speed" (1937, p. 445). In contrast, the changes in movement duration that we found appear to indicate that timing relations may change as a function of increased skill acquisition.

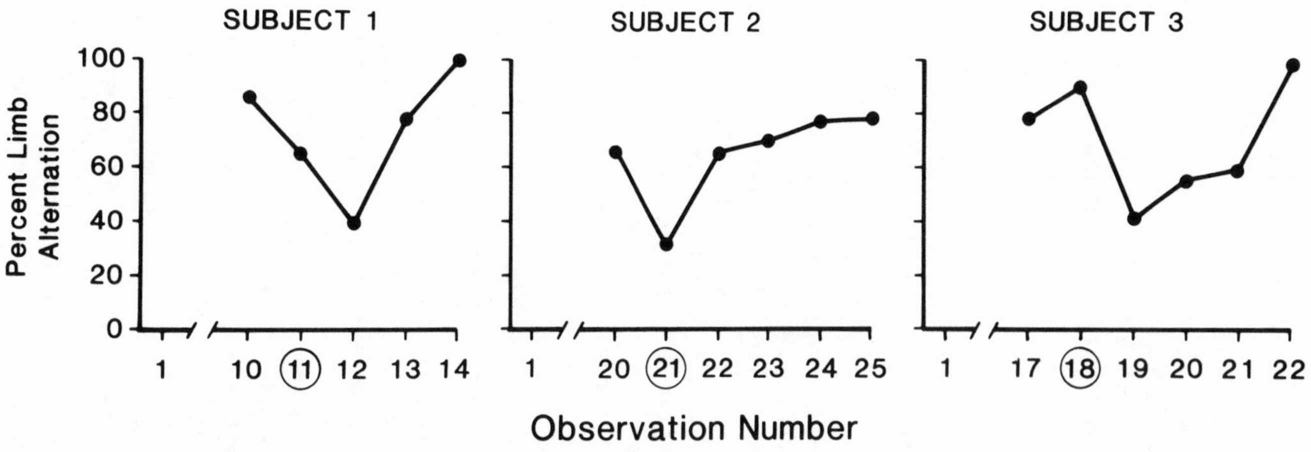

FIG. 3. Changes in percent limb alternation during the the acquisition of prone, self-produced locomotion. (Percent alternation is calculated by dividing the number of alternating limb movements [i.e., hand, knee is counted as an alternation whereas hand, hand is not] by the total number of limb movements. The numbered observation that is circled indicates the first occurrence of forward progression.)

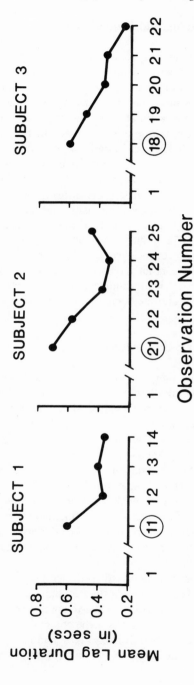

FIG. 4. Changes in limb onset lag during the acquisition of prone, self-produced locomotion. (The onset lag is calculated by taking the difference between the onset times of two sequential limb movements. The numbered observation that is circled indicates the first occurrence of forward progression.)

Relations Among Limb Timing and Sequencing

Relations among limb timing and sequencing were considered next. The timing pattern of crawling is affected by both limb onset lag and the duration of limb movements. To gain a more integrated sense of limb timing and sequencing, a mean lag/limb-duration ratio was calculated by dividing the onset lag of two sequential movements by the duration of the first movement. This ratio reflects the relative point during a limb movement at which a successive movement occurs. In other words, do successive limb movements tend to begin at the beginning, middle, or end of the previous limb movement, and will the relative point at which a successive limb movement begins change during the process of locomotor-skill acquisition? The mean lag/limb-movement duration ratios for each subject are plotted across the successive visits, and are shown in Figure 5. As can be seen, there is a steady decrease in the mean lag/limb-duration ratio for each of the three subjects. The relative timing among the sequential limb movements appears to change across observations such that the lags became shorter in duration. Also, there is an increase in the frequency of successive limbs moving at the same time, which indicates that with increased skill successive limbs began to move nearer the beginning of a previous limb movement.

Interpretation of Locmotor-Skill Measures

There is little question that these findings must be interpreted with caution until they can be confirmed with a larger sample of infants. However, I believe that these preliminary findings are provocative. The limb-timing data reveal a fairly regular decreasing function for several variables. These include mean onset lags, the variance of limb-movement duration, and the mean lag/limb-movement duration ratio. This pattern of findings suggests that there is steady improvement in the timing of sequential limb movements with increasing locomotor experience and skill acquisition. At the same time, the form of movement data, indicative of which limbs were moved, showed discontinuous patterns of coordination. Discontinuity was reflected in the fluctuations of the correlations between the angular displacement of the hip and knee joints, and for the percent of hand and knee alternation. In brief, the limb-timing data showed steady continuous improvement with skill acquisition, while the limb-sequence data showed discontinuity or reorganization with skill acquisition.

Some insight into what factors may influence the timing and phasing of bilateral limb and cross-lateral limb (i.e., right arm and left leg) movements may be gained by first considering some findings in the contemporary and early motor development literature. Recent research from the dynamic systems perspective has convincingly shown that the seemingly jerky, disorganized movements of

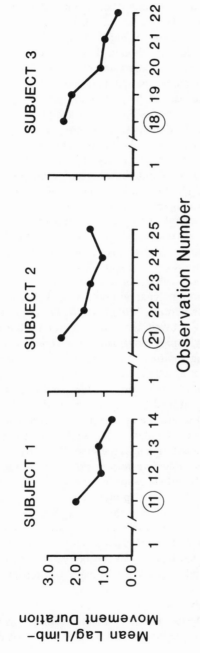

FIG. 5. Changes in mean limb onset lag/limb-movement duration during the acquisition of prone, self-produced locomotion. (The lab/limb-movement duration is calculated by dividing the onset lag by the duration of the successive limb movement. The numbered observation that is circled indicates the first occurrence of forward progression.)

very young infants appear to share some fundamental elements of coordination seen in more mature actions. For example, Thelen (Thelen & Fisher, 1982, 1983) found that kinematic elements of leg kicking in newborns share features with movements made by adults. Although these relations between infant and adult movement features were generally thought to hold for single limb movements, it has recently been demonstrated that some, but not all, space-time behaviors of one limb can be affected by perturbations to the opposite limb (i.e., adding weights) in infants as young as 6 weeks of age (Thelen, Skala, & Kelso, 1986). Despite some kinematic similarity in the movements of bilateral limbs in infants and adults, the tighly coupled phasing of both bilateral and cross-lateral limbs, as seen in adult locomotion, becomes only gradually evident in young infants. For example, prior to 5 months of age, young infants rarely show alternation in spontaneous leg kicking; after 5 months of age, however, the phase relations among the sequencing and timing of the two legs becomes tightly coupled as seen by the bilateral symmetry of alternating leg kicks (Thelen, 1985). Thelen (1986) has also shown that 6- to 7-month-old infants, when supported while their feet make contact with a motorized treadmill, will make instantaneous alternating stepping movements. She concluded that symmetrical, alternating stepping movements were not learned, but appeared to "fall out" or were elicited by the supporting dynamic context in which these infants were placed (i.e., the motorized treadmill). Moving from two to four limbs, almost 50 years ago McGraw (1939) showed that cross-lateral limb coordination was clearly evident in reflexive swimming movements in newborns, but this coordination became highly disorganized at approximately 4 months of age. She did not observe the reappearance of purposeful, coordinated swimming until after the onset of "independent erect locomotion," or walking, in the same infants.

None of the examples examined thus far have involved sustained interlimb coordination of opposite side arms and legs in a situation involving weight-bearing and the maintenance of balance. These factors are essential for the successful acquisition of crawling and creeping. Recently, Goldfield (1987) argued that one of the most potent factors responsible for the transition from rocking fore and aft on hands and knees to forward progression in creeping is the asymmetry that is introduced by hand preference. He found that once infants begin to creep they also begin to demonstrate a strong hand preference. Goldfield reports that when infants fell forward from a seated to a prone posture, the nonpreferred hand was more likely to be used fo support while the preferred hand was typically extended forward to propel the body in creeping. This relation between hand preference and interlimb coordination is intriguing and helps to explain the shift from bilateral symmetry to bilateral asymmetry, but the problem of discontinuity in interlimb coordination remains.

How can continuous patterns of improvement in limb movements occur for some parameters (i.e., timing relations) at the same time that there are regressions and progressions in the sequencing or phasing of bilateral and cross-lateral limb movements? Additionally, what factors may underlie the shifts in reorganization of limb sequences such that bilateral asymmetries appear in sequential limb movements prior to consistent bilateral limb symmetry?

I can only speculate here, and my speculation relies heavily on the assumption that there are complex interactions between two important categories of movement control. The first category concerns the biological properties of movement, such as the neurological and anatomical constraints on limb movements as recently specified by the dynamic systems perspective. The second category concerns psychological factors, such as infants' intentions to initiate and perform movements, and their growing appreciation of a practical knowledge about how the limbs move and what can be accomplished with such movement.

At an early stage the infant may know when to act, but may not know how. With the exception of early reflexes (i.e., the tonic neck reflex, the swimming reflex, and the crawling reflex), there is no true behavioral precursor to cross-lateral coordination between the legs and the arms, especially in weight-bearing and balance situations. The elegant demonstrations of early limb alternations and movements that are kinematically similar to adult forms gives insight into the remarkable continuity of some actions. However, how the infant comes to control and invoke these coordinated movements, and to use them as efficient means to achieve ends in the appropriate situation, is not well understood, but may provide insight into discontinuties in motor development. I would like to suggest that, in addition to emergent dynamic properties that have been proposed to act as rate-limiting factors in discontinuous phase-shifts in motor development (Fogel & Thelen, 1987; Thelen, 1987), psychological factors, such as conscious efforts to control limb movements and learning and decision-making processes that specify which movements an infant may invoke in a given situation, may also bring about discontinuties in motor-skill acquisition. For example, very young infants can learn and remember the contingency between a leg kick and the movement of a mobile when a string attached to the mobile is also tied to the infant's foot (Rovee-Collier & Fagen, 1981). When watching an infant who is struggling to crawl, one cannot help but notice what appear to be conscious efforts to control new movements. Infants at early phases of skill-acquisition often look back and forth between their limbs and the goal they are attempting to reach. At an intermediate phase in skill-acquisition, some infants will first move a limb out of the alternation sequence, say by moving the left knee after moving the right knee, but then move the left knee back, and then proceed to move the left hand, as if to correct for an error in the alternation sequence. We also need to incorporate higher-level psychological considerations for a full account of infant locomotion. Such an account will have to deal with why babies are motivated or make a decision to move in order to obtain a goal in the first place, or why a newly walking baby reverts to crawling or creeping when a desired object is at stake. Dynamic-system principles, as currently formulated, do not address such questions. Yet I feel that when the full story is told, we will find that such factors interact with those factors described in the dynamic systems tradition, to effect the movement products that we see.

Some advocates of the dynamic systems approach to motor development (e.g., Newell, 1986; Thelen, 1987) have acknowledged the presence of psychological factors in motor behaviors in terms of task constraints. However, specific dynamic systems properties have not yet been clearly spelled out for such additional constraining factors. Nevertheless, we certainly acknowledge deliberate attentional factors in such mature skill acquisition as learning to drive a car or learning to ski. Commonly, we assume that the acquisition of these skills involves considerable attentional effort; with time, these skills become automatized, freeing up resources for other tasks (like dodging people and trees). I am puzzled about why we have denied such factors for developmental milestones like crawling and walking. If the discontinuous patterns of hip-knee coordination and percent alternation of hand-knee movements are considered (see Figures 1 and 3) in light of such psychological factors, an alternative interpretation of these data may be that one skill component regresses as another skill component is being mastered, perhaps because conscious attempts to acquire control of the movement may be in play. During such attempts, attentional diversion from an incompletely automatized action may result. That is, during skill acquisition, infants may very well be learning just how to move their limbs (e.g., alternation of the hands and knees) in order to bring about a desired result (e.g., moving quickly through space to obtained a desired object).

The consideration of such psychological factors is complementary to a dynamic systems approach, and hopefully will yield greater insights into the holistic nature of motor and intellectual development in infancy.

RELATING LOCOMOTOR-SKILL MEASURES AND SPATIAL, COGNITIVE, AND PERCEPTUAL MEASURES

The locomotor-skill measures that I described above tell only one part of the story of motor development. These measures are useful for describing different aspects of locomotor-skill acquisition and for revealing interesting changes in limb coordination with development. What remains, however, is to directly relate the locomotor-skill measures to specific spatial-cognitive and perceptual-performance measures. The implicit assumption is that once locomotor skills are acquired and become coordinated and automatized, infants are free to pay direct attention to a number of important correspondences between their own movements and related changes in the visual surround. These correlations would be especially important for the appreciation of depth and distance relations, as well as for the appreciation of spatial relations that is required for the maintenance of spatial orientation during navigation. Consequently, individual variation in interlimb coordination may produce individual differences in spatial functioning, similar to the pattern of results of the spatial orientation study described earlier.

We are studying this possibility by collecting locomotor data and spatial-cognitive and perceptual data from the same infants in a larger longitudinal study. This combined data base will permit us to more precisely examine relations between locomotor development and spatial cognitive and perceptual functioning. I believe that this approach is crucial for providing the best information on how motor skill acquisition mediates or organizes the acquisition of intellectual abilities in infancy.

SUMMARY AND FUTURE DIRECTIONS

In this chapter I have offered a review of the early motor development research that was directed at the study of the acquisition of crawling and creeping and that attempted to link early motor skill development to later intellectual development. I argued why these early attempts were not successful, and I described problems underlying this initial lack of success in finding relations between motor development and intellectual development. Since we are now in a better position to avoid most of these problems, I have argued that it is important to once again reexamine the existence of relations between motor development and specific intellectual functions (i.e., in the spatial-cognitive domain). Researchers are now better equipped, both conceptually and methodologically, to examine whether specific relations exist between motor development and certain kinds of intellectual and emotional functioning. I have suggested that both biological and psychological factors contribute to locomotor-skill acquisition, and the specific intellectual and social-emotional consequences of such motor skills.

In addition to a conceptual framework, I offered some research strategies that are beginning to document that the onset of locomotor skills serves to maintain, facilitate, and induce certain kinds of intellectual functioning. Moreover, I have suggested that the most informative strategy may be to collect both locomotor-skill measures and specific intellectual measures from the same infants at the same time. To this end, I have described a series of measures that are still in the process of development and refinement, but do seem to hold promise as they begin to capture some of the complex and interesting changes in interlimb dynamics and coordination that occur during the different phases of the acquisition of crawling. We are now collecting these and other locomotor-skill measures. At the same time, we are collecting additional spatial-cognitive and perceptual performance measures from infants at different stages of locomotor-skill acquisition. One hopes that this work will provide insight into the two parallel domains of motor development and intellectual development and how they relate during infancy. The study of the relations between motor and intellectual processes is essential for understanding how infants learn to act on the world in which they live, and how this activity mediates the acquisition of certain types of knowledge. The importance of this area of investigation was first recognized by the early motor development researchers more than 50 years ago. They promoted the view that motor activity was a direct manifestation of intelligence and that individual differences in intelligence was a consequence of motor activity. Today's motor development researcher continues to recognize the importance of understanding how motor behavior is related to intellectual capacities, but we have new conceptions to guide our investigations of both motor and intellectual development and their interrelations. One of these conceptions is that, rather than simply reflecting intelligence, the acquisition of motor skills provides a means for infants to acquire knowledge about their world. The task still remains, however, to document how infants master common motor skills such as sitting, reaching, crawling, and walking, and how infants use these activities to learn about the world of people, objects, time, space, and causality.

REFERENCES

Acredolo, L. P. (1978). The development of spatial orientation in infancy. *Developmental Psychology, 14,* 224–234.
Acredolo, L. P., Adams, A., & Goodwyn, S. W. (1984). The role of self-produced movement and visual tracking in infant spatial orientation. *Journal of Experimental Child Psychology, 38,* 312–327.
Acredolo, L. P., & Evans, D. (1980). Developmental changes in the effects of landmarks on infant spatial behavior. *Developmental Psychology, 16,* 312–318.
Ainsworth, M. D. S., Blehar, M., Waters, E., & Wall, S. (1978). *Patterns of attachment.* Hillsdale, NJ: Erlbaum.
Ames, L. B. (1937). The sequential patterning of prone progression in the human infant. *Genetic Psychology Monographs, 19,* 409–460.
Bayley, N. (1933). Mental growth during the first three years: A developmental study of 61 children by repeated tests. *Genetic Psychology Monographs, 1,* 1–92
Bayley, N. (1935). The development of motor abilities during the first three years. *Monographs of the Society for Research in Child Development, 1,* 1–26
Bayley, N. (1949). Consistency and variability in the growth of intelligence from birth to eighteen years. *Journal of Genetic Psychology, 75,* 165–196.
Benson, J. B. (1987a, April). The acquisition of locomotor skills: New means for learning about the world. In M. Haith (Chair), *Perception and action: The acquisition of skill.* Symposium conducted at the meetings of the Society for Research in Child Development. Baltimore, MD.
Benson, J. B. (1987b, April). New lessons on how infants learn to crawl. In E. Thelen (Chair), *Crawling and walking: New perspectives in motor development.* Symposium conducted at the meetings of the Society for Research in Child Development, Baltimore, MD.

Benson, J. B., Bertenthal, B. I., & Campos, J. (in preparation). Locomotor experience and spatial development.

Benson, J. B., & Uzgiris, I. C. (1985). Effect of self-initiated locomotion on infant search activity. *Developmental Psychology, 21,* 923–931.

Benson, J. B., Welch, L., Campos, J., & Haith, M. M. (1985, July). *The development of crawling in infancy.* Presented to the International Society for the Study of Behavioral Development, Tours, France.

Bertenthal, B. I., & Campos, J. J. (1984). A reexamination of fear and its determinants on the visual cliff. *Psychophysiology, 21,* 413–417.

Bertenthal, B. I., Campos, J. J., & Barrett, K. C. (1984). Self-produced locomotion: An organizer of emotional, cognitive and social development in infancy. In R. N. Emde & R. J. Harmon (Eds.), *Continuities and discontinuities in development* (pp. 175–210). New York: Plenum.

Bremner, J. G., & Bryant, P. E. (1977). Place versus response as the basis of spatial errors made by young infants. *Journal of Experimental Child Psychology, 23,* 162–171.

Bowlby, J. (1973). *Attachment and loss: Separation, anxiety and anger* (vol. 2). New York: Basic Books.

Bullinger, A. (1987, April). Action as tutor for the infant's tools of exploration. In M. Haith (Chair), *Perception and action: The acquisition of skill.* Syposium conducted at the meetings of the Society for Research in Child Development, Baltimore, MD.

Burrnside, L. (1927). Coordination in the locomotion of infants. *Genetic Psychology Monographs, 2,* 283–372.

Cairns, R. B. (1983). The emergence of Developmental Psychology. In W. Kessen (Ed.), *Handbook of child psychology Vol 1 History, Theory and Methods.* (4th ed., pp. 41–102). New York: John Wiley.

Campos, J. J., Hiatt, S., Ramsey, D., Henderson, C., & Svejda, M. (1978). The emergence of fear on the visual cliff. In M. Lewis & L. Rosenblum (Eds.), *The development of affect* (pp. 149–182). New York: Plenum Press.

Campos, J. J., Svedja, M. J., Campos, R. G., & Bertenthal, B. I. (1982). The emergence of self-produced locomotion: Its importance for psychological development in infancy. In D. D. Bricker (Ed.), *Intervention with at-risk and handicapped infants: From research to application* (pp. 195–216). Baltimore: University Park Press.

Decarie, T. G. (1969). A study of the mental and emotional development of the thalidomide child. In B. M. Foss (Ed.), *Determinants of infant behavior* (Vol. 4, pp. 167–187). London: Methuen.

Dennis, W., & Dennis, M. G. (1940). The effect of cradling practice on the age of walking in Hopi children. *Journal of Genetic Psychology, 56,* 77–96.

Emde, R. N., Gaensbauer, T., & Harmon, R. (1976). Emotional expression in infancy: A biobehavioral study. *Psychological Issues* (vol. 10, Whole No. 37). New York: Interational Universities Press.

Feldman, H. (1833). *Observations on the normal functioning of the human body.* Bonne: C. Georgie.

Fischer, K. W. (1980). A theory of cognitive development: The control and construction of hierarchies of skills. *Psychological Review, 87,* 477–531.

Fogel, A., & Thelen, E. (1987). Development of early expressive and communicative action: Reinterpreting the evidence from a dynamic systems perspective. *Developmental Psychology, 23,* 747–761.

Fraiberg, S. (1959). *The magic years.* New York: Charles Scribner's Sons.

Gallistel, C. R. (1980). *The organization of action: A new synthesis.* Hillsdale, NJ: Earlbaum.

Gesell, A. (1928). *Infancy and human growth.* New York: McMillan.

Gesell, A. (1929). Maturation and infant behavior pattern. *Psychological Review, 36,* 307–319.

Gesell, A. (1933). Maturation and the patterning of behavior. In C. Muchison (Ed.), *A handbook of child psychology* (pp. 209–235). Worcester, MA: Clark University Press.

Gesell, A. (1939). Reciprocal neuromotor interweaving: A principal of development evidenced in the patterning of infant behavior. *Journal of Comparative Neurology, 70,* 161–180.

Gesell, A. (1945). *The embryology of behavior.* New York: Harper.

Gesell, A. (1954). The ontogenesis of infant behavior. In L. Carmichael (Ed.), *Manual of child psychology* (2nd ed., pp. 335–373). New York: Wiley.

Gesell, A., & Ames, L. B. (1940). The ontogenetic organization of prone behavior in human infancy. *Developmental Medicine and Child Neurology, 14,* 336–341.

Gesell, A., & Thompson, H. (1929). Learning and growth in identical infant twins: An experimental study by the method of co-twin control. *Genetic Psychology Monographs, 6,* 1–120.

Gesell, A., & Thompson, H. (1934). *Infant behavior: Its genesis and growth.* New York: McGraw-Hill

Gesell, A., & Thompson, H. (1941). Twins T and C from infancy to adolescence: A biogentic study of individual differences by the method of co-twin control. *Genetic Psychology Monographs, 24,* 3–121.

Gibson, J. J. (1979). *The ecological approach to visual perception.* Boston: Houghton-Mifflin.

Goldfield, E. C. (1987, April). Symmetry and asymmetry in the transition from rocking to crawling. In E. Thelen (Chair), *Crawling and walking: New perspectives in motor development.* Symposium conducted at the meetings of the Society for Research in Child Development, Baltimore, MD.

Goldfield, E. C., & Michel, G. F. (1986). The ontogeny of infant bimanual reaching during the first year. *Infant Behavior and Development, 9,* 81–89.

Gottlieb, G. (1976). Conceptions of prenatal development: Behavioral embryology. *Psychological Review, 83,* 215–234.

Gottlieb, G. (1983). The psychobiological approach to developmental issues. In M. M. Haith & J. C. Campos (Eds.), *Handbook of child psychology. Vol. 2. Infancy and developmental psychobiology* (pp. 1–26). New York: John Wiley.

Haith, M. M. (1980). *Rules that babies look by.* Hillsdale, NJ: Lawrence Erlbaum.

Hay, J. G. (1985). *The biomechanics of sports techniques.* Englewood Cliffs, NJ: Prentice-Hall.

Jones, M. C. (1926). The development of early behavior patterns in young children. *Pedagogical Seminary, 33,* 537–585.

Kaufman, L. (1979). *Perception: The world transformed.* New York: Oxford University Press.

Kelso, J. A. S., & Clark, J. E. (Eds.). (1982). *The development of movement control and coordination.* New York: Wiley.

Klinnert, M., Campos, J. J., Sorce, J., Emde, R., & Svejda, M. (1982). Emotions as behavior regulators: Social referencing in infancy. In R. Plutchik & H. Kellerman (Eds.), *Emotions in early development* (Vol. 2, pp. 57–86). New York: Academic Press.

Kopp, C. B. (1979). Perspectives on infant motor system development. In M. Bornstein & W. Kessen (Eds.), *Psychological development from infancy: Image to intention* (pp. 9–35). Hillsdale, NJ: Erlbaum.

Kuhn, T. S. (1962). *The structure of scientific revolutions.* Chicago: University of Chicago Press.

Mahler, M. S., Pine, F., & Bergman, A. (1975). *The psychological birth of the child.* New York: Basic Books.

McCall, R. B., Eichorn, D. H., & Hogarty, P. S. (1977). Transitions in early mental development. *Monographs of the Society for Research in Child Development, 42,* (3, serial no. 171).

McGraw, M. B. (1935). *Growth: A study of Johnny and Jimmy.* New York: Appleton-Century.

McGraw, M. B. (1939). Swimming behavior of the human infant. *Journal of Pediatrics, 15,* 485–490.

McGraw, M. B. (1941). Development of neuro-muscular mechanisms as reflected in the crawling and creeping behavior of the human infant. *Journal of Genetic Psychology, 58,* 83–111.

McGraw, M. B. (1943). *The neuromuscular maturation of the human infant.* New York: Columbia University Press.

McGraw, M. B. (1946). Maturation of behavior. In L. Carmichael (Ed.), *Manual of child psychology*. New York: Wiley.

Newell, K. M. (1986). Constraints on the development of coordination. In H. T. A. Whiting & M. G. Wade (Eds), *Motor skills acquisition in children: Aspects of coordination and control* (pp. 341–371). Amsterdam: North-Holland.

Piaget, J. (1952). *The origins of intelligence in children.* New York: International Universities Press.

Piaget, J. (1954). *The construction of reality in the child.* New York: Basic Books.

Rader, N., Bausano, M., & Richards, J. (1980). On the nature of the visual-cliff-avoidance response in human infants. *Child Development, 51,* 61–68.

Richards, J., & Rader, N. (1981). Crawling-onset age predicts visual cliff avoidance in infants. *Journal of Experimental Psychology: Human Perception and Performance, 7,* 382–387.

Richards, J., & Rader, N. (1983). Affective, behavioral and avoidance responses on the visual cliff: Effects of crawling onset age, crawling experience and testing age. *Psychophysiology, 20,* 633–642.

Rosenblith, J. F., & Sims-Knight, J. E. (1985). *In the beginning: Development in the first two years.* Monterey, CA: Brooks-Cole.

Rovee-Collier, C. K., & Fagen, J. W. (1981). The retrieval of memory in early infancy. In L. P. Lipsett (Ed.), *Advances in infancy research* (pp. 225–254). Norwood, NJ: Ablex.

Scientific American. (1987). "Overview: Growing Up—Del and Rey, Johnny and Jimmy, and nature versus nurture." *257,* 30–32.

Sherrington, C. S. (1906). *The integrative action of the nervous system.* New York: Scribner's.

Shinn, M. W. (1900). *The biography of a baby.* New York: Houghton-Mifflin.

Shirley, M. M. (1931). *The first two years: A study of twenty-five babies I. Postural and locomotor development.* Minneapolis: University of Minneapolis Press.

Shirley, M. M. (1933). Locomotor and visual-manual functions in the first two years. In C. Murchison (Ed.), *The handbook of child psychology* (pp. 236–279). Worcester, MA: Clark University Press.

Spitz, R. (1965). *The first year of life.* New York: International Universities Press.

Stelmach, G. E. (1976). *Motor control: Issues and trends.* New York: Academic Press.

Super, C. (1976). Environmental effects on motor development: The case of "African infant precocity." *Developmental Medicine and Child Neurology, 18,* 561–567.

Terman, L. M. (1925). *Genetic studies of genius: Vol. 1. Mental and physical traits of a thousand gifted children.* Stanford, CA: Stanford University Press.

Thelen, E. (1984). Learning to walk: Ecological demands and phylogenetic constraints. In L. P. Lipsett (Ed.), *Advances in infancy research* (Vol. 3, pp. 213–260). Norwood, NJ: Ablex.

Thelen, E. (1985). Developmental origins of motor coordination: Leg movements in human infants. *Developmental Psychobiology, 18,* 1–22.

Thelen, E. (1986). Treadmill-elicited stepping in seven-month-old infants. *Child Development, 57,* 1498–1506.

Thelen, E. (1987). The role of motor development in developmental psychology: A view of the past and an agenda for the future. In N. Eisenberg (Ed.), *Contemporary topics in developmental psychology* (pp. 3–33). New York: Wiley.

Thelen, E., & Fisher, D. M. (1982). Newborn stepping: An explanation for a "disappearing reflex." *Developmental Psychology, 18,* 760–775.

Thelen, E., & Fisher, D. M. (1983). The organization of spontaneous leg movements in newborn infants. *Journal of Motor Behavior, 15,* 353–377.

Thelen, E., & Fogel, A. (in press). Toward an action-based theory of infant development. In J. Lockman & N. Hazen (Eds.), *Action in social context.* New York: Plenum.

Thelen, E., Kelso, J. A. S., & Fogel, A. (1987). Self-organizing systems and infant motor development. *Developmental Review, 7,* 39–65.

Thelen, E., Skala, K. D., & Kelso, J. A. S. (1987). The dynamic nature of early coordination: Evidence from bilateral leg movements in young infants. *Developmental Psychology, 23,* 179–186.

Trettien, A. W. (1900). Creeping and walking. *The American Journal of Psychology, 12,* 1–57.

Turvey, M. T. (1977). Preliminaries to a theory of action with reference to vision. In R. Shaw & J. Bransford (Eds.), *Perceiving, acting and knowing* (pp. 211–265). Hillsdale, NJ: Erlbaum.

Uzgiris, I. C. (1976). Organization of sensorimotor intelligence. In M. Lewis (Ed.), *Origins of intelligence* (pp. 123–163). New York: Plenum Press.

Watson, J. B. (1919). Psychology from the standpoint of a behaviorist. Philadelphia: J. B. Lippincott.

Watson, J. B., & Watson, R. R. (1921). Studies in infant psychology. *Scientific Monthly, 13,* 493–515.

Wellman, B. L. (1931). Physical growth and motor development and their relation to mental development in children. In C. Murchison (Ed.), *A handbook of child psychology* (pp. 242–277). Worcester, MA: Clark University Press.

White, B. L., Castle, P., & Held, R. (1964). Observations of the development of visually directed reaching. *Child Development, 35,* 349–364.

Zelazo, P. R. (1983). The development of walking: New findings and old assumptions. *Journal of Motor Development, 15,* 99–137.

Zelazo, P. R., Zelazo, N. A., & Kolb, S. (1972). "Walking" in the newborn. *Science, 176,* 314–315.

AUTHOR NOTES:

Portions of this chapter were presented at the Motor Development Research Consortium Meetings at the University of Indiana, Bloomington, September 1987. This work is supported by research grants from the National Institute of Child Health and Development (HD/MH #22093) and the March of Dimes Birth Defects Foundation (MOD #12-188). Many of the thoughts and ideas expressed in this chapter were formed during stimulating intellectual exchanges with Joseph Campos during my tenure as an NIMH postdoctoral trainee (MH #09295). I thank both Joe Campos and Marshall Haith for their postdoctoral sponsorship from 1983 to 1986. I warmly thank Marshall Haith, Esther Thelen, Jane Clark, and Denise Arehart for their very helpful comments on earlier drafts of this paper. Finally, I would like to acknowledge the terse yet helpful comments made by an anonymous reviewer.

8

ARE GESELL'S DEVELOPMENTAL PRINCIPLES GENERAL PRINCIPLES FOR THE ACQUISITION OF COORDINATION?

K. M. Newell
R. E. A. van Emmerik

ABSTRACT

In this paper we consider whether Gesell's developmental principles, particularly those of developmental direction, reciprocal interweaving, and self-regulation, might be regarded as general principles for the acquisition of coordination. It appears that there are a number of parallel descriptive trends in the acquisition of phylogenetic and ontogenetic activities, and these commonalities are due to the confluence of constraints imposed on action. There are, however, a number of task conditions in both phylogenetic and ontogenetic activities that produce exceptions to the descriptive principles identified by Gesell. These demonstrated exceptions to the developmental motor sequence hold significant consequences for the development of a general theory of action that is not specific to activity type or maturational age.

One of the enduring concepts in motor development is the notion that there is a fundamental movement sequence that emerges during the early years of life. Indeed, no matter what the theoretical viewpoint of development, there is a general agreement that there is a relatively invariant intra- and inter-task sequence to the onset of the fundamental activities of posture, locomotion, and prehension during infancy and early childhood. This notion is in large part predicated on the careful systematic observation of infants by early workers in the field of motor development such as Bayley (1935), Gessell (1929), McGraw (1943), and Shirley (1931), and the supplementation of these observations through the more recent charting of the milestones of fetal movement progressions (e.g., de Vries,

Visser, & Prechtl, 1983), which can now be conducted with the aid of modern technological advances. Departures from the infant developmental motor sequence have been reported (e.g., Robson, 1970, Touwen, 1971), but typically these exceptions to the motor sequence rule, as it were, are downplayed in both descriptions and explanations of the acquisition of the fundamental movement patterns, and, by and large, treated erroneously (as we will argue subsequently) as isolated aberrations.

The fundamental movement patterns of posture, locomotion, and prehension are usually classified as phylogenetic activities because they are in that general group of activities that are viewed as essential to the survival of the species. Moreover, the commonality of the emergence of the movement forms across all infants from all cultures provides intuitive *face validity* to an endogenous maturational account of the motor development sequence. The champion of the maturational cause to development in general and motor development in particular was Arnold Gesell (1929, 1946). Others such as Myrtle McGraw (1943) held views that were variations on this maturational theme.

Gesell saw growth and development as unitary with the process of growth mediated by innate processes that are laid down by genes. This intuition recognized the dynamic field like processes that constrain physiochemical systems such as the human species, where "field-like" refers to those neuromuscular and biochemical processes which operate within the body's soft tissue as a result of concentration differences, gradients, asymmetries, and so on; but Gesell's perspective also promoted the prescriptive properties of the genetic code in terms of accounting for the sequential growth process that was evident, for example, in the development of the fundamental movement sequence. In Gesell's maturational theory, this dynamic process of growth was governed by a number of behavioral principles of development.

The central question addressed in this paper is whether one might consider Gesell's developmental principles, particularly those of developmental direction, reciprocal interweaving, and self-regulation, as general principles for the acquisition of coordination. Bernstein (1967) considered coordination to reflect an activity that guarantees that a movement has homogeneity, integration, and structural unity. The acquisition of coordintion was defined by Bernstein as the process of mastering the redundant degrees of freedom (e.g., joints, muscles, motor units) of the moving organism. Operationally, we can view coordination as the function that constrains the potentially free variables into a behavioral unit (Kugler, Kelso, & Turvey, 1980; Newell, 1985). By general principles of the acquisition of coordination, we mean that Gesell's tenets of development may also relate to the acquisition of ontogenetic activities throughout the life span. Ontogenetic activities are those which emerge during ontogeny due to the short-term demands of society. These activities are not general to the species and include activities such as handwriting and piano playing. Thus the developmental principles advanced by Gesell could cut across the categories of both phylogenetic and ontogenetic activities and may not be confined to the early phase of the life-span continuum.

The question of the generality of Gesell's developmental principles has not been broached previously, in large part we suspect, because the traditional skill-learning approach to the study of ontogenetic activities has essentially eliminated the problem of the acquisition of coordination due to the selection of a very narrow range of task constraints employed for experimentation (see Newell, 1985, for an elaboration of this argument). One consequence of this experimental limitation is that the acquisition of new patterns of coordination have not been a focus of study in adult motor learning. Furthermore, and perhaps in part due to the omission of the study of the acquisition of coordination in adults, different theories exist for the acquisition of phylogenetic and ontogenetic activities, and there is little connection between the field of motor development and that of motor learning or skill acquisition. This activity-based theoretical distinction is consistent with the general trend of theoretical propositions in the movement domain to be very task specific (Newell, 1989).

There have been some new empirical thrusts of late in the adult skill-learning domain, however, and a few studies have been published that examined directly the acquisition of new patterns of coordination in adults as they learn to meet the demands of a given set of task constraints. In our view, the findings from these studies show a number of similarities to those evident in the development of the fundamental movement patterns in infants as reported by Gesell and other developmentalists. It is this insight that initiated the question that guides the discussion of this chapter.

To help outline an answer to our question, we will first introduce and review the essence of the principles of behavioral development as postulated by Gesell. We will then examine the evidence in the adult motor-skill acquisition literature that bears on and provides possible parallels to Gesell's behavioral developmental principles. In the final section of the paper, we discuss what the establishment of a descriptive common ground in these two domains could mean for the possibility of a general theory of action that would encompass and help break down the well-engrained traditional distinction of phylogenetic and ontogenetic activities.

GESELL'S PRINCIPLES OF BEHAVIORAL DEVELOPMENT

Gesell (1946, 1952) advanced six behavioral principles from his general maturational theory of development. This maturational position postulated that the basic forms and sequences of ontogenesis are determined by endogenous rather than exogenous factors. Furthermore, the environment, whether considered as internal or external, supported and reflected the behavior form, but it does not engender the ontogenetic sequence. Maturation is the term that Gesell used to reflect this intrinsic patterning of behavior.

The six behavioral developmental principles outlined by Gesell are not equally relevent to the question posed in this chapter regarding the acquisition of coordination. Accordingly, each principle is given differential weighting in light of its relevance for the issues at stake here. In the subsequent section of the paper, we will draw on the relevant adult data to provide an immediate basis for comparison of the evidence in domains that are rarely contrasted.

Principle of Motor Priority and Fore-Reference.

The essential point of this principle is that the functional capacity of the motor system is laid down in advance of actual experience and utilization. Gesell notes that in embryogenesis, muscle function precedes neural; motor nerves are functional before sensory; and proprioception sensitivity antedates exteroception. Thus, Gesell proposed that virtually all activities involve the motor system and have a motor origin.

Principle of Developmental Direction.

Motor development involves increasing differentiation of the action system that follows the somatic and behavioral organizational lines of cephalo-caudal, proximo-distal, and ulnar-radial. These directional trends have been well illustrated in the development of the fundamental activities of posture, locomotion, and prehension. For example, the infant progressions in grasping configuration are seen to advance from gross palmar, to ulnar, medial, and radial digits (Halverson, 1931). These directional advances in motor control occur in successive phases with variations that create a spiral progressive-regressive character to the sequence of motor development. In essence, Gesell was promoting a *functional* developmental direction to motor development that was parallel in principle to the *structural* directional trends that had been advanced previously in embryology (Jackson, 1914; Kingsbury, 1924).

Principle of Reciprocal Interweaving.

Gesell noted that there is a duplexity to much of the anatomy and nervous system of the organism. Many organs are paired, and there is functional duplexity in, for example, the reciprocal antagonism of flexor and extensor muscles, in excitation and inhibition of biochemical and behavioral processes, and in many other aspects of the system. The task of development is to bring these opposites into effective coordination. Gesell argued that this process was not linear and that reciprocal interweaving is evidenced ontogenetically by successive shifts in the ascendancy of one function in the pair of organs under consideration over the other, with progressive integration and modulation of the resultant behavior patterns.

The classic example of this principle for Gesell was the postural transformation in the development of upright posture and walking that could be characterized into 23 stages with reference to abduction, adduction, bilaterality, unilaterality, ipsilaterality, and crossed laterality. Figure 1 shows Gesell's expressive schematic of the progressive-regressive nature of the patterning of prone behavior during the first year of life. It should be noted that this image of the development of motor skills is very much an "image" in the sense that it is not based on a data set that provides strong empirical support for the progressive-regressive trends of the development of the fundamental motor skills.

Principle of Functional Asymmetry.

The sequence of reciprocal interweaving does not lead eventually to perfect symmetry. Indeed, Gesell proposed that there is a functional role to the resultant asymmetry that is evident in all aspects of behavior. The classic asymmetry that is magnified in infant posture is the tonic neck reflex, but the inevitable dominance of one hand, foot, and eye over its paired opposite was also viewed as an advantage for stable behavior.

Principle of Self-Regulation.

Gesell viewed the developing action system as in a state of formative instability combined with a progressive movement toward stability. The system is self-regulatory in that in establishing new behavior it adheres to the stability inherent in the system. In other words, the variations in behavior that create instability are constrained by the mutual influence of stable elements of the system. Gesell views this fluctuation between stability and instability in the preservation of the organism as a reflection of the self-regulatory properties of the system.

Principle of Optimal Realization.

The behavior growth of the organism tends toward maximum realization irrespective of the perturbations or insults that are imposed on the system. Thus, even in the face of significant breaches in the normal cycle of growth, compensatory or substitutive, growth allows the system to tend toward optimal realization.

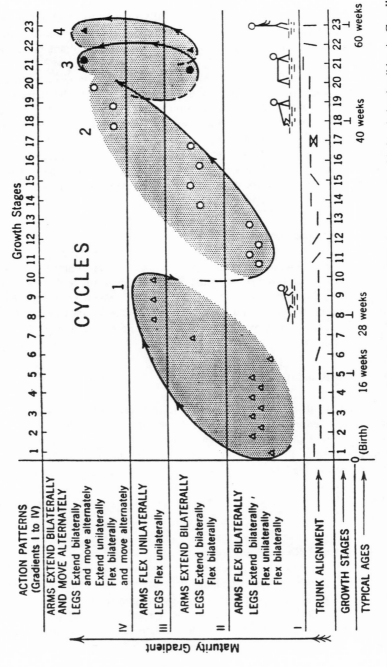

FIG. 1. Growth cycles in the patterning of prone behavior (adapted from "The ontogenesis of infant behavior," by A. Gesell in L. Carmichael (Ed.), *Manual of child psychology.* Copyright © 1946 by John Wiley and Sons. Reprinted by permission.)

PARALLEL BEHAVIORAL PRINCIPLES IN
ONTOGENETIC ACTIVITIES

We now examine from a broader perspective Gesell's principles of developmental direction, functional asymmetry, reciprocal interweaving, and self-regulation, since these tenets are the most directly relevant to problems of motor control, and the question under examination in this paper. Indeed, it is apparent that there are a number of parallels between these so-called developmental principles and the trends evident in the changes of the behavioral patterns in the acquisition of ontogenetic activities, irrespective of the age or maturational state of the performer. We now outline some of the evidence that supports this point of view.

Directional Trends in the Acquisition of Ontogenetic Activities.

The movement form of the beginner or less well practiced motor skill performer is often qualitatively distinct from that of the skilled performer. It is not simply that the expert scores higher than the beginner on some externally defined task criterion (which she typically does), but rather that the relative motion patterns that emerge from the configuration of the torso and limbs tend to exhibit different topological relationships as a function of skill level. This is particularly noticeable if one contrasts the movement form of an individual on the first few attempts in a given activity with the form that is expressed as a reflection of a skilled performance (Newell, 1985).

Many observations of change in qualitative movement form with increments of skill are anecdotal, but there are now some findings from empirical studies that exhibit systematic trends in the changes of coordinated movement patterns. Indeed, there is preliminary evidence that cephalo-caudal, proximo-distal, and ulnar-radial directional principles identified by Gesell for infant motor development may also be observed in the acquisition of ontogenetic activities by adult subjects. We will focus on that evidence that has emerged from our laboratory.

In a recent series of studies, we have been examining how adults learn to coordinate their limb segments to produce cursive script (van Emmerik & Newell, 1989, in press; Newell & van Emmerik, 1989). We had adults use their nondominant limb as a method to establish a relatively unpracticed limb linkage for the task constraints at hand. A general finding was that in naturally dominant right-handed subjects there was a trend to write from the shoulder of the nondominant left limb. Subjects locked the more distal finger, wrist, and elbow joints and effected the pen output from the shoulder. Figure 2 shows the relative motion plots of pairs of limb links for the dominant and nondominant limb in a single subject writing his signature. The highly regular diagonal relative motion patterns for the left (nondominant) limb in Figure 2B for the pen-wrist and

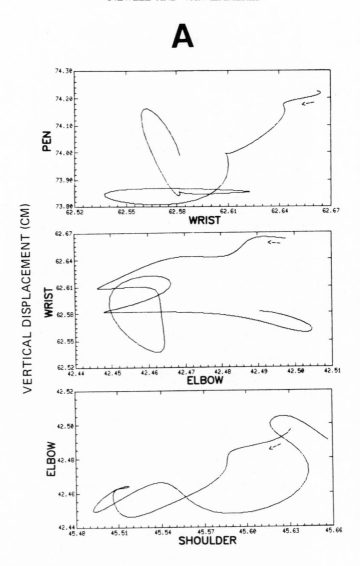

FIG. 2. Position-position plots of pairs of pen and joint movements for individual trials of dominant (A) and nondominant (B) signature production (adapted from "The acquisition of coordination: Preliminary analysis of learning to write," by K. M. Newell and R.E.A. van Emmerik, 1989, *Human Movement Science, 8.* Copyright 1989 by Elsevier Science Publishers. Reprinted by permission.)

B

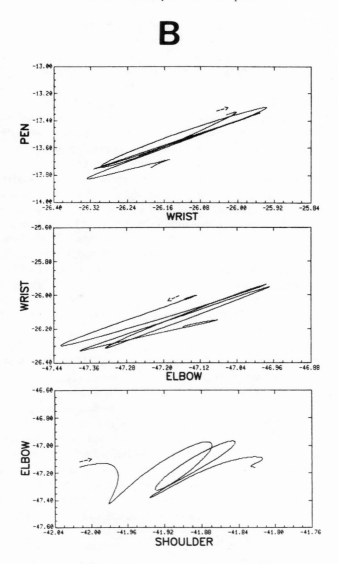

VERTICAL DISPLACEMENT (CM)

wrist-elbow indicate high phase-locking between these units. The diagonal patterns were absent in the right (dominant limb), which reflects a decoupling of pen, wrist, elbow, and shoulder in producing the cursive script (Figure 2a). This proximal shift occurred in the unpracticed (nondominant) limb even though the subjects were producing script that was the natural size for writing their signature in a checkbook or generating a draft of a manuscript—a writing size that is for the dominant limb normally driven by motions at the fingers and wrists. This same set of topological limb relationships was not apparent in naturally dominant left-handers due to the differences in the directional constraint of writing for right- and left-handers (van Emmerik & Newell, in press).

The naturally dominant right-handers were given some 10,000 trials of practice in writing their signature and producing segments of cursive *e*'s over a 3-month period. This practice period induced a small change in the topological properties of the arm link relative motion at the shoulder joint, suggesting that control was in effect shifting to the more distal segments. The amount of practice employed, however, was not enough to generate the limb relationships evident in the highly practiced dominant limb. This finding is consistent with the significantly long practice period required for children in early childhood to learn to write, although clearly there are other factors mediating the pace with which children learn to appropriately coordinate their limb segments in the task of writing.

We have found similar proximo-distal practice effects with adults learning to play the game of darts with their nondominant limb (McDonald, van Emmerik, & Newell, 1989). In this study, subjects had 5 days of 120 trials per day practice of learning to throw darts with their nondominant limb and 2 days of 120 practice trials per day with the dominant limb. This amount of practice produced a reduction in the contribution of the shoulder joint to the dart throw in the dominant limb in much the same way as we reported for the nondominant limb handwriting. These proximo-distal shifts in the pattern of coordination in the dominant limb did not take as much practice to effect as it appears to be necessary for the task of either dart throwing or handwriting with the nondominant limb, although it is reasonable to project that further practice with either limb would have led to additional topological changes in the organization of limb dynamics.

It should be noted that the findings from the studies briefly outlined above are related to arm movements and tasks in which the hand is manipulating an object. A test of these directional trends in limb coordination patterns under a broader range of task constraints is clearly in order. However, there are good grounds upon which to expect the directional trends to hold up under a considerable range of task conditions. For example, consider the practicing typist or piano player who gradually learns to consistently and effectively employ the more radial digits of their hands in depressing the keyboard. In summary, there are empirical and intuitive grounds to project that the directional trends identified by Gesell for the emergence of the fundamental movement patterns will be similarly found in the acquisition of a range of ontogenetic activities, independent of the age of the performer.

Reciprocal Interweaving in Ontogenetic Activities.

The principle of reciprocal interweaving is intimately linked to the principle of developmental direction. The successive shifts in the progressive ascendancy of one element of a pair of organs occur within the backdrop of the general directional trends of cephalo-caudal, proximo-distal, and ulnar-radial development. This relationship is illustrated in Gesell's growth cycle for prone progression that was displayed in Figure 1.

Given that there have been few studies of the changes in the qualitative aspects of the coordination pattern as a function of practice, we have no direct evidence of the cyclical nature of the changes in the topological properties of limb organization in ontogenetic activities. A further problem, of course, is that there appears to be so few adult skill learning studies that have required a practice period that is sufficiently long in duration to allow examination of the cylical nature of performance. The principle of reciprocal interweaving is consistent, however, with the generally advanced anecdotal descriptions of performance changes that occur as a function of practice. Adults often exhibit progressions and regressions in both the production of movement form and the resultant task-oriented behavioral outcome while practicing a task. Indeed, Fuchs (1962), building on the earlier work of Paul Fitts, proposed the progression-regression hypothesis to account for the systematic changes that occurred as a function of practice and stress, respectively, in terms of the signal cue (position, velocity, acceleration) that was being used to guide the tracking performance. However, these types of behavioral change in adult skill learning have not been generally analyzed with respect to their cyclical reciprocal nature.

The reciprocal properties of muscle activity reflect another level of analysis at which Gesell observed and promoted the principle of reciprocal interweaving. Gesell interpreted Sherrington's (1906) law of reciprocal innervation in muscle synergisms as fundamental to movement control. The general view was that effective movement resulted from the inhibition of one set of muscles while the opposing set of muscles are in excitation. In short, co-contraction of opposing muscle pairs (or groups) is usually seen as an ineffective reciprocal relationship for efficient motor control.

Gesell interpreted the gradual ascendancy of one muscle pair in ontogenesis as an example of reciprocal interweaving. Indeed, Gesell proposed that it was the progressive nature of this ascendancy over sets of muscles that gave rise to the reciprocal nature of the movement form observed at the behavioral level in the motor development sequence. It is evident, however, that similar trends in the agonist-antagonist or synergistic relations between muscles occur while adults are learning ontogenetic activities.

The general findings from electromyographic (EMG) studies examining the muscle activity of adults learning motor skills reveal that: (a) there is a reduction of overall muscle activity as a function of practice; (b) there is a reduction of co-contraction and a more finely tuned synergistic relation between opposing pairs of muscles (Basmajian, 1978). Prolonged practice can even lead to the generation of momentum periods during which time neither muscle in the relevant muscle-pair synergy is active (Hubbard, 1960). The learned patterning of the muscle synergy is, therefore, congruent with the principle of reciprocal interweaving evident in the developmental cycle of behavior.

It should be noted, however, that practice on a given task will not always result in the elimination of co-contraction in opposing groups of muscles. Certain task constraints, such as a rapid 100-ms movement that is brought to a stop voluntarily by the performer, ensure that co-contraction of opposing muscle groups will eventuate. In summary, although not many studies have examined changes in the EMG signal as a function of extended practice on a task and the resultant acquisition of skill, there is sufficient evidence to point to parallels with Gesell's interpretation of reciprocal interweaving in muscle action in the development of prone progression.

Functional Asymmetry in Ontogenetic Activities.

The functional asymmetry that Gesell identified in infant motor development is evident in adult performance of ontogenetic activities. For example, the tonic neck reflex is still present and demonstrable in adults, particularly under demanding task constraints (Fukuda, 1961; Hellebrandt, Schade, & Carns, 1962). The dominance of one hand, foot, and eye over its paired opposite probably only strengthens over the life-span. Thus, asymmetry is present at the macro-biomechanical level of performance and in the neural substrate as evident in reflexive action. The functional nature of these asymmetries, however, has not been a significant issue for theories of the ontogenetic development of skill.

The acquisition of ontogenetic activities clearly engenders functional asymmetries in action, although these have not been studied in any detail. For example, adults typically exhibit preferred directions of motion as reflected, for example, in drawing a given shape. This kind of functional asymmetry is beyond the bounds of the examples provided by Gesell, but it may well be that there are common principles driving these asymmetries that are evident at different stages of the life span.

Self-Regulation in Ontogenetic Activities.

Gesell proposed that the self-regulatory properties of the system were reflected in the fluctuation between stability and instability. He did not develop this fieldlike dynamic account of the development of phylogenetic activities beyond the behavioral developmental principles outlined here. Field-theory approaches to biology were common in the first half of the 20th century (e.g., Weiss, 1939), but they became dormant in the 1950s and 1960s due to the strong claims of the mechanistic genetic approaches of biology. Field-theory approaches to biology and psychology have regained some ground, however, and the physical biology perspective of the coordinative structure theory of motor control (Kugler et al., 1980; Kugler & Turvey, 1987) holds some descriptive commonalities to the self-regulation ideas expressed by Gesell. For example, Kugler and Turvey propose that the exploration of perceptual-motor workspaces is guided by the structural stabilities and instabilities of evolving flow field processes (Kugler & Turvey, 1987; Turvey & Kugler, 1984). The stability and instability of the flow processes is modeled in terms of the gradient and equilibrium regions of the perceptual-motor workspace using the techniques of nonlinear dynamics and stability theory. There are strong implications of this dynamical approach to action for the motor development domain (Kugler, 1986; Kugler, Kelso, & Turvey, 1982; Thelen, Kelso, & Fogel, 1987), and these linkages are actively being pursued on the empirical front.

Summary.

The foregoing brief outline of some parallels between Gesell's developmental behavioral principles and the descriptive trends evident in adults learning ontogenetic activities holds a number of interesting implications for theory development in both phylogenetic and ontogenetic activities. It needs to be reiterated that further empirical work would be desirable to support the claim of parallel descriptive principles in the acquisition of phylogenetic and ontogenetic activities. However, there is clearly sufficient evidence to make the theoretical pursuit of this descriptive parallel of the coordinative mode changes in phylogenetic and ontogenetic activities an interesting proposition.

THE PARALLELS IN PHYLOGENETIC AND ONTOGENETIC ACTIVITIES RECONSIDERED

The identification of a relatively invariant sequence to the development of the fundamental movement patterns during infancy was established some 50 years ago through the work of developmentalists attempting to chart the milestones of the onset of the fundamental movement patterns (Bayley, 1935; Gesell, 1929; McGraw, 1943; Shirley, 1931). This work, and the subsequent interpretation of it, has highlighted the *regularity* in the developmental sequence through infancy, rather than the *variability* of motor behavior. Thus, as Connolly (1986) has argued, the trend in motor development has been to neglect variations within individuals, between individuals, and between behaviors.

A further outgrowth of the acceptance of the invariant nature of the motor development sequence has been to give *prima facie* evidence to the maturation theory of Gesell (1929, 1946). As it was intimated in the opening paragraph of this paper, the exceptions to the motor development sequence has been downplayed inspite of the fact that the sustained exhibition of stereotypic behavior at any stage of the lifespan, both within and between individuals, would probably be viewed as abnormal. The most common between-subject variation, of course, is the variation in the timing of the onset of a given movement pattern in the motor development sequence. This variation in the rate of movement pattern onsets is magnified in comparisons of cross-cultural influences on motor development (Super, 1981), but it is also apparent between individuals within a given culture. Thus, there are distributional properties associated with the developmental motor sequence, but these variational features of behavior are not problematic for maturation theory.

More damaging to maturational theory, particularly if one assumes a preformationist view of maturation, are variations in the emergence of the order of the movement patterns that constitute the motor development sequence. These variations in sequence order may be due to omissions, commissions, and reversals of the movement forms of the developmental motor sequence. For example, Robson (1970) reported that some infants did not crawl as a precursor to the onset of independent upright locomotion. Reversals in the order of appearance of movement patterns in the developmental postural sequence have also been reported by Touwen (1971). Similarly, the child-handling practices of different cultures (Bril, 1986) can lead to the introduction of new movement forms to the motor development sequence. The study of feral children also suggests that the infant motor development sequence does not remain invariant in the face of atypical environmental constraints. Thus, there have been a number of published examples of variations in the emergence of movement forms in the motor development sequence.

The above examples, together with others that exist in the literature, tend to get passed off as insignificant in traditional accounts of the motor development sequence, in the sense that these exceptions to the motor development sequence are rarely discussed. We would propose, however, that these departures from the "normal" motor development sequence should be taken as a serious challenge for Gesell's essentially preformationist maturational view of motor development. Furthermore, it is quite evident that a more varied and significant manipulation, than heretofore conducted, of the various sources of constraint to the development of action would provide additional grounds to challenge both Gesell's description and explanation of the motor development sequence.

There are three primary sources of constraint to action: namely, environmental, organismic, and task constraints (Newell, 1986). In the general sense, constraints are boundary conditions that limit the motion of a given entity or property. The organism holds a variety of structural and functional constraints to action that have been analyzed at a variety of levels of analysis (Newell, 1984a). Furthermore, it is useful to distinguish between environmental constraints that reflect the ambient conditions to the task and the more local and focal task constraints that include: (1) the goal of the task; (2) rules specifying or constraining the response dynamics; and (3) implements or machines that specify or constrain the response dynamics. These sources of constraint interact to channel the emergent dynamics of the child in action. The traditional developmental polemic of maturation versus learning or endogenous versus exogenous may be reflected in the organismic and environmental constraints distinction. However, a key ingredient that has been missing from many traditional and contemporary analyses of motor development is a consideration of task constraints (Newell, 1984b, 1986).

A particular problem for theoretical accounts of the motor development sequence is that they are predicated on observations made from a very narrow set of task constraints. In other words, the motor development sequence and the various resultant tests of motor ability that have been generated on the basis of it have been established on a particular set of task constraints that have been explicitly or implicitly created by the observer or tester. The established set of task constraints may or may not be optimal for eliciting a given movement pattern at the earliest chronological age—which is the direct goal of much of this infant motor development work. Indeed, it seems reasonable to propose that most conditions for examining infant motor development are probably not optimal, and, therefore, the resultant outcome (namely, the established motor development sequence) may be as much experimenter as child limited.

One example of the potential impact of task constraints on the motor development sequence is some recent work on the development of prehensile grip configurations from our laboratory. In one study (Newell, Scully, McDonald, & Baillargeon, in press), we showed that infants 4–9 months of age differentiated their grip configurations in a systematic way according to the size and shape properties of the object presented. These data suggest that the traditional description of an orderly sequence to the development of prehension (e.g., Halverson, 1931) is too conservative and inflexible to capture the functionally adaptive prehensile behavior of infants to changing task constraints. Furthermore, our prehensile work with preschoolers suggests that grip configurations are driven to a large degree by the body scale of the object (Newell, Scully, Tenenbaum, & Hardiman, 1989).

The significance of the foregoing discussion of exceptions and limitations to the motor development sequence is that some of the descriptive principles that constitute the heart of Gesell's maturational theory may be very task specific. In other words, principles such as that of developmental direction may not be *general* action-related descriptive principles. Rather, they may well be task specific, or at best, reflective of a narrow category of task constraints. It might be anticipated that our account of the parallel descriptive trends evident in adults learning ontogenetic activities tends to undermine the potential of a task constraints interpretation to the motor development sequence. The position advanced here is just reverse, however, and the claim is that many of the descriptive parallels evident in phylogenetic and ontogenetic activities are primarily due to the common task constraints that drive the interaction of the organism with the environment. Such a proposition holds considerable relevance for theories of motor development and skill acquisition.

Consider, for example, the Gesellian principle of developmental direction. This principle was drawn with respect to an anatomical functional definition after the early anatomical structural descriptions of embryology (Jackson, 1914; Kingsbury, 1924). Thus the directional principles of cephalo-caudal, proximo-distal, and ulnar-radial are organismically driven without any reference to environmental or task constraints. It is our projection that these anatomical directional trends emerge in both phylogenetic and ontogenetic activities only because of the confluence of constraints at play in the organismic, environmental, and task interaction (Newell, 1984b, 1986). In other words, these directional trends are not direct reflections of the organismic constraints and prescriptions of maturation as implied by Gesell.

A broader manipulation of task constraints would expose the limitations of the anatomically based directional trends of Gesell. For example, a task in which a subject holds with the hand a fixed object and has to move his or her body in a systematic way to meet a task demand driven by the shoulder-joint configuration would probably reverse the proximo-distal trend in the control of the coordination mode. Similarly, a task in which a subject was to perform a novel handstand with the legs above the head may well reverse the cephalo-caudal trend. If the reversal of Gesell's developmental directional principles could be revealed through the above, or similar manipulations of task constraints, then this would provide strong evidence against the notion that the developmental principles are driven by maturational processes, particularly if such directional trends could be reversed at any point in the life-span cycle. Of course, if a broader range of task manipulations failed to engender a change in the directional trends, then this would provide stronger evidence for Gesell's maturational position than we now have. The latter outcome seems, however, to be an unlikely prospect, but no matter how the data fall out, it can be seen that there are many benefits to be gained from a stronger test of the influence of task constraints on motor development.

The task-specific or functional nature of limb organization has already been revealed in postural perturbation studies. Although a proximo-distal sequence in limb adjustments has been demonstrated in postural tasks (Friedli, Hallett, & Simon, 1984), there is evidence that the nature of the compensatory response can be reversed according to the specific functional demands of the task constraints. The mechanical demands of maintaining one's posture in relation to the center of gravity seems to be a more general constraint then the specific directional reorganization of limb-link relationships (Cordo & Nashner, 1982; Marsden, Merton, & Morton, 1981, 1983).

Although the above arguments have been directed toward the principle of developmental direction, we believe that a fuller consideration of the confluence of constraints on action will also hold relevance to the other developmental principles of Gesell. For example, the notion of reciprocal interweaving at both the macro coordination level and the more micro muscle synergy level can surely be influenced by the direct manipulation of task constraints. This proposal is also likely to operate across activity type and age-related boundaries.

In summary, it is proposed that the sensitivity of certain of the developmental principles of Gesell to task-constraint manipulations and their generality across the life-span holds significant implications for theoretical notions about motor development and the acquisition of skill in ontogenetic activities (Newell, 1986). We now turn to a brief discussion of some of these theoretical implications. Interestingly, it can be argued that the promotion of a general theoretical relevance of the task-constraint perspective for action is linked to Gesell's developmental principle of self-regulation.

THEORETICAL IMPLICATIONS OF THE COMMONALITIES AND EXCEPTIONS TO GESELL'S DEVELOPMENTAL PRINCIPLES

The foregoing account of the commonalities and exceptions of certain of Gesell's developmental principles in phylogenetic and ontogenetic activities holds a number of significant theoretical implications for the fields of both motor development and skill acquisition. We now consider a number of these theoretical issues with a view to their significance for formulating a general theory of action that is neither activity nor age specific. We begin by reconsidering Gesell's (1929, 1946) maturational theory.

The observation that some of the developmental principles identified by Gesell have also been observed in the acquisition of ontogenetic activities leads to a reconsideration of the place of maturational theory in motor development. The fact that certain of the developmental principles are evident in the learning of ontogenetic activities throughout the life-span suggests that Gesell's descriptive account of motor development may not be driven by a maturational explanation.

After all, it is doubtful if a maturational explanation would be advanced for the more rapid time scale over which a number of the parallel changes occur in ontogenetic activities (e.g., McDonald et al., 1989). Thus, the parallel descriptive trends evident in phylogenetic and ontogenetic activities should provide prima facie evidence against a maturational theory for even the development of phylogenetic activities. This theoretical challenge is only strengthened when one considers the theoretical relevance of the demonstrated exceptions to the motor development sequence and the strong role that task constraints play in influencing the resultant qualitative and quantitative dynamics of action (Newell, 1984b, 1986).

It is evident that Gesell's developmental principles for motor development are descriptions that fit a relatively large and common ground of task constraints that confront children in action. Thus the principles that relate to the development of action tend only to break down in both phylogenetic and ontogenetic activities under a broad manipulation of task constraints. These exceptions suggest that a strong preformationist view of maturation and motor development does not hold. This criticism of maturation theory (and the preformationist view, in particular) is not new, but it needs to be reiterated because it is apparent that interpretations of the relatively invariant order to the motor development sequence still dominate and are taken directly, or indirectly, as evidence for a prescriptive account of maturation theory. This trend is evident inspite of the early existence of competing views on maturation (Coghill, 1929), the introduction of Waddington's (1957) probablistic approach to maturation through the epigenetic landscape, and Connolly's (1970, 1986) highlighting of the significance of these positions for motor development. In summary, there are considerable problems with a number of Gesell's developmental principles, although it is clear that motor development needs to handle directly the issue of phylogenetic constraints (cf. Thelen, 1984).

A perspective on action that appears capable in principle of handling the commonalities and exceptions to the behavioral principles in both phylogenetic and ontogenetic activities is that of the coordinative structure theory (Kugler, 1986; Kugler et al., 1980, 1982; Kugler & Turvey, 1987). This perspective is based on: (a) a Gibsonian (1979) position to the role of information in supporting activity; (b) a thermodynamical perspective to accommodate the fact that organisms are open systems that allow the flow of energy to help organize the micro-macro conversions in harnassing the many degrees of freedom that need to be constrained (after Bernstein, 1967); and (c) a theoretical strategy that seeks to minimize the role of computational requirements through pursuing a natural law-based approach to the general action problem of linking dynamics and information. A central element of this perspective that has direct relevance to the commonalities and exceptions of Gesell's developmental principles is the proposal that constraints eliminate certain configurations of response dynamics, with the resulting pattern of coordination a reflection of principles of self-organizing optimality of the biological system, rather than specifications from some prescriptive symbolic knowledge structure.

A significant point that emerges from the coordinative structure perspective is that the contribution of task constraints to driving the organism-environment interaction have been underemphasized in traditional and contemporary theories of motor development (see Newell, 1984b, 1986). The functional nature of action needs to be reemphasized in understanding the adaptive properties of the organism to the constraints imposed. This is not to imply that there are no phylogenetic or maturational constraints to action. Clearly there are. The significant point is that assessments of motor development are made with reference to the confluence of constraints that exist on the organism. In the same way that a completely endogenous maturational perspective to motor development cannot be sustained, it is the case that a single source of constraint cannot be isolated in analyzing action. This is particularly the case if one adopts the Gibsonian (1979) affordance strategy of interpreting constraints from the perspective of their functional nature for the organism, rather than solely on extrinsic grounds. On this view, the organism-environment interaction cannot be viewed as an interaction in an analysis of variance sense, in which the factors of the design are by definition independent. The definitions of the organismic and environmental constraints are truly mutually related in the ecological approach to perception and action.

In summary, an empirical perspective is required that more vigorously and systematically manipulates the constraints to action in both phylogenetic and ontogenetic activities (Newell, 1986). A potential outcome of this approach is that the traditional distinction between phylogenetic and ontogenetic activities may be reformulated along the lines of a constraints view to action undergirded by an analysis of the gradients and equilibrium regions that support the perception-action cycle (Kugler & Turvey, 1987). It should be recognized that Gesell's developmental principle of self-regulation is a property that is consistent with the emerging physical biology view of both motor development and the acquisition of skill in general.

CONCLUDING REMARKS

The answer, then, to the central question of this paper, as in most academic questions, is yes and no. On the affirmative side, certain of the developmental principles identified by Gesell can also accommodate the changes in coordination mode evidenced by adults learning a range of ontogenetic activities. It appears that these parallel descriptive trends in the acquisition of phylogenetic and ontogenetic activities are due to a relatively common set of constraints to action. On the contradictory side, there are a number of task conditions that can produce exceptions to the descriptive principles identified by Gesell in both phylogenetic and ontogenetic activities. These exceptions may be less common in everyday action than the general developmental principles promoted by Gesell, but as we have argued, it is the demonstrated exceptions to the motor-sequence rule that hold significant consequences for the development of a general theory of action that is not specific to activity type or maturational age.

REFERENCES

Basmajian, J. V. (1978). *Muscles alive: Their functions revealed by electromyography* (4th ed.). Baltimore: Williams and Wilkins.

Bayley, N. (1935). The development of motor abilities during the first three years. *Monograph of the Society for Research on Child Development, 1,* 1–26.

Bernstein, N. (1967). *The coordination and regulation of movement.* New York: Pergamon.

Bril, B. (1986). Motor development and cultural attitudes. In H. T. A. Whiting & M. G. Wade (Eds.), *Themes in motor development* (pp. 297–314). Boston: Martinus Nijhoff.

Coghill, G. E. (1929). *Anatomy and the problem of behavior.* Cambridge: Cambridge University Press.

Connolly, K. (1970). Skill development: Problems and plans. In K. Connolly (Ed.), *Mechanisms of motor skill development* (pp. 3–17). New York: Academic Press.

Connolly, K. J. (1986). A perspective on motor development. In M. G. Wade & H. T. A. Whiting (Eds.), *Motor development in children: Aspects of coordination and control* (pp. 3–22). Boston: Martinus Nijhoff.

Cordo, P., & Nashner, L. (1982). Properties of postural adjustments associated with rapid arm movement. *Journal of Neurophysiology, 47,* 287–302.

Emmerik, R. E. A. van, & Newell, K. M. (in press). The influence of task organismic constraints on intralimb kinematics and pen-point kinematics in a drawing task. *Acta Psychologica.*

Emmerik, R. E. A. van, & Newell, K. M. (1989). The relationship between pen-point and joint kinematics in handwriting and drawing. In C. Y. Suen, R. Plamodan, & M. L. Simner (Eds.), *Computer and human recognition in handwriting* (pp. 231–248). Singapore: World Scientific Publishing Company

Friedli, W. G., Hallett, M., & Simon, S. R. (1984). Postural adjustments associated with rapid voluntary arm movements. I. Electromyographic data. *Journal of Neurology, Neurosurgery, and Psychiatry, 47,* 611–622.

Fuchs, A. (1962). The progression-regression hypothesis in perceptual-motor skill learning. *Journal of Experimental Psychology, 63,* 177–192.

Fukuda, T. (1961). Studies on human dynamic postures from the viewpoint of postural reflexes. *Acta Oto-Laryngological* (Supplement 161).

Gesell, A. (1929). Maturation and infant behavior pattern. *Psychological Review, 36,* 307–319.

Gesell, A. (1946). The ontogenesis infant behavior. In L. Carmichael (Ed.), *Manual of child psychology* (pp. 295–331). New York: Wiley.

Gesell, A. (1952). *Infant development.* New York: Harper and Brothers.

Gibson, J. J. (1979). *The ecological approach to visual perception.* Boston: Houghton Mifflin.

Halverson, H. M. (1931). An experimental study of prehension in infants by means of systematic cinema records. *Genetic Psychology Monographs, 10,* 107–283.

Hellebrandt, F. A., Schade, M., & Carns, M. L. (1962). Methods of evoking the tonic neck reflexes in normal human subjects. *American Journal of Physical Medicine, 41,* 90–139.

Hubbard, A. W. (1960). Homokinetics: Muscular function in human movement. In W. R. Johnson (Ed.), *Science and medicine in exercise and sports* (pp. 5–23). New York: Harper & Row.

Jackson, C. M. (1914). Morphogenesis. In C. M. Jackson (Ed.), *Morris' human anatomy* (pp. 9–25). Philadelphia: Blakistons.

Kingsbury, B. F. (1924). The significance of the so-called law of cephalocaudal differential growth. *Anatomical Record, 27,* 305–321.

Kugler, P. N. (1986). A morphological perspective on the origin and evolution of movement patterns. In M. G. Wade & H. T. A. Whiting (Eds.), *Motor development in children: Aspects of coordination and control* (pp. 459–525). Boston: Martinus Nijhoff.

Kugler, P. N., Kelso, J. A. S., & Turvey, M. T. (1980). On the concept of coordinative structures as dissipative structures: 1. Theoretical lines of convergence. In G. E. Stelmach & J. Requin (Eds.), *Tutorials in motor behavior* (pp. 3–47). Amsterdam: North-Holland.

Kugler, P. N., Kelso, J. A. S., & Turvey, M. T. (1982). On the control and coordination of naturally developing systems. In J. A. S. Kelso & J. E. Clark (Eds.), *The development of movement control and coordination* (pp. 5–78). New York: Wiley.

Kugler, P. N., & Turvey, M. T. (1987). *Information, natural law, and the self-assembly of rhythmic movement.* Hillsdale, NJ: Erlbaum.

Marsden, C. D., Merton, P. A., & Morton, H. B. (1981). Human postural responses. *Brain, 104,* 513–534.

Marsden, C. D., Merton, P. A., & Morton, H. B. (1983). Rapid postural reactions to mechanical displacement of the hand in man. *Advances in Neurology, 39,* 645–659.

McDonald, P. V., Emmerik, R. E. A. van, & Newell, K. M. (1989). The effects of practice on limb kinematics in a drawing task. *Journal of Motor Behavior, 21,* 245–264.

McGraw, M. B. (1943). *The neuromuscular maturation of the human infant.* New York: Columbia University Press.

Newell, K. M. (1984a). Physical constraints to the development of motor skills. In J. R. Thomas (Ed.), *Motor development during preschool and elementary years* (pp. 105–120). Minneapolis: Burgess.

Newell, K. M. (1984b). *The development of coordination: Significance of task constraints.* Paper presented at the meeting of the American Association for the Advancement of Science, New York, NY.

Newell, K. M. (1985). Coordination, control and skill. In D. Goodman, R. B. Wilberg, & I. M. Franks (Eds.), *Differing perspectives in motor learning, memory and control* (pp. 295–317). Amsterdam: North-Holland.

Newell, K. M. (1986). Constraints on the development of coordination. In M. G. Wade & H. T. A. Whiting (Eds.), *Motor development in children: Aspects of coordination and control* (pp. 341–360). Boston: Martinus Nijhoff.

Newell, K. M. (1989). On task and theory specificity. *Journal of Motor Behavior, 21,* 92–96.

Newell, K. M., & Emmerik, R. E. A. van (1989). The acquisition of coordination: Preliminary analysis of learning to write. *Human Movement Science, 8,* 17–32.

Newell, K. M., Scully, D. M., McDonald, P. V., & Baillargeon, R. (1989). Task constraints and infant prehensile grip configurations: Asymmetry in perceiving and acting. *Developmental Psychobiology.*

Newell, K. M., Scully, D. M., Tenenbaum, F., & Hardiman, S. (1989). Body scale and the development of prehension. *Developmental Psychobiology, 22,* 1–13.

Robson, P. (1970). Shuffling, hitching, scooting, or sliding: Some observatiaons in 30 otherwise normal children. *Developmental Medicine and Child Neurology, 12,* 608–617.

Sherrington, C. S. (1906). *The integrative action of the nervous system.* New Haven, CT: Yale University Press.

Shirley, M. M. (1931). *The first two years: A study of twenty-five babies: Vol. 1. Postural and locomotor development.* Minneapolis: University of Minnesota Press.

Super, C. M. (1981). Cross-cultural research on infancy. In H. C. Triandis & A. Heron (Eds.), *Handbook of cross-cultural psychology: Developmental psychology* (Vol. 4). Boston: Allyn and Bacon.

Thelen, E. (1984). Learning to walk: Ecological demands and phylogenetic constraints. In L. P. Lipsitt & C. Rovee-Collier (Eds.), *Advances in infancy research* (pp. 213–260). Norwood, NJ: Ablex.

Thelen, E., Kelso, J. A. S., & Fogel, A. (1987). Self-organizing systems and infant motor development. *Developmental Review, 7,* 39–65.

Touwen, B. C. L. (1971). A study of the development of some motor phenomena in infancy. *Developmental Medicine and Child Neurology, 13,* 435–446.

Turvey, M. T., & Kugler, P. N. (1984). An ecological approach to perception and action. In H. T. A. Whiting (Ed.), *Human motor actions: Bernstein reassessed* (pp. 373–412). Amsterdam: North-Holland.

de Vries, J. I. P., Visser, G. H. A., & Prechtl, H. F. R. (1983). Fetal motility in the first half of pregnancy. In H. F. R. Prechtl (Ed.), *Continuity of neural functions from prenatal to postnatal life* (pp. 46–64). Oxford: Blackwell.

Waddington, C. H. (1957). *The strategy of the genes.* London: George, Allen & Unwin.

Weiss, R. (1939). *Principles of development.* New York: Henry Holt.

AUTHOR NOTE:

This work was supported in part by the National Institute of Health Award HD 21212.

9

THE MEASUREMENT AND EVALUATION OF SKILL WITHIN THE DYNAMICAL SYSTEMS PERSPECTIVE

Graham E. Caldwell
Jane E. Clark

ABSTRACT

The measurement and evaluation of skill within the dynamical systems perspective requires the use of different measures from those used in previous paradigms investigating skill (i.e., information processing theory). In this paper, we examine a selection of these measures for their utility in assessing motor skill. Both measures of movement outcome and measures of the movement itself are considered. Movement outcome measures explored include: mechanical efficiency; movement economy; mechanical task cost; total body impulse; effectiveness; and mechanical energy transfer. Measures of the movement itself are categorized into kinematic and kinetic measures. In addition to the traditional uses of kinematic measures of the position, velocity, and acceleration of the body and its segments' movement, we discuss several different methods such as phase portraits as potential measures of skillfullness. Kinetic measures considered include: muscle moments, segmental mechanical energies, and both joint and muscle power. For each of these measures, we present examples of their utility to the measure of skill and its development. From the dynamical systems perspective, these measures provide new ways of looking at motor skillfulness.

In a 1985 review, MacKenzie and Marteniuk asked "What is motor skill?" Correctly, they pointed out that the number of answers to that question is probably limited only by the number of extant experimental paradigms. For example, their behavioral perspective has led them to define motor skill in terms of the relationship between internal representations (i.e., action plans) formu-

165

lated to solve a movement problem and the implementation of those plans into a movement. The skilled mover is characterized as one who can readily adapt his/her action plan to a particular set of conditions in order to achieve the intended movement outcome. Such a definition is typical of those found in an information processing perspective (Schmidt, 1988). However, as MacKenzie and Marteniuk pointed out, the answer to "what is motor skill?" depends on one's research paradigm. Not surprising then is a very different definition offered by Saltzman and Kelso (1987) who work within the **dynamical systems** paradigm inspired by the writings of the Russian physiologist Nicolai Bernstein (1967). To these authors, motor skill is a one-to-one correspondence between the functional demands of the task and the dynamics underlying the movement.

Definitions of motor skill do more than define skill; they also define the way motor skills are measured and evaluated. For example, in the information processing paradigm, defining motor skills in terms of matching the movement to the intended outcome has led to an emphasis on the measurement of the movement's temporal and spatial accuracy. On the other hand, the emphasis in the dynamical systems paradigm on the movement dynamics has led to the measurement of other kinematic and kinetic variables. But while a good deal of experimental work has gone into the measurement of skill within the information processing paradigm, similar work has been slow in forthcoming from those within the dynamical systems perspective. This is not altogether unusual since the information processing paradigm has been employed in the motor domain for more than three decades (cf. Fitts, 1954), while the dynamical systems paradigm was introduced less than a decade ago.

Therefore the purpose of this paper is to explore the use of some variables that might provide insight into the measurement and evaluation of skill within the dynamical systems paradigm. However, before examining these variables, we review key elements of the dynamical systems paradigm and its relevance for those studying the development of motor skills. (For a more thorough review of dynamical systems, the reader is referred to Thelen, Kelso, & Fogel, 1987; Thelen, 1989).

OVERVIEW

The Dynamical Systems Paradigm

Decades ago Bernstein (1940/1984) recognized that the execution of the simplest movements requires the coordination of a large number of diverse elements. The difficulty posed by the vast number of individual elements to be coordinated and controlled came to be called the "degrees of freedom" problem. For the so-called prescriptive models in which order and regulation resulted from internal representations (i.e., motor programs or action plans), the system's degrees of freedom posed a formidable computational problem. It was Bernstein who pointed the way to the solution to the degrees of freedom problem and for many inspired the current theorizing in what is called dynamical theory (Kelso, Saltzman & Tuller, 1986), dynamical pattern theory (Schöner & Kelso, 1988), or, as preferred here, dynamical systems theory (Thelen, Kelso, & Fogel, 1987). Bernstein argued that free variables of the motor system are not individually controlled but are "collected" into larger units called "synergies" (Gelfand, Gurfinkel, Tsetlin, & Shik, 1971), "collectives" (Gelfand & Tsetlin, 1971), or "coordinative structures" (Easton, 1972; Turvey, 1977). This collective unit of action assembles to meet the task demands facing a particular system.

The many degrees of freedom that must be regulated in human movement are not limited to the elements of the motor system. Human motor performance results from the combined effect of many biological subsystems (Fig. 1). Metabolic systems interact with the neural and muscular systems as well as the cognitive system. Within dynamical systems theory, the movement behavior observed is seen as emerging from the collective interaction of these ever changing subsystems. An important property of dynamical systems is that these subsystems will self-organize (Nicolis & Prigogine, 1977; Prigogine & Stengers,

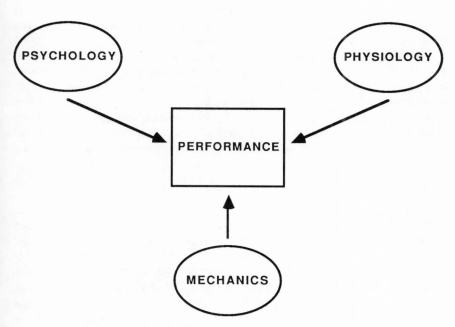

FIG. 1. Human subsystems affecting performance.

1984). That is, because of system nonlinearities and constraints, an order or a pattern will emerge out of the dynamics of the collective elements (Schöner & Kelso, 1988). This order is constrained both internally and externally. Internally, it is constrained by the state of the body's subsystems; externally, it is constrained by the task that is to be executed and by the environment within which the movement takes place.

To understand how movements are organized and regulated and eventually how they become skillful, we must come to understand the emerging movement patterns and the constraints which give rise to them. To describe these patterns, two types of variables are used: coordination and control. Coordination variables (or order parameters) are essential to characterize the movement pattern (Kugler, Kelso & Turvey, 1980). They reflect the spatial and temporal order that emerges from the dynamical systems. One example of a coordination variable is the relative phase relationship between two system elements that are moving cyclically. This relationship might be one in which the right hand is 180° out-of-phase with the action of the left hand (Haken, Kelso, & Bunz, 1985). By knowing the phasing relationship and the position of one hand, the other hand's position is both time and space can be determined.

Control variables represent nonessential elements that do not embody the movement pattern itself (Kugler et al., 1980). However, it is the scaling of control variables that may change the pattern of coordination that emerges (Kelso et al., 1986). Control variables, or constraints, as they are sometimes called, can be either external or internal to the system. In the example of two-handed cyclical action, the frequency at which the two hands oscillate is a control variable (Kelso, 1984). If the frequency is scaled to a critical value, the coordination of the two hands will shift from being in an asymmetrical 180° out-of-phase relationship to one in which the two hands are symmetrical, or in-phase. While hand frequency is an internal control variable, adding a weight to one of the hands would be an example of an external constraint or control variable. If that weight is increased to a critical value, it too might be seen to change the two limbs' coordination.

Skilled Action

Within the dynamical systems paradigm, skilled action is defined in terms of the optimality of the control variables to meet the task requirement (Kelso, 1982). To the extent that the control variables can affect the movement coordination, then skill also refers to optimality in coordination. In either case, optimality is defined in terms of the task goal or function. Therefore, definition of the task goal is an important determinant of what we would call motor skill. Is carrying a cup of coffee to your desk without spilling it a motor skill? It is if you consider how difficult such a task might be for a 3-year-old child or an adult with

Parkinson's disease. Just because something is easy for you does not mean it is not a skilled movement. Perhaps Greg Louganis (Olympic gold medalist in diving) finds diving off the 3-m board as easy as carrying a cup of coffee, yet many people would consider 3-m diving a skillful act. The definition of motor skill should not be based on how few people can do something, but rather it should be based on how one meets the task's goal. The distinction that is usually made is one in which the task goals differ. For example, driving a car at 55 mph in rush hour without hitting other cars is less rigorous than driving a car at 130 mph in a Grand Prix race and covering the distance faster than anyone else. One's sense of whether a performance is skillful lies *both* in the task's goal and in the optimality of the control variables necessary to achieve the goal. Such an orientation to motor skill places an emphasis not only on the performer but on the task as well.

The Development of Skilled Action

The development of skill is the process of finding the optimal value of the control variables that will meet the task demands. According to Bernstein (1940/1984), this process is in part one of learning to exploit the system's degrees of freedom. The first stage of skill development is one in which there is a freezing of the degrees of freedom. This, according to Saltzman and Kelso (1983), is likened to the problem of balance faced by the novice cyclist, which can be solved by the constraints on instability provided by training wheels. These constraints serve to reduce the degrees of freedom and at the same time provide a rough approximation of the task goal and an environment in which the bicyclist can find the supporting dynamics for the task. The training wheels provide an extended time over which to explore the task dynamics. As one progresses toward skillfulness, the constraints can be selectively changed and the degrees of freedom increased—that is, the training wheels can be removed.

Of course, some control variables are not so much sought as given to the performer. An example that immediately comes to mind is the increasing length of the body segments with bodily growth. Around 2 years of age, a toddler is about half his or her adult standing height. By adulthood, dramatic increases in total height as well as individual segment lengths have the potential for changing the constraints on the emerging movement pattern. How these growth-related constraints (including other variables such as weight gain, changes in body composition, and body proportions, to name a few) will affect motor skill is an important but as yet unanswered question.

There is some recent work that demonstrates the efficacy of using the dynamical systems perspective in understanding movement organization and regulation and may well point the way to understanding motor skill acquistion. In this work, infants are studied as they acquire upright bipedal locomotion. Using the phasing relationship between the two limbs as the coordination variable, Thelen has shown the importance of the infant's weight gain as a control variable in the so-called disappearance of infant stepping coordination. By manipulating the weight constraints on the infants' legs, Thelen has been able to show that alternating step coordination could "reappear" or disappear (Thelen & Fisher, 1982; Thelen, Fisher, & Ridley-Johnson, 1984; Thelen, Fisher, Ridley-Johnson, & Griffin, 1982). Similarly, she has shown that a motor-driven treadmill can provide an extrinsic force to the legs that results in an alternating stepping action in 7-month-old infants who do not display this type of interlimb coordination otherwise (Thelen, 1986).

For Thelen and others who study motor behavior within the dynamical systems perspective, the identification of variables that will reveal the control and coordination of the movement is critical. What are these variables and how are they to be interpreted? In the sections to follow, we explore a number of variables that might provide insights into motor skillfulness and its development. In particular, we look for those variables which might serve as measures of coordination and control.

THE MEASUREMENT OF SKILL

There are any number of techniques that can be used to measure skilled movement. Generally the methods fall into one of two categories: (1) measuring the movement's outcome, and (2) measuring the movement itself. The former method, measuring the movement outcome, has been the traditional approach to quantifying skill by those in the behavioral or information processing perspective. Examples include measuring accuracy (error scores) or speed of the movement (time measures). There are other movement outcomes that may be measured through the use of more sophisticated biomechanical and physiological techniques, many of which have rarely been applied to the study of motor skills. Mechanical efficiency, for example, provides an index of how efficient a movement might be given the work output derived from the work input. These types of outcome measures may point the way to possible underlying changes in the control variables (and therefore coordination) with developing skillfulness. There are a number of these measures that might be useful, and we discuss a selection of them as well as the potential information afforded by each.

Similarly, the measurement of the movement itself has until recently been almost the sole province of those in the field of biomechanics. Using a variety of techniques based on principles of Newtonian mechanics, information can be obtained concerning both descriptive and causal movement parameters. Kinematic analysis of segmental action throughout the time history of the motion is an example of the type of measurement that might be undertaken. Such an analysis provides information about both control and coordination variables. For example, measures of movement amplitude or velocity may reveal changes in a control variable, whereas measures of the relationship *between* two kinematic variables can reveal how the movement is coordinated.

In the following sections we examine several methods of quantifying *skill* or *proficiency* in movement, first from an *movement outcome* approach and then from a *movement process* approach. Within each we describe and discuss the utility of the measure from the dynamical systems perspective.

MOVEMENT OUTCOME MEASURES OF SKILLED MOTION

In many tasks there is an identifiable outcome that indicates successful performance, such as the fastest time in a 10-km road race or the lowest score in a golf match. Associated with such performances are other less obvious movement outcomes, which may be used to clarify the reasons for success. Researchers have attempted to quantify many such outcomes in order to understand differences in performance levels between individuals (Norman, Sharratt, Pezzack, & Noble, 1976; Sparrow & Irizarry-Lopez, 1987; Williams & Cavanagh, 1983). A survey of the current techniques used by biomechanists and physiologists shows that although some measures identify specific reasons for task success, other measures combine metabolic and mechanical variables and therefore tend to confuse mechanical and physiological performance. It is important to recognize the integration of all interrelated human systems in the production of skilled performance. Indeed, limits of one system (e.g. mechanical) may be viewed as constraints within which the other systems (e.g. physiological, psychological) must operate. While these interrelationships are important, the ability to assess clearly the performance of each separate system is critical in analyzing how to change and improve performance. Some currently used outcome measures provide a clear picture of the separate systems while some do not differentiate between individual systems.

Mechanical Efficiency

The learning of some motor skills, if not explicitly stated, implicitly requires that the performer move as proficiently as possible. What would be an objective measure of skill proficiency in such a task? One measure that has been proposed and applied to such skills is *mechanical efficiency.* Sparrow and Irizarry-Lopez (1987) used this measure to assess proficiency of adults learning to crawl on hands and feet on a motor-driven treadmill. These authors examined both mechanical and metabolic work during the learning phase of this crawling task to permit calculation of the mechanical efficiency of this movement. The concept of mechanical efficiency has been borrowed from the field of engineering. Machines may be compared by this variable, which describes their ability to convert one form of energy to another. The mechanical work output of the system is divided by the work input (fuel consumption) and expressed as a percentage to evaluate the amount of work successfully transformed by the machine (Eq. 1). A perfectly efficient machine (an impossible ideal) is one that converts 100% of its input work into useful output work. Machines are compared by their efficiency ratings, with the "better" machine having a higher efficiency value.

$$\text{Mechanical Efficiency} = (W_o \div W_i) \times 100\% \qquad \textbf{Eq. 1}$$

where W_o is work output and W_i is work input.

The efficiency concept has been applied to gross human motion by considering the performer as a "machine" that converts metabolic energy (input) into mechanical energy (output). This is an intuitively attractive model because the human metabolic system is directly responsible for extracting useful energy from foodstuffs, and the mechanical energy generated during a motion sequence is produced by muscular contractions fueled by the metabolic system. Furthermore, techniques exist for the measurement of both metabolic and mechanical work. Supposedly a more "efficient" or skilled movement pattern would be one that produced more mechanical work for a given amount of metabolic work (or the same mechanical output for less metabolic input). This approach is attractive because it integrates two important human movement subsystems in the assessment of movement skill. From the dynamical systems perspective, this may provide a method of assessing both mechanical and metabolic constraints on a performer during a movement sequence. In terms of assessing coordination, there is an implicit assumption that a performer with a high mechanical efficiency would be considered better coordinated.

Unfortunately, the application of this approach to quantify the proficiency of human movement is not straightforward. The overall value of mechanical efficiency for a performer depends on two separate considerations: the ability to convert chemical energy to useful metabolic energy (i.e., metabolic efficiency), and the ability to generate useful mechanical work that contributes to the performance (i.e., mechanical proficiency). For example, it has been shown that two runners may achieve a running velocity of 19 km/hr with mechanical efficiencies of 34% and 26% respectively (Norman et al., 1976). However, the first runner required a mechanical work rate of 89 cal/kg/min while the second required only 76 cal/kg/min. Is the first runner more skilled because of his higher mechanical efficiency value, or is the second runner more skilled because he can achieve the same performance goal (running speed) while generating less mechanical power? If skilled movement is thought of in mechanical terms, mechanical efficiency is an inappropriate measure due to its metabolic component.

The information from the mechanical and metabolic components in its calculation can be used individually to examine the performer's movement constraints. In this case the *task function* would be important in assessing which of the runners was more "skilled." If the task was expressed as running velocity, the runners are equally skilled. Expressing the task in terms of metabolic cost minimization or mechanical work maximization would lead to different appraisals of the performers' skill levels. These differences may be due in part to the fact that the runners may have different metabolic capabilities, and therefore have different constraints on their performance levels. Developmentally, the use of metabolic cost or mechanical work also might prove useful. While a 9-year-old runner may not attain the same running velocity of the taller and stronger adult, measurement of the mechanical efficiency of his or her running performance compared to an adult may reveal that size-for-size the two performers are equal. Such comparisons could offer insight into the role of size and strength (i.e., control variables) in motor performance.

Movement Economy

The issue of ambiguity between mechanical and metabolic systems is a problem for mechanical efficiency measures. A less ambiguous measure is the term movement *economy,* in which the metabolic cost of running at a given speed is used to assess a runner's skill level (Williams, 1985). Other authors have shown metabolic reductions during certain performances such as the aforementioned crawling study of Sparrow and Irizarry-Lopez (1987), which illustrated that the metabolic cost of this motion declined as practice time (and presumably skill level) increased. These are examples of the *principle of economy* or *minimum energy* (in this case metabolic energy). However, as this measure is indicative of the metabolic cost and is not a direct measure of mechanical work performed, it is only an indirect indicator of movement technique and coordination. Its value is critically dependent on a performer's metabolic capacity, and may be related to factors other than the movement technique alone. Another problem with this measure as an indicator of mechanical performance is that metabolic and mechanical systems of the performer may become attuned to each other as a function of practice. The performer's metabolic cost may be lowest when a well-practiced pattern of movement is used. Deviation to *any different* mechanical pattern (even if it were a more proficient one) may cause the athlete to expend more metabolic energy until his nervous system can access the appropriate muscles more easily (i.e., "build" the new coordinative structure). For example, a middle-distance runner may train at shorter distances for much of his career, developing a mechanical style and metabolic expenditure level related to that particular style. Later in his career he may run longer distances to compensate for loss of speed. These longer races will change the relative role of the metabolic system in overall performance, and he likely will alter his mechanical style to be more appropriate for these longer distances. Initially this change in mechanical style may be associated with a higher metabolic cost that later is reduced as his mechanical and metabolic systems become attuned. To our knowledge, this possibility has not been addressed in any experimental protocol. This concept may offer interesting possibilities for examining transitions from one behavior to another that are based on underlying changes in a control variable (i.e., the metabolic system). The interaction between various human subsystems is undoubtedly important, although it may be a source of confusion when trying to assess mechanically proficient movement. However, for tasks that are critically dependent on metabolic processes, economy is a convenient measure of skilled motion.

Mechanical Task Cost

There are some measures of movement outcome that are more closely related to the mechanical aspects of the motion, and may be applied unambiguously to performers having quite different constraints (body size, metabolic capacity, etc.). An example of such a mechanical measure is *mechanical task cost* (MTC), defined as the amount of mechanical work necessary to move one kilogram of mass a distance of one meter, and which is expressed in joules/kg/m (Winter, 1979). Presumably the skill level of subjects will be related to the ability to perform a given task while minimizing this mechanical task cost. For example, of the two runners in the Norman et al. (1976) study, the runner with the lowest mechanical work rate had the lowest MTC. MTC can be considered the mechanical equivalent of the physiologically based economy term. However, the MTC is not dependent on the metabolic capabilities of the performer, while economy may be dependent on his/her mechanical attributes. Note that consideration of MTC leads to a different decision than either economy or mechanical efficiency on the relative skill level of the two runners. Because it is purely mechanical, this can be viewed as a measure of coordination independent of other constraint parameters. Its use will be most attractive in movements in which the physical technique of the motion dominates the overall performance outcome. However, its use is somewhat controversial due to the many ways in which mechanical work can be calculated and interpreted (Williams & Cavanagh, 1983). For example, a study on preferred running technique indicated that nonpreferred styles may or may not generate more mechanical work, depending on which of two work terms were used in making this judgment (Chapman, Caldwell, Herring, Lonergan & Selbie, 1987). Further discussion of the ways in which mechanical work may be calculated and interpreted is found below.

Total Body Impulse

Other indices in addition to MTC are available for quantifying the total mechanical cost of an activity. *Total body impulse* (TBI) has been described as a measure that more accurately reflects the muscular cost of a movement, because it includes the mechanical effect of isometric contractions that perform no measurable mechanical energy change (Eq. 2). Since isometric contractions do not result in a change in energy, their effect is not seen in mechanical work calculations.

$$\text{TBI} = \Sigma \int | M_{ij} | \, dt \qquad \textbf{Eq. 2}$$

M_{ij} represents the resultant joint moment at joint i at time j. Each moment is integrated ($\int$) over the time course of the movement, and all joint integrals are then summed (Σ). Mechanical impulse at a joint relates kinetic expenditure to move kinematics through the Impulse-Momentum relation (Eq. 3). Impulse at a joint results in changes in segment momentum and velocity, and is useful in determining specific muscle group activity throughout a performance.

$$\int M \, dt = \Delta I \omega \qquad \textbf{Eq. 3}$$

M represents the resultant joint moment, I the segment moment of inertia, and ω the segment angular velocity. The moment is integrated ($\int$) over the complete time of the movement.

The efficacy of using TBI is seen in the above mentioned study of preferred running style (Chapman et al., 1987). If one considers that a preferred running style results from years of trying and discarding nonpreferred styles, it is apparent that this process is the development of skilled movement in much the same manner that a child discards inappropriate motion while learning to walk. Although two different measures of mechanical work were unable to clearly distinguish between preferred and nonpreferred running styles, the TBI for the preferred technique was less than for any nonpreferred style. Because TBI is an indicator of muscular involvement, it seems to indicate that preferred technique in running is associated with minimization of muscle use. However, while TBI (and MTC) is a useful barometer of overall muscular work, it is lacking somewhat as a good measure of coordination because it does not account for nonmuscular sources of mechanical work. Coordination is the interaction of control variables that may be either internal or external, while muscular forces are only one particular type of internal variable.

Effectiveness

Another index for overall mechanical proficiency is *effectiveness*, a term used to describe the ability of cyclists to apply pedal forces that are properly directed to provide propulsive force (Eq. 4). The force vector (F) that a cyclist applies to a pedal has two orthogonal components: one is the effective force, F_E, which is directed at a 90° angle to the crank axis of rotation and is responsible for production of the torque that moves the cyclist and bike. The other component (F_F) is directed through the crank axle and is therefore unable to aid in torque production. The relative size of F_E and F_F is dependent upon the direction at which the cyclist applies the total force vector F. Effectiveness is the ratio of F_E to F, and will be higher for a cyclist who is able to apply force in a direction beneficial to torque production throughout the cycling motion.

$$\text{Effectiveness} = (F_E \div F) \times 100\% \qquad \textbf{Eq. 4}$$

This is an excellent example of a term that links mechanical performance with the goal of the movement task, and therefore is useful in assessment of cyclist skill level (LaFortune & Cavanagh, 1983). Similarly, effectiveness could provide a valuable measure for exploring children's tricycle and bicycle skills. Over 50 years ago, in her study of the twins Johnny and Jimmy, McGraw (1935) commented on her difficulty in teaching one of the twins to pedal a tricycle. Despite all of McGraw's efforts, she seemed unable to help the child with this task. This was all the more interesting because he seemed to have the necessary strength to move the tricycle, as he was able to run at this age. Using a measure such as effectiveness, the ratio of forces (effective and otherwise) could reveal a better understanding of why the child could not pedal the tricycle.

As with other single index terms, effectiveness suffers from the inability to describe *why* the cyclist may be ineffective, and gives no information at the segmental level. It also gives no information about individual control parameters and how they are coordinated. It does, however, give an excellent overall indication of coordination level that can be used to differentiate between individuals in a task-specific manner. Extension of this technique to other activities in combination with segmental kinetics could extend its use as a more general tool for skill assessment. For example, it could be applied to jumping and its development, because the direction of force application is critical to the distance or height jumped.

Mechanical Energy Transfers

All of these movement outcomes measures may be criticized, for though they offer a concise description of mechanical cost, they reduce the intricacies of a complex performance to a single index. Such distillation of information cannot help but ignore important aspects of the event useful in determination of skill level. Although they can be indicative of overall mechanical performance, taken by themselves they are *not* useful in determination of specific reasons why one subject is more skilled than another. Other measures can be combined with these movement outcome measures to explain specific mechanisms of skilled motion. To more clearly illustrate the mechanisms of skill differences, these measures should be able to explain differences in coordination and therefore address both internal and external parameters. Many of the outcome measures reflect muscular cost only, and as such do not consider nonmuscular sources of work. However, there are several techniques that permit the assessment of mechanical energy usage from both internal and external sources. These techniques are based on the classic equations of motion as expressed by Newton in the late 17th century, which may be used to quantify force and/or energy variations from a number of different internal and external sources.

One such measure is derived from estimation of mechanical work through segmental energy changes observed during a motion. Although there are several methods of calculating mechanical work from these energy data, the basic approach is to calculate the instantaneous potential (PE), kinetic (KE), and rotational (RE) energies for all involved body segments during a movement sequence (Eq. 5, 6, and 7):

$$PE_{ij} = m_i g h_{ij} \qquad \text{Eq. 5}$$

$$KE_{ij} = 0.5 \, m_i v_{ij}{}^2 \qquad \text{Eq. 6}$$

$$RE_{ij} = 0.5 \, I_{gi} \omega_{ij}{}^2 \qquad \text{Eq. 7}$$

where m_i and I_{gi} represent the mass and mass moment of inertia of the ith segment, and h_{ij}, v_{ij}, and ω_{ij} represent the height, velocity, and angular velocity of ith segment at the jth time period. PE is the energy related to the height of a segment, while KE and RE are related to linear and rotational velocity of the segment, respectively. These three variables represent possible mechanical results of internal and external forces that act on a segment, and can be used to deduce contributions from these various sources. The energy levels of all segments of interest may be calculated from film data and expressed as energy time histories. Examples of these energy time histories during walking are depicted in Figure 2.

An example of other energy profiles for walking may be found in Figure 3. By summing the PE, KE, and RE components within a segment at any point in time, the total segmental energy (SE) can be found (Eq. 8 and Fig. 3a). In a similar fashion, the SE profiles may be summed to give a measure of the energy pattern of the total body as a whole (Eq. 9 and Fig. 3b).

$$SE_{ij} = PE_{ij} + KE_{ij} + RE_{ij} \qquad \text{Eq. 8}$$

$$TBE_j = \Sigma \, SE_{ij} \qquad \text{Eq. 9}$$

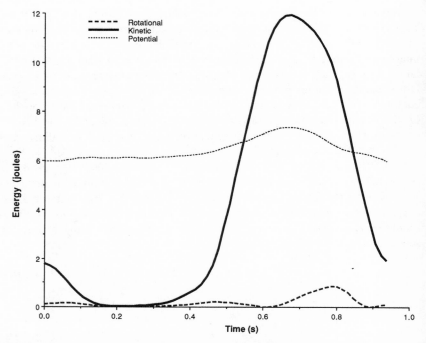

FIG. 2. Time histories of translational kinetic (KE), potential (PE), and rotational kinetic (RE) energies for the shank segment during a walking cycle.

Mechanical work can be calculated from these energy data in several different ways, each of which makes different assumptions concerning the transfer of energy between and within segments (Pierrynowski, Winter & Norman, 1980). In each case work is defined as the sum of the absolute changes in energy over the time of the movement (Eq. 10). In other words, mechanical work generated is manifested as changes in the energy levels of the body and its segments. The difference in work calculations is based on which energy profiles from Equations 5 through 9 are involved in the work estimate.

$$W = \Sigma \mid E_j - E_{j-1} \mid \qquad \textbf{Eq. 10}$$

One method of calculating work is to apply Equation 10 separately to each of the segmental energy components PE, KE, and RE, and to sum these individual work components for all segments (Eq. 11). Work calculated in this fashion has an underlying assumption of no interaction of energy components either within or between segments and has been termed "pseudowork" (W_N) (Norman et al., 1976). This work term has been criticized as an unrealistically high value that is an overestimate of true muscular cost (Williams & Cavanagh, 1983), because

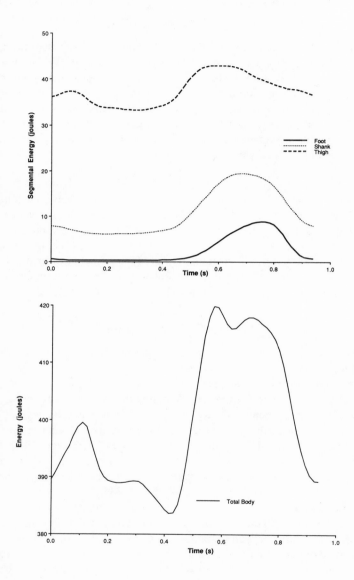

FIG. 3. (a) Time history of the total segmental energy (SE) of the foot, shank, and thigh segments during a walking cycle. (b) Time history of the total body energy (TBE) during walking.

some of the work generated is actually due to exchanges of PE and KE within segments and/or energy transferred between structurally connected segments.

$$W_N = \Sigma \ (W_{Pi} + W_{Ki} + W_{Ri}) \qquad \text{Eq. 11}$$

An alternative work estimate can be calculated assuming that energy components (PE, KE, RE) may be exchanged within segments (W_W), by applying Equation 9 to the SE time history of each segment, and then summing these segmental work values (Equation 12). Because the PE, KE, and RE components are summed at each time interval to calculate SE, offsetting fluctuations in the component profiles may occur without changing the SE level. These energy exchanges within a segment are therefore removed from this work calculation based on changes in SE levels over time.

$$W_W = \Sigma \ \Sigma \ | \ SE_{ij} - SE_{ij-1} \ | \qquad \text{Eq. 12}$$

The final method of calculating mechanical work assumes that transfers of energy are possible both within and between segments (W_{WB}), and has been calculated by applying Equation 10 to the total body energy profile (Winter, 1979; Eq. 13). The TBE profile is a summation of all SE time histories, so that offsetting flucuations in SE profiles may produce no changes in the TBE time history. The offsetting SE profiles are indicative of between-segment transfers, and are therefore factored out of the TBE profile and the subsequent work estimate W_{WB}.

$$W_{WB} = \Sigma \ | \ TBE_j - TBE_{j-1} \ | \qquad \text{Eq. 13}$$

While this latter assumption is essentially correct, this particular method of calculating W_{WB} is somewhat contentious in that it allows energy transfers between segments that are not physically connected (Wells, 1988; Williams & Cavanagh, 1983). Other methods of calculating this work term allowing transfers between adjacent segments only are found in Williams and Cavanagh (1983) and Caldwell, Forrester, Phillips, and Clark (1989). These calculation methods are more appropriate than the original method proposed by Winter (1979; Eq. 13), although the most accurate work estimate would be one that allows transfers between adjacent segments *and* between nonadjacent segments connected by two-joint muscles (Aleshinsky, 1986; Wells, 1988).

An important aspect of the energy approach is the recognition that not all mechanical work is directly associated with muscular action. Energy changes are associated with three specific mechanisms: muscular work (as measured by W_{WB}), the exchange of PE, KE, and RE within a segment, and the transfer of energy between segments. The work terms W_N, W_W, and W_{WB} can be used to calculate the amount of within (ET_W) and between-segment energy transfer (ET_B) for the entire body (Pierrynowski et al., 1980; Eq. 14 and 15).

$$ET_W = W_N - W_W \qquad \textbf{Eq. 14}$$

$$ET_B = W_W - W_{WB} \qquad \textbf{Eq. 15}$$

While much has been written regarding the total body work term W_{WB} as a measure of muscular cost, the information contained in the two transfer terms ET_W and ET_B may be useful within the dynamical systems perspective. These transfers are outcome measures that reflect mechanical work accomplished with little or no metabolic cost. An example that illustrates this concept of energy transfers performing mechanical work is seen in the movement of a simple pendulum. If a frictionless pendulum is held in its highest horizontal position, it will have its maximum PE (highest height) and its minimum KE (0 joules because its velocity is 0 m/s). When released from this position it will swing downward, gaining KE while losing PE. Note that this is a conservative system in that the total energy (PE + KE) remains constant. At the bottom of its arc the pendulum will have maximal KE and minimal PE. As the pendulum swings upward towards its other maximal height the process is reversed, as it gains PE and loses KE. In the perfect frictionless pendulum, this exchange of PE and KE will repeat itself indefinitely, sustaining the pendulum's motion with no input of external mechanical work. In this case all the work is done through the energy exchange mechanism, clearly without other "costs" (pendulums don't have muscles!).

In the context of dynamical systems, energy transfers may be regarded as a measure of what the performer gets "for free" from the chosen movement technique (Kelso, 1982). For example, Norman, Caldwell, and Komi (1985) report that world-class cross-country ski racers exhibit significantly more within-segment energy exchange than do less skilled skiers while performing the diagonal stride technique. Implicated in this type of energy transfer is the use of gravitational force rather than muscular force during certain phases of the motion sequence. An advantage of the energy approach is that the work values and energy transfers can be expressed at the level of *individual* segments as well as at the whole body level. This allows one to specify more precisely the interactions of muscular and nonmuscular energy sources, and to link these energy sources more closely with causal mechanisms of task performance. In the case of the cross-country skiers, the elite skiers were found to have higher within-segment energy exchanges than their less-skilled counterparts not only in overall levels, but also in segments associated with a specific propulsive mechanism (the transfer of momentum of the swing leg) that results in differences in horizontal velocity.

The interaction of potential and kinetic energy components should not be taken as the only possible indication of proficiency difference. The transfer of energy between segments is another manner in which athletes may realize higher segmental energy levels without the use of musculature acting directly on that segment (Phillips, Roberts, & Huang, 1983; Robertson & Winter, 1980). Between-segment transfer results from the linked segment nature of the human skeleton. In certain types of movement patterns the difference in skill level between individuals may be indicated by between-segment transfers rather than within-segment transfers, depending on the nature of the task function. Although little work has addressed the degree of between-segment transfer associated with skill level, there have been differences reported in other activities. For example, preliminary energy data on adult subjects walking or running across a wide range of locomotion velocities demonstrate differences in between-segment transfer patterns that are related to the form of locomotion rather than velocity *per se* (Caldwell et al., 1989). An interesting question might be how these segmental transfer patterns appear in the transition from walking to running seen during children's gait development. One can speculate on other developmental questions regarding both within-segment energy exchanges and between-segment transfers. Are transfer patterns germane to the activity in question, and do they remain relatively stable as developmental level increases, or are distinct changes in energy transfer patterns seen as one progresses through developmental levels? It should be stressed once more that any differences observed should be interpreted in relation to completion of task goals that are specific to the motion under study.

The mechanical energy analysis is attractive for those studying skill in the dynamical systems paradigm, since one of the essential tenets of this theory is that movement patterns emerge from the flow of energy in and out of the system's components (Kugler et al., 1980). With this type of analysis, the contributions of both muscular and nonmuscular sources of energy during a motion sequence can be assessed. For an interesting discussion of energetics and dynamical systems with respect to skilled movement, the reader is referred to Beek and Beek (1988). The energy transfer and exchange measures may allow one to examine external control parameters, and appreciate the coordination of these external parameters with other internal variables. Different movements will be characterized by the specific combinations of within- and between-segment transfer *possibilities*. For example, the relative contribution of between-segment transfer to the movements of high jumping and cross-country skiing will be quite different. Proficiency in any one movement may be assessed by the ability of the performer to utilize the appropriate nonmuscular sources of energy transfer. A highly skilled performer may be the one who can use transfer energy in the most advantageous manner. This may be related to mechanical and/or metabolic energy constraints, or to more specific mechanical events occurring within the motion sequence. Within the dynamical systems framework the ability to examine both internal and external control variables associated with energy is an important tool in assessing coordination.

Summary

The use of movement outcome measures is useful in that it allows one to quickly compare two performances with some objectivity. The researcher must be aware of the limitations and assumptions underlying the measure being used, and must be able to relate the measure to the causes of the specific motion being studied. The term *mechanical efficiency,* although widely used, is somewhat confusing because it relies on both mechanical and metabolic capabilities of the performer, when in many instances it is the proficiency of the mechanical motion alone we wish to assess. The terms *economy, mechanical task cost, total body impulse,* and *effectiveness* have each been used to assess mechanical proficiency, and all may be useful for answering questions about specific tasks. However, all of these terms are limited when addressing questions of coordination, because they fail to identify the operative control variables and the manner in which they interact. In this regard the *mechanical energy analysis* may be most useful, because it allows the calculation of muscular and nonmuscular sources of energy. *Energy transfer* terms may be estimated for individual segments and joints, and therefore allow more precise definition of control variables and their coordination. Seldom have these measures been applied to developmental questions, and may serve as useful techniques in understanding the way in which coordination changes with developmental time.

MOVEMENT PROCESS MEASURES OF SKILLED MOTION

Consider an analysis of the walking patterns produced by two subjects—one an 18-month-old who has been walking unaided for 5 months, the other a 3-year-old who has been walking for almost 2 years. Based on the time of walking and no other maturational factors, it would not be surprising if the 3-year-old displayed a more proficient walking performance when assessed with any of the previously discussed outcome measures. However, if we wish to understand *why* and *how* the 18-month-old's gait differed from the older child, then we need to use measures that inform us about the movement itself, that is, movement process measures. More and different information may be obtained from the movement process measures than found through the outcome measures. For example, the child may have a lower mechanical efficiency index than an adult, but the index itself does not provide information about what the source of the inefficiency may be. From measures of the movement itself, it may be possible to isolate the segmental action that is contributing to the child's inefficiency. The movement process measures of skilled motion employ mechanical variables to identify and explain the motion sequence. However, as with the movement outcome measures, it is important to interpret these mechanical variables in the context of successful completion of the movement task. Without this link, the measure of skill gives an incomplete assessment of the movement under consideration. In many cases it may be appropriate to combine the results of a movement outcome analysis by exploring more specific measures of the movement processes as they vary in time.

Kinematic Analyses

Kinematic analyses provide an accurate and precise description of a movement without establishing the cause of the movement. The position, velocity, and acceleration of the body and its segments can be calculated from kinematic analyses. A kinematic description of walking, for example, might include time histories of the linear and/or angular position, velocity, and acceleration of such body segments as the foot, shank, or thigh, or of intersegmental joints such as the ankle, knee, or hip. Figure 4a is a time history of the shank's position during the walking cycle (toe-off to toe-off). Figure 4b is the time history of the shank's velocity over the same cycle. For this walking cycle, these two time histories provide information about the range of motion through the step cycle as well as the magnitude and time of the peak shank velocity in the forward and backward direction. Indeed any or all the position, velocity, and acceleration variables could be considered measures of possible control variables.

Kinematic analyses also may yield information about coordination. Since a coordination variable is one in which a relationship between component elements is described, then clearly relationships between position, velocity, and acceleration variables could be considered as potential coordination variables. For example, Clark, Phillips, & Petersen (1989) used the timing relationship between joint reversals (hip and knee) and peak angular velocities to study the coordination patterns for vertical jumping. Another example of a coordination measure is the footfall relationship between the two legs in walking. Walking football patterns are: right foot, left foot, right foot, and so on (Fig. 5). The coordination measure between the two legs can be expressed as a temporal or spatial ratio. That is, if one divides the time between the right footfall and left by the time between the right footfall and the next right footfall, a ratio of 0.5 is found. In other words, 50% of the way through the right leg's step cycle, the left foot starts (or ends) its step cycle. Expressed in angular phasing notation, the limbs are said to be 180° out-of-phase with each other. Developmentally, this interlimb coordination has been found in the early kicking patterns of infants (Thelen, 1985) and at the onset of walking (Clark, Whitall, & Phillips, 1988).

Recently, intralimb coordination has been described using kinematic variables (Clark, Truly, & Phillips, 1989; Truly, 1988). Here the kinematic variables of a segment's position and velocity are first plotted against each other. In Figure 6, the shank's normalized position and velocity are plotted for the same cycle as in

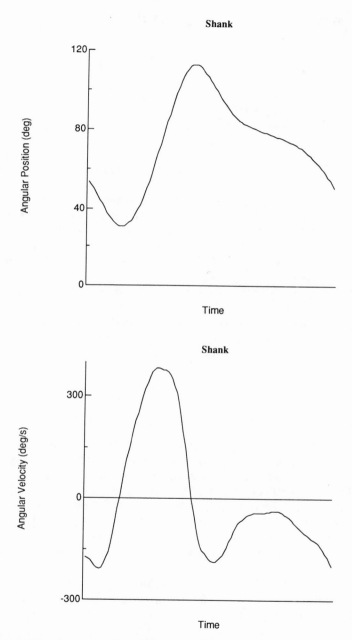

FIG. 4. (a) Time history of the angular position of the shank during a walking cycle. (b) Time history of the angular velocity during a walking.

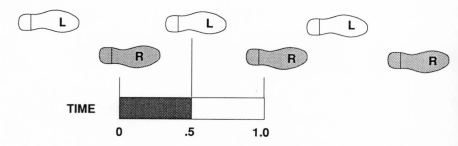

FIG. 5. Spatial and temporal pattern of interlimb footfall during walking.

Figure 4. This type of plot is called a *phase portrait*. Any one point on the plot describes both the shank's position and velocity at that moment in the step cycle. One method to determine the manner in which the shank's motion is coordinated with that of the thigh is to identify the occurrence of a selected event in the thigh's action (such as reversal from backward to forward rotation) on the shank's phase portrait. The point of this reversal is marked on the phase portrait in Figure 6 by the letter T. A measure of coordination can be calculated by expressing this point's normalized Cartesian coordinates as equivalent polar coordinates, consisting of a *radius* and *phase angle*. In this way the kinematic state (position and velocity) of one segment (shank) may be related to the occurrence of a significant kinematic state (reversal) of another segment (thigh). More details on this measure of coordination may be found in Kelso et al. (1986).

Kinetic Analyses

While kinematic analysis techniques provide a precise description of the movement, *kinetic analyses* permit the causal nature of the motion to appear as well. From kinetic analyses, one may study the *interactions* between the internal and external forces that dictate the kinematic description. This is important for the study of control and coordination for two reasons. First, because of the linked segment nature of the human musculoskeletal system, the motion of most body segments is dictated by muscles at more than one joint. It is therefore critical to assess kinetic inputs at all joints to appreciate how these inputs interact to produce the observed kinematic motion. Second, these muscular forces are augmented by external forces such as gravity and ground reactions. Dynamical systems theory stresses the emergence of movement patterns from the interaction of both internal and external forces, so the ability to identify these forces is critical to the understanding of coordination. Although kinetic segmental analyses have been used in biomechanical studies for some time, relatively few authors in the field of motor development have made use of these powerful

ADULT (LB301)

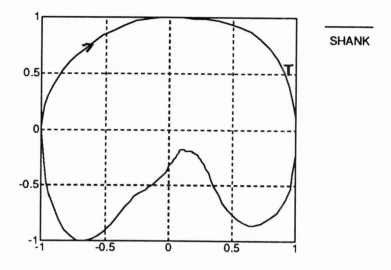

NORM. POSITION

FIG. 6. Phase plot depicting normalized angular position and velocity for the shank. Same trial as in Figure 4. The letter *T* denotes the occurrence of thigh reversal.

research techniques. Here we examine three segmental kinetic analysis techniques, namely *inverse dynamics, mechanical energy,* and *mechanical power,* each of which could reveal information about the causes of the movements we observe.

Inverse Dynamics. One kinetic segmental analysis that might prove useful is termed *inverse dynamics analysis,* first applied to human movement in the study of walking by Bresler and Frankel (1950). In this technique the forces and torques (moments) acting on each body segment are combined in a set of equations that permit the calculation of *joint reaction forces* and *resultant joint torques* at each joint (Eq. 16 and 17, and Figure 7).

$$\Sigma F = m\,a \qquad\qquad \textbf{Eq. 16}$$

$$PJF + DJF + EF + mg = m\,a \qquad\qquad \textbf{Eq. 16a}$$

$$\Sigma T = I\,\alpha \qquad\qquad \textbf{Eq. 17}$$

$$PM + DM + (r \times ma) + (r \times mg) + (1 \times DJF) + (d \times EF) = I \, \alpha$$

Eq. 17a

F is force; m is segment mass; I is the segment moment of inertia; a is the acceleration of the segmental center of mass; α is the segmental angular acceleration; PJF and DJF are the joint reaction forces at the proximal and distal ends of the segment, respectively; EF is an externally applied force; PM and DM are the resultant joint moments at the proximal and distal joints, respectively; the bracketed terms in Equation 17a are the moments associated with the respective force terms; and r, l, and d are distances from the various force terms to the joint center (refer to Fig. 7).

The resultant joint moments (PM and DM in Eq. 17a) are the moments produced by the muscles (and ligaments) controlling each joint. The interplay of moment-time histories for joints that function together during a movement may be regarded as a measure of coordination (see Fig. 8). Since the CNS sends electrical impulses to the muscles, they are the mechanism through which the CNS must structure the coordination of movement. The resultant joint moments may yield greater insight to understanding the rules by which the CNS operates than kinematic data, which are a result of both internal and external influences. Furthermore, these joint moments act together with moments due to external (d $\times$ EF in Eq. 17a), gravitational (r $\times$ mg), inertial (r $\times$ ma), and distal joint (1 $\times$ DJF) forces acting on each segment. It is the combination of these kinetic variables that produces the segmental pattern of motion. Study of the interrelation of each component torque can reveal the fine balance the performer establishes between internal and external forces involved in the movement sequence.

An example of how inverse dynamics can be used to understand the development of motor skills is the work on infant kicking by Thelen and her colleagues (Jensen et al., 1988; Jensen et al., 1989; Schneider et al., 1988). Here the issue is how the infant manages to balance the forces of gravity and inertia with those produced by their own muscular contractions. Calculation of resultant joint torque and other component moments has revealed that babies as young as 2 months of age display considerable coordination between nonmuscular forces and their own muscular contractions in leg-kicking movements. By plotting the time histories of nonmuscular and muscular moments acting about the leg joints, a picture of segmental coordination can be seen to emerge.

Another example of the use of joint moments as a measure of coordination is seen in the way in which one throws a ball. A well-timed, sequential application of joint moments from the more proximal joints to the more distal joints results in a high ball velocity at release. Generation of joint moments in an inappropriate sequence results in a lower ball velocity and in an unsmooth motion pattern. A kinematic analysis will quantify the latter two phenomena, but a kinetic analysis

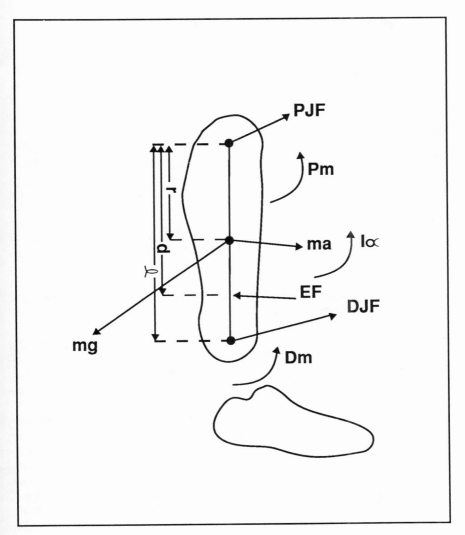

FIG. 7. Segmental free body diagram illustrating forces, torques, and geometrical information. Refer to Equations 16–17a. NB: Vertical indicated by mg.

of the joint moments is required to fully elucidate the implicated muscle groups. An analysis of the joint reaction, gravitational, and inertial forces acting on each segment may further enhance our understanding of the motion sequence. Indeed, coupled with previous descriptive studies of the development of throwing such as those by Roberton and her colleagues (Roberton, 1977, 1978; Roberton &

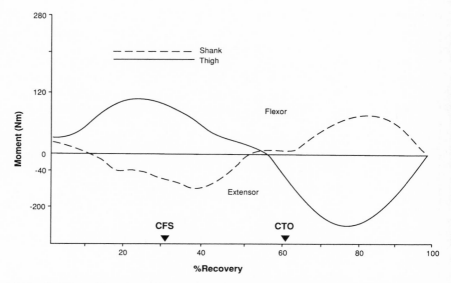

FIG. 8. Time histories of resultant joint torques during recovery phase in running. Adapted from Chapman, Lonergan, and Caldwell (1984).

Langendorfer, 1980), the joint movement histories might possibly provide insight into the interplay between muscular and nonmuscular forces with the changing developmental patterns observed. For example, considerable descriptive evidence has documented a qualitative sequence in the humeral action of the throwing arm. An inverse dynamics analysis of the shoulder might well indicate why this particular sequence is found in development.

An inverse dynamics analysis also may provide a clearer picture of the role of growth in motor skill development. Jensen (1981) has shown that with growth comes changes in the body's mass and its distribution. These changes will affect the magnitude of inertial and gravitational terms in the force and torque equations (Eq. 16a and 17a) and consequently will affect the joint torques produced. From the dynamical systems perspective, these changes represent changes in the body's constraints that may affect the coordination of a movement. Indeed, Jensen (1981) has shown that growth changes over a 12-month period have the potential for dramatically affecting children's performance of movements that have a substantial rotational component.

The interrelation of separate kinetic influences may be appreciated further by observing the manner in which angular segmental movement is produced during the swing phase of running (Chapman, Lonergan, & Caldwell, 1984). The movement of the thigh or shank is produced by a delicate balance of offsetting muscular and nonmuscular torques. The effect of one kinetic source alone can be of sufficient magnitude to produce six revolutions of the thigh about the hip joint! It is the tempering effect of four other competing sources that results in the much less drastic angular change observed during running. These kinetic sources demonstrate the importance of considering all internal and external forces in the overall coordination scheme. The dynamical systems perspective accentuates this importance and is an ideal framework for analyzing coordination of such diverse control elements.

Mechanical Energy. Earlier in this paper we discussed the use of mechanical energy techniques for the assessment of whole body, joint-specific, and segment-specific mechanical work in terms of muscular or nonmuscular origins. The segmental energy time histories from which these work measures are derived contain much valuable information in their own right. The interaction of potential, kinetic, and rotational energy profiles for a specific segment indicate *when* in the movement cycle, and to what extent, energy exchanges are occurring within the segment. Furthermore, the profiles of individual segmental energies may be used to assess energy transfers between segments as a function of time during the motion sequence. These time-dependent measures are valuable because they allow specific energy changes to be affiliated with causal mechanisms of task function.

Consider Figure 9a, which is an *energetic phase plot* of the motion of a frictionless pendulum, which plots kinetic energy (KE) against potential energy (PE). The frictionless pendulum is an example of a completely conservative system, requiring no external work to sustain its motion. In this plot the exchange of PE and KE is characterized by an inverse relationship between the two energy forms. Note that an input of external energy at any time would tend to drive this relation away from its straight-line inverse form. Examples of energy phase plots for three different body segments during walking are shown in Figures 9b–d. These plots display the interaction between PE and KE within the shank, thigh, and trunk during one complete walking cycle. The shank segment (Fig. 9b) is essentially nonconservative during walking, in that its KE rises and falls without appreciable change in PE. This means that kinetic energy changes (mechanical work) in the shank's motion are caused by muscular forces. In contrast, the trunk segment (Fig. 9d) acts in a very conservative manner in that KE and PE are inversely related. Changes in energy of the trunk are at least in part due to an exchange of energy between its kinetic and potential components. The thigh segment (Fig. 9c) has a more complex energetic phase plot, displaying both periods of energy exchange and periods of muscular force generation.

Clearly, such as analysis of infant locomotion could be very beneficial. Is the infant able to exploit the transfer of energy as well as the mature walker? By observing segmental energetics the profile of all sources of energy may be

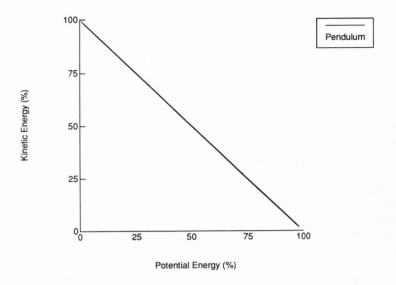

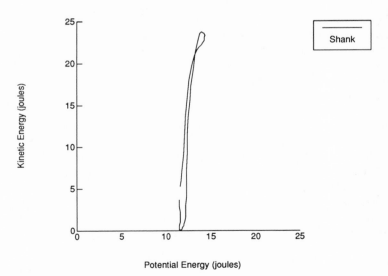

FIG. 9. Energetic phase plots for the motion of (a) a frictionaless pendulum, (b) shank during walking; (c) the thigh during walking; and (d) the trunk during walking.

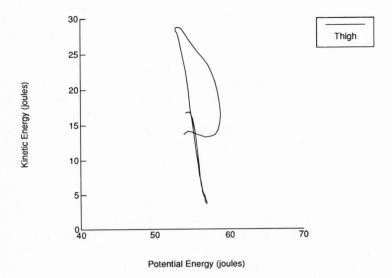

Potential Energy (joules)

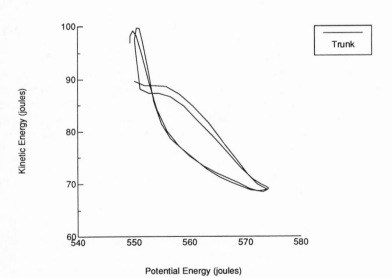

Potential Energy (joules)

revealed. Again, as Kelso (1982) so aptly stated: *what do we get for free?* Is the infant able to capitalize on relatively low-cost energy sources, or must energy be generated by muscular forces?

Mechanical Analysis. Another method of calculating mechanical work is through segmental *mechanical analysis,* also known as the *joint work* approach. Calculation of segmental energy is accomplished through the process of integration of segmental powers with respect to time. Mechanical work can then be calculated from the changes in segmental energies. More important, for the present discussion, the power analysis allows a more detailed description of the segmental motion because it determines the mechanisms behind the observed changes in energy levels. Power is defined as the rate of change in energy, so that any changes is segmental energy levels must be due to one or more specific sources of power. In general there are four separate power sources that influence the magnitude of a segment's energy. The joint work approach identifies energy changes to be the result of *muscle moment power* (MMP), in which muscle groups generate, absorb, or transfer energy, and *joint force power* (JFP), in which energy is transferred between segments through the joint centers rather than through the muscles (Robertson & Winter, 1980; Eq. 18 and 19; see Fig. 10).

$$JFP_{ij} = F_{ij} \, V_{ij} \qquad\qquad \textbf{Eq. 18}$$

$$MMP_{ij} = M_{ij} \, \omega_{ij} \qquad\qquad \textbf{Eq. 19}$$

F_{ij} is the joint reaction force at one of the joints of the ith segment; V_{ij} is the linear velocity of that same joint center; M_{ij} is the resultant moment applied at that joint to the ith segment; and ω_{ij} is the segmental angular velocity. All variables are instantaneous values at the jth time interval. Segmental energy variations may be attributed to MMP and JFP at both the proximal and distal joints that define a segment, so that four separate mechanisms of energy changes may be appreciated (Eq. 20 and 21).

$$IP_{ij} = JFP_{ij,p} + MMP_{ij,p} + JFP_{ij,d} + MMP_{ij,d} \qquad\qquad \textbf{Eq. 20}$$

$$SE_{ij} = \int IP_{ij} \, dt \qquad\qquad \textbf{Eq. 21}$$

An important feature of this analysis technique is that the sign of the MMP power terms are indicative of concentric, eccentric, or isometric muscular contractions. Therefore, power profile analysis may be an excellent tool for skill assessment because it allows the calculation of an overall work term yet permits one to more fully appreciate the muscular and nonmuscular interactions that are responsible for the overall mechanical work production. The power analysis has

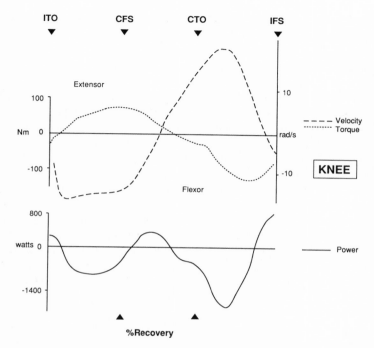

FIG. 10. Time histories of resultant joint torque, angular velocity, and muscle moment power for the knee during running. Adapted from Chapman and Caldwell (1983).

been used to study many activities, such as walking (e.g., Robertson & Winter, 1980), running (e.g., Chapman & Caldwell, 1983), and jumping (Bobbert & van Ingen Schenau, 1988), but has seldom been applied to the study of skill level *per se*. One exception to this is a study of skilled and unskilled weight lifters (Enoka, 1988). This technique is especially attractive for the study of coordination because of its ability to express time varying characteristics of both internal and external control parameters. The timing of individual joint powers has been used to demonstrate various aspects of the coordination evident in normal human walking (Winter, 1983).

One application of power analysis to the development of motor skill has been suggested by Jensen (1988). Using the developmental levels for the standing long jump hypothesized by Clark and Phillips (1985), Jensen selected subjects representing developmentally immature, intermediate, and mature levels of jumping. She then calculated the relative muscle power at the hip, knee, and ankle. Preliminary results suggest that there may be developmental differences in the power profiles or kinetic strategies employed by these young jumpers, whereas the kinematic parameters of displacement and velocity revealed no such differences.

Summary

The measures of the movement itself offer important windows to study the control and coordination of skilled movement and its development. Of all the measures discussed, kinematic analyses have been employed most frequently by those seeking to measure and evaluate skill. New ways of using kinematic measures, such as phase portraits and phase angles, were discussed for their potential as measures of skillfulness. Less well known and rarely used in measuring motor skill and its development are the kinetic analyses of movement. Three types of kinetic analyses were discussed: inverse dynamics, mechanical energy, and power analysis. The advantage of the kinetic analyses over the other measures discussed is that they provide information about the cause of a movement. That is, each of the kinetic analyses provides some clue as to the forces that produced the movement. How and when the CNS controls and coordinates both the muscular and nonmuscular forces may be at least partially understood with the use of kinetic analyses.

SUMMARY

From the dynamical systems perspective, the study of motor skill and its development requires the use of measures different from those found in other paradigms (e.g., the information processing paradigm). Our purpose was to examine some of these measures for their utility in assessing motor skill. Variables that yield information about movement outcomes as well as the movement itself were discussed. Each of the variables presented contributes a different type of information about motor skill. Selection of the variable or variables to use is dependent on the researcher's questions. For example, if we seek answers about control parameters we might study the kinematics of one particular segment. However, if we seek answers about the coordination of this segment with another, then we might explore the use of phase angles. Furthermore, kinetic analyses of these segmental motions can clarify the role of muscular and nonmuscular forces in both control and coordination.

While our focus has been on the utility of these variables in measuring and evaluating motor skills within the dynamical systems perspective, it is clear that some of these variables have been developed for use in answering questions outside this perspective. Clearly these variables can be used by those studying motor skillfulness using other theoretical paradigms. Indeed, future efforts to understand skill will not only bring new techniques and variables, but new paradigms as well.

As our review has noted, very few of these variables have been used in the study of motor skill and its development. It is our hope that by understanding the potential information afforded by each of these measures, developmentalists will begin to utilize those measures which may better help them to understand motor skill.

REFERENCES

Aleshinsky, S. Y. (1986). An energy "sources" and "fractions" approach to the mechanical energy expenditure problem—IV. Criticism of the concept of "energy transfers within and between links." *Journal of Biomechanics, 19,* 307–309.

Beek, P. J. & Beek, W. J. (1988). Tools for constructing dynamical models of rhythmic movements. *Human Movement Science, 7,* 301–342.

Bernstein, N. A. (1967). *The co-ordination and regulation of movements.* London: Permagon Press.

Bernstein, N. (1984). Biodynamics of locomotion. In H. T. A. Whiting (Ed.), *Human motor actions: Bernstein reassessed* (pp. 171–222). New York: North-Holland. (Original work published 1940).

Bresler, B., & Frankel, J. P. (1950). The forces and moments in the leg during level walking. *American Society of Mechanical Engineers, 48-A-62,* 27–35.

Bobbert, M. F., & van Ingen Schenau, G. J. (1988). Coordination in vertical jumping. *Journal of Biomechanics, 21,* 249–262.

Caldwell, G. E., Forrester, L. W., Phillips, S. J., & Clark, J. E. (1989, June). *Segmental energy contributions in walking and running.* A paper presented at the International Congress of Biomechanics, University of California at Los Angeles, Los Angeles.

Chapman, A. E., & Caldwell, G. E. (1983). Factors determining changes in lower limb energy during swing in treadmill running. *Journal of Biomechanics, 16,* 69–77.

Chapman, A. E., Caldwell, G. E., Herring, R. M., Lonergan, R. M., & Selbie, W. S. (1987). Mechanical energy and the preferred style of running. In B. Jonsson (Ed.), *Biomechanics X* (pp. 875–879). Champaign-Urbana, IL: Human Kinetics.

Chapman, A. E., Lonergan, R. M., & Caldwell, G. E. (1984). Kinetic sources of lower limb angular displacement in the recovery phase of sprinting. *Medicine & Science in Sports & Exercise, 16,* 382–388.

Clark, J. E., & Phillips, S. J. (1985). A developmental sequence of the standing long jump. In J. E. Clark & J. H. Humphrey (Eds.), *Motor development: Current Selected Research* (Vol. 1, pp. 73–85). Princeton, NJ: Princeton Book.

Clark, J. E., Phillips, S. J., & Petersen, R. (1989). Developmental stability in jumping. *Developmental Psychology, 25,* 929–935.

Clark, J. E., Truly, T., & Phillips, S. J. (1989, July). *A dynamical systems approach to understanding the development of intralimb coordination in locomotion.* A paper presented at the NATO Advanced Study Institute on Infancy, Rouen, France.

Clark, J. E., Whitall, J., & Phillips, S. J. (1988). Human interlimb coordination: The first 6 months of independent walking. *Developmental Psychobiology, 21,* 445–456.

Easton, T. A. (1972). On the normal use of reflexes. *American Scientist, 60,* 591–599.

Enoka, R. M. (1988). Load-and skill-related changes in segmental contributions to a weightlifting movement. *Medicine & Science in Sports & Exercise, 20,* 178–187.

Fitts, P. M. (1954). The information capacity of the human motor system in controlling the amplitude of movement. *Journal of Experimental Psychology, 47,* 381–391.

Gelfand, I. M., Gurfinkel, V. S., Tsetlin, M. L., & Shik, M. L. (1971). Some problems in the analysis of movements. In I. M. Gelfand, V. S. Gurfinkel, S. V. Fomin, & M. L. Tsetlin (Eds.), *Models of the structural-functional organization of certain biological systems* (pp. 329–345). Cambridge, MA: MIT Press.

Gelfand, I. M., & Tsetlin, M. L. (1971). Mathematical modeling of mechanisms of the central nervous system. In I. M. Gelfand, V. S. Gurfinkel, S. V. Fomin, & M. L. Tsetlin (Eds.), *Models of the structural-functional organization of certain biological systems* (pp. 1–22). Cambridge, MA: MIT Press.

Haken, H., Kelso, J. A. S., & Bunz, H. (1985). A theoretical model of phase transitions in human hand movements. *Biological Cybernetics, 51,* 347–356.

Jensen, J. L. (1988, June). *Changing intersegmental dynamics in the development of body projection skills.* Paper presented at the annual meeting of the North American Society for the Psychology of Sport and Physical Activity, Knoxville, TN.

Jensen, J. L., Ulrich, B. D., Thelen, E., Schneider, K., & Zernicke, R. F. (1988, November). *Posture-related changes in lower-limb intersegmental dynamics in spontaneous kicking in 3-month-old infants.* Paper presented at the annual meeting of the Society for Neuroscience, Toronto, Canada.

Jensen, J. L., Ulrich, B. D., Thelen, E., Schneider, K., & Zernicke, R. F. (1989, April). *Limb dynamics of infant kicking in supine and vertical postures.* Paper presented at the biannual meeting of the Society for Research in Child Development, Kansas City, KS.

Jensen, R. K. (1981). The effects of 12-month growth period on the body moments of inertia of children. *Medicine & Science in Sports & Exercise, 13,* 238–242.

Kelso, J. A. S. (Ed.). (1982). *Human motor behavior: An introduction.* Hillsdale, NJ: Erlbaum.

Kelso, J. A. S. (1984). Phase transitions and critical behavior in human bimanual coordination. *American Journal of Physiology: Regulatory, Integrative, Comparative Physiology, 246,* R1000–R1004.

Kelso, J. A. S., Saltzman, E. L., & Tuller, B. (1986). The dynamical perspective on speech production: Data and theory. *Journal of Phonetics, 14,* 29–59.

Kugler, P. N., Kelso, J. A. S., & Turvey, M. T. (1980). On the concept of coordinative structures as dissipative structures: I. Theoretical lines of convergence. In G. E. Stelmach & J. Requin (Eds.), *Tutorials in motor behavior* (pp.3–47). New York: North-Holland.

LaFortune, M. A., & Cavanagh, P. R. (1983). Effectiveness and efficiency in bicycle riding. In H. Matsui & K. Kobayashi (Eds.), *Biomechanics VIII-B* (pp. 928–936). Champaign-Urbana, IL: Human Kinetics.

MacKenzie, C. L., & Marteniuk, R. G. (1985). Motor skill: Feedback, knowledge, and structural issues. *Canadian Journal of Psychology, 39,* 313–337.

McGraw, M. B. (1935). *Growth: A study of Johnny and Jimmy.* New York: Appleton-Century.

Nicolis, G., & Prigogine, I. (1977). *Self organization in non-equilibrium systems: From dissipative structures to order through fluctuations.* New York: Wiley.

Norman, R. W., Caldwell, G. E., & Komi, P. V. (1985). Differences in body segment energy utilization between world-class and recreational cross-country skiers. *International Journal of Sports Biomechanics, 1,* 253–262.

Norman, R. W., Sharratt, M. T., Pezzack, J. C., & Noble, E. G. (1976). Re-examination of the mechanical efficiency of horizontal treadmill running. In P. V. Komi (Ed.), *Biomechanics V-B* (pp. 87–93). Baltimore: University Park Press.

Phillips, S. J., Roberts, E. M., & Huang, T. C. (1983). Quantification of intersegmental reactions during rapid swing motion. *Journal of Biomechanics, 16,* 411–417.

Pierrynowski, M. R., Winter, D. A., & Norman, R. W. (1980). Mechanical energy transfer in treadmill walking. *Ergonomics, 23,* 147–156.

Prigogine, I., & Stengers, I. (1984). *Order out of chaos: Man's new dialogue with nature.* New York: Bantam.

Roberton, M. A. (1977). Stability of stage categorizations across trials: Implications for the "stage theory" of overarm development. *Journal of Human Movement Studies, 3,* 49–59.

Roberton, M. A. (1978). Longitudinal evidence for developmental stages in the forceful overarm throw. *Journal of Human Movement Studies, 4,* 167–175.

Roberton, M. A., & Langendorfer, S. (1980). Testing motor development sequences across 9–14 years. In D. Nadeau, W. Halliwell, K. Newell, & G. Roberts (Eds.), *Psychology of Motor Behaviour and Sport—1979* (pp. 269–279). Champaign, IL: Human Kinetics.

Robertson, D. G. E., & Winter, D. A. (1980). Mechanical energy generation, absorption and transfer amongst segments during walking. *Journal of Biomechanics, 13,* 845–854.

Saltzman, E., & Kelso, J. A. S. (1983). Toward a dynamical account of motor memory and control. In R. A. Magill (Ed.), *Memory and control of action* (pp. 17–38). New York: North-Holland.

Saltzman, E., & Kelso, J. A. S. (1987). Skilled actions: A task-dynamic approach. *Psychological Review, 94,* 84–106.

Schmidt, R. A. (1988). *Motor control and learning: A behavioral emphasis* (2nd ed.). Champaign, IL: Human Kinetics.

Schneider, K., Zernicke, R. F., Ulrich, B. D., Jensen, J. L., & Thelen, E. (1989). *Control of lower limb intersegmental dynamics during spontaneous kicking in 3-month-old human infants.* Manuscript submitted for publication.

Schöner, G., & Kelso, J. A. S. (1988). Dynamic pattern generation in behavioral and neural systems. *Science, 239,* 1513–1520.

Sparrow, W. A. (1983). The efficiency of skilled performance. *Journal of Motor Behavior, 15,* 237–261.

Sparrow, W. A., & Irizarry-Lopez, V. M. (1987). Mechanical efficiency and metabolic cost as measures of learning a novel gross motor task. *Journal of Motor Behavior, 19,* 240–264.

Thelen, E. (1985). Developmental origins of motor coordination: Leg movements in human infants. *Developmental Psychobiology, 18,* 1–22.

Thelen, E. (1986). Treadmill-elicited stepping in seven-month-old infants. *Child Development, 57,* 1498–1506.

Thelen, E. (1989). Self-organization in developmental processes: Can systems approaches work? In M. Gunnar & E. Thelen (Eds.), *Systems and development: The Minnesota Symposium on Child Psychology* (Vol. 22, pp. 77–117). Hillsdale, NJ: Erlbaum.

Thelen, E., & Fisher, D. M. (1982). Newborn stepping: An explanation for a "disappearing reflex." *Developmental Psychology, 18,* 760–775.

Thelen, E., Fisher, D. M., & Ridley-Johnson, R. (1984). The relationship between physical growth and a newborn reflex. *Infant Behavior and Development, 7,* 479–493.

Thelen, E., Fisher, D. M., Ridley-Johnson, R., & Griffin, N. (1982). The effects of body build and arousal on newborn infant stepping. *Developmental Psychology, 158,* 447–453.

Thelen, E., Kelso, J. A. S., & Fogel, A. (1987). Self-organizing systems and infant motor development. *Developmental Review, 7,* 39–65.

Truly, T. L. (1988). *Getting the system started: Intralimb coordination for gait initiation in newly walking infants.* Unpublished thesis. University of Maryland, College Park, MD.

Turvey, M. T. (1977). Preliminaries to a theory of action with reference to vision. In R. Shaw & J. Bransford (Eds.), *Perceiving, acting and knowing: Toward an ecological psychology* (pp. 211–265). Hillsdale, NJ: Erlbaum Press.

Wells, R. P. (1988). Mechanical energy costs of human movement: An approach to evaluating the transfer possibilities of two-joint muscles. *Journal of Biomechanics, 21,* 955–964.

Williams, K. R. (1985). The relationship between mechanical and physiological energy estimates. *Medicine & Science in Sport & Exercise, 17,* 317–325.

Williams, K. R., & Cavanagh, P. R. (1983). A model for the calculation of mechanical power during distance running. *Journal of Biomechanics, 16,* 115–128.

Winter, D. A. (1979). A new definition of mechanical work done in human movement. *Journal of Applied Physiology: Respiratory, Environmental, Exercise Physiology, 46,* 79–83.

Winter, D. A. (1983). Biomechanical motor patterns in normal walking. *Journal of Motor Behavior, 15,* 302–330.

AUTHOR NOTES:

We wish to thank L. W. Forrester, J. L. Jensen, and T. L. Truly for helpful reviews of this manuscript. Address correspondance to G. E. Caldwell, Dept. of Kinesiology, University of Maryland, College Park, MD., 20742.

10

TOWARD AN ECOLOGICAL THEORY OF MOTOR DEVELOPMENT: THE RELEVANCE OF THE GIBSONIAN APPROACH TO VISION FOR MOTOR DEVELOPMENT RESEARCH

Jürgen Konczak

ABSTRACT

The first part of this paper reviews three aspects of Gibson's concept of direct perception: optical flow field theory (ecological optics), the concept of affordances, and the role of vision as a kinesthetic sensory system (perception of ego-movement). Complementing this review is a discussion of recent psychophysical and psychophysiological research, critical to or in support of Gibsonian theory. The second part of the article places Gibson's ecological model into the perspective of a global theory of perception and action, and outlines its relevance for motor development research. The issue of body-scaled information is presented as one possible approach for conducting motor development research in an ecological framework. The paper concludes with the implementation of the Gibsonian model to a theory of action that offers an explanatory construct for the study of the development of human motor coordination.

We perceive only while we act.
—Whewell, 1840

We hold unequivocally that perception without motor consciousness is impossible.
—Ladd, 1898

As motor development researchers, we have tended to focus predominantly on the motor aspect of human coordination and have neglected its perceptual basis. Since the 1960s, stage theories dominated the thinking in motor development.

The results were numerous projects attempting to validate stagelike models for an array of motor skills (e.g., Roberton, 1977). Despite the demonstrated success of such an approach, stage models are only descriptive constructs of developmental patterns.

In recent years, ecological theories have attracted attention among motor development researchers. Proponents of such models claim that they represent explanatory constructs, and that motor coordination and its development could only be understood in the context of ecological paradigms—paradigms that address the interrelationship between the organism and the environment (Kugler, Kelso, & Turvey, 1982; Turvey, 1974, 1977). One of these theories is J. J. Gibson's (1979) model of ecological perception. His theory has paralleled the introduction of an ecological model to motor behavior, the Bernstein (1967) perspective to motor control. In order to determine whether in fact these theories are explanatory, we need to examine the basic premises of both theories.

J. J. Gibson (1966) opposed "little-man-in-the-brain" theories of perception. In his opinion, the assumption of a "little man" sitting in the brain, looking at the physiological image of the retina, does not help to explain visual perception. The use of a homunculus model might explain how human perception operates, but then the question arises of how the "little man's" perceptual system works. Ultimately, this approach leads to infinite regress, and nothing is gained.

In the same way, Bernstein suggested that the degrees of freedom for movement are not entirely regulated by a "homunculus" in the brain. He was convinced that a single, central agency cannot handle the overwhelming number of decisions that are necessary for controlling the states of all individual muscles to produce an infinite variety of possible movements. Moreover, such a system would require an enormous amount of perceptual information for on-line and feedback control of the performed movements. In his alternative model, Bernstein (1967) proposed that muscles are not controlled individually, but by means of muscle synergies or *coordinative structures*. Such an organization reduces the number of central decisions that need to be made. He and his proponents in the United States (Kugler, 1986; Kugler, Kelso, & Turvey, 1982) suggested that the manifest patterns of coordination are due to the changing constraints imposed on action. In their view, coordination is not exclusively the result of genetic or learned prescriptions as maturation or learning theories have assumed. Moreover, the emergence of new behaviors is the result of the interaction of *organismic* and *environmental constraints*. These constraints are not deterministic in their nature, and they do not prescribe a certain course of development. They permit the emergence of particular movement patterns, rather than determining it (Newell, 1986). Development is not caused by these constraints; rather they exclude possible forms of behavior.

Nevertheless, this system of constraints cannot operate without perceptual information. To modulate or tune coordinative structures, a perceptual system must be able to provide information for motor control without intervention from homunculuslike agencies in the brain. Gibson's (1966, 1979) ecological theory on vision suggested such a model of *direct perception*. According to Gibson, perceptual information is not interpreted solely by higher brain centers. This view parallels the view of proponents of the Bernstein perspective, who are opposed to a perceptual system that exclusively decides what segments of information are given to control a coordinative structure (Fitch, Tuller, & Turvey, 1982). Thus, Bernstein's model of coordinative structures and Gibson's theory of ecological perception can be regarded as complementary building blocks of a unified *theory of perception and action*.

This paper will focus on the perceptual component of this global theory of perception and action. The first part reviews Gibson's concept of direct perception; the second part attempts to put his theory into the context of a perception-action theory and outlines the relevance of this theoretical construct for motor development. Specifically, the first section addresses three different aspects of direct perception.

First, a brief synopsis of the optic flow field theory is provided. Second, I present the implications of this model for visual kinesthesis (perception of ego-movement) and for the concept of affordances (perception of objects). Third, I review psychophysiological research and discuss its compatibility with Gibson's physical model of perception.

In line with the work of Kugler et al. (1982), the second section of this paper proposes a theory of perception and action, based on Gibson's ecological approach to vision and the Bernstein perspective of motor control. First, the principles of an ecological theory of motor development are outlined. Second, the issue of body-scaled information is presented as an example of how motor behavior/motor development research can be conducted within an ecological framework.

THE CONCEPT OF DIRECT PERCEPTION

Ecological Optics and the Perception of Depth

Gibson's (1979) ecological approach to visual perception demonstrated his own "fresh start" to model the phenomenon of vision. Traditional theories on perception (empiricism, nativism, rationalism, Gestalt theory, information theory) had based their models of visual perception on the two-dimensional image of the retina. This assumption led to the important question of how it was possible to perceive the world in three dimensions when the available retinal images represented only two dimensions? The answer to this question has been the central focus of perceptual theory since the Enlightenment. The dilemma of the lost dimension led all traditional theories to the assumption that the third dimension must be *mediated* via some additional perceptual mechanisms. The empiricist Berkeley (1784/1969) suggested that the perceptual judgment of objects in space depends entirely on the observer's associations with prior experience. Spatial vision without the reference to experience was impossible. The idealistic (nativistic) position states that perception of depth was only possible because of innate ideas (schemata) of space and time (Kant, 1784/ 1979). Von Helmholtz (1868/1962), the founder of modern physiological optics, proclaimed that the two retinal images are combined in the brain by a "mental act," and that the third dimension is reestablished by using perceptual cues. These cues are provided by the image itself and by the very activity of the oculomotor apparatus. A list of such cues for depth is given in most psychology textbooks: motion parallax,[1] convergence and accommodation of the lenses, apparent size, linear perspective (monocular cues), along with binocular disaparity and convergence (binocular cues).

Gestalt theorists offered a holistic approach to perception. They thought that three-dimensional vision was possible due to the spontaneous organization of sensory inputs to the brain. The primary data of perception were specific structures or Gestalten, not single stimuli on the retina (Köhler, 1942).

These contrasting views of perception formed the theoretical antecedents for modern theories on vision. The prevailing information-theoretic models are still largely influenced by Helmholtz's physiological optics. The basis of their research remains the retinal image. They also acknowledge the existence of independent depth cues. The electrophysiological research conducted under this paradigm focuses on how the neural network accomplishes the processing of the visual input (for reviews see Livingstone & Hubel, 1988, and Maunsell & Newsome, 1987). Contemporary psychophysical approaches to perception, such as constructivist (Rock, 1984) or connectionist (Marr, 1982) theories, assume that some type of mental operations are necessary to establish a percept from the data of the occurrent visual input.

In Gibson's view, the assumption of a two-dimensuonal retinal image was erroneous. It led to one of the greatest fallacies in the history of psychology— that we are able to "see" the retinal picture. He felt that the concept of space is merely a geometrical abstraction that has no significance for perceptual theory. The doctrine that we cannot perceive the outer world unless we have a concept of space (either innate or gained by experience) is "nonsense"; it does not explain perception and only creates a "theoretical mess" (Gibson, 1979, p. 3). In his view the process of perception is *direct;* it is not *mediated* by any retinal, neural, or mental images. The physical concept of space does not apply to perception; it is a myth,—"the third dimension is not lost in the retinal image since it was never in the environment to begin with" (Gibson, 1979, p. 148).

Because physical optics could not provide the answers to his questions,

Gibson (1961) proposed a new science of vision, *ecological optics*. There are several important distinctions between the two optical theories. Physical optics conceives of light as radiant, propagating outward from a source. Ecological optics describes light as ambient, focusing to a point in a medium. Radiant light depends on a source; ambient light is simply there. It illuminates the environment (its source is largely irrelevant). Radiant light is electromagnetic energy; ambient light is determined by the surface layout of the environment; it carries ecological information.

In physiological optics, which subscribes to the physical model of light, the basis of visual perception is the stimulation of photoreceptors by photons of light. For Gibson these sensations of light are not fundamental to perception, because we *see* the environment or facts about the environment, but we never *see* photons or waves of radiant energy (Gibson, 1979). Photons generate a sensation at the photoreceptor, but not a perception of the visual world. Gibson acknowledged that the *stimulation* of the retina is the *necessary* condition for perception, but it is not sufficient, because it does not provide the data for perception. In contrast, *stimulus information* from the ambient array of light is a *sufficient* condition for vision, because the ambient light is structured by the surface layout of the environment. Hence it is capable of providing information about the environment. Theoretically, ambient light can be unstructured. For example, an empty medium like air or a fog-filled room has unstructured ambient light. Although it stimulates the photoreceptors, it contains no ecological information about the environment. The distinction between *stimulus* and *stimulus information* stands in sharp contrast to other information-based theories of visual perception. In Gibson's view these theories simply used the wrong model to explain

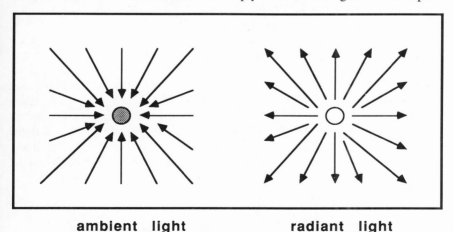

ambient light　　　　　　**radiant light**

FIG. 1. The basic features of radiant and ambient light.

vision. We do not perceive stimuli, but we perceive illuminated surfaces in the environment. Physical optics cannot account for the complexity of the optic array of light. Because this model reduces the visual input to photons of light, it is unable to explain how light can carry optical information that specifies the environment.

The work of David Lee and his coworkers has lent theoretical and experimental support to the Gibsonian concept of direct perception. In agreement with Gibson, Lee and Thomson (1982) stated that the issue of the missing depth perception represents a nonproblem. They argued that the traditional consideration of the time-frozen, cameralike image of the retina as the perceptual basis is actually a special case that rarely occurs in daily perception. In real life human observers are constantly moving their eyes, their heads, and bodies. As a result of this activity the visual input to the eye is not constant, but a time-varying, spatially structured array of light, which is characterized as the *optic flow field*.

The optic flow field provides spatial information about the animal's movement to the environment. It also provides temporary information necessary for timing its actions, and three-dimensional information about the environment itself. Lee and Thomson (1982) revealed theoretically that the positions of all visible texture elements in the environment are optically specified in terms of the organism's velocity (see also Lee, 1980). Their finding implied that the dynamic structure of the optic flow field provides information about the relative distances, sizes, and orientations of surfaces and objects in the environment. In other words, the three-dimensional, spatial information the observer needs to obtain depth perception is always available to the observer—it just needs to be picked up.

This theory of *information-pick-up* is supported by psychophysical research. Rogers and Graham (1979) conducted an experiment in which subjects looked at computer-generated, random-dot patterns of an oscilloscope. In two different conditions, the visual stimulus was transformed either by movements of the observer or by moving the display on the screen. As a result, the retinal images of the dot pattern moved relative to the amplitude of the screenmovements. These perspective transformations produced a reliable and consistent impression of a three-dimensional surface in the absence of other depth cues. This finding underlined Helmholtz's (1925) claim of the importance of motion parallax for depth perception, but it also supported Gibson's (1966, 1979) idea that the deformation and acceleration of the ambient array are sufficient for three-dimensional vision. The fact that the subjects perceived the two-dimensional dot pattern as a three-dimensional surface indicated that they were able to pick up this type of information.

The Perception of Affordances

So far I have described the differences between ambient and radiant light and their relevance for the perception of depth. Radiant light cannot carry ecological

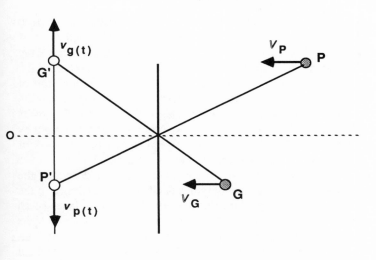

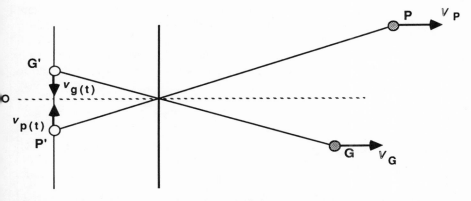

FIG. 2. Illustration of how movement in the environment generates an optic flow field. The schematic eye is considered to be stationary, with the environment moving toward it with the velocity V (top), or away from it (bottom). G and P denote texture elements of surfaces in the environment. Ambient light, reflected from these texture elements, passes through the nodal point of the lens and gives rise to the retinal images G' and P'. These optic texture elements move outward along radial flow lines when the environment moves toward the observer (top), and inward, if the environment moves away from the eye (redrawn and modified from Lee & Thomson, 1982, p. 414).

information, while ambient light has this ability, if it is structured by the surface layout of the environment. The environment is determined by the solid surfaces and a medium in which the observer lives (normally air). We perceive the surfaces in the environment because we register the *stimulus information* in the ambient array of light. But how does the reception of *stimulus information* of surfaces translate to the perception of an object? Gibson (1979) argued that the perception of the surface of an object is synonymous with the perception of its *affordance*. "Perhaps the composition and layout of surfaces constitute what they afford" (Gibson, 1979, p. 127). This assumption implies that the "values" or "meanings" of objects in the environment are perceived directly.

The term *affordance* was introduced by Gibson himself. It describes the functional utility of particular environmental objects taken with reference to the perceiver and his or her action capabilities (Mark, 1987). An affordance of an object is determined by the properties of its substance (e.g., its texture) and its surfaces (e.g., its shape, size). For example, a flat, rigid surface that is horizontal in relation to the observer affords support; if this surface is large enough, it might afford walking or other forms of locomotion. This surface of support can be called ground or floor. It is a "stand-on-able," but it may also be a "walk-on-able." If, in addition to this surface, another surface is assumed, which is raised to approximately knee level, then this surface affords to be "sit-on-able." Note that the object is being perceived according to this affordance. The fact of being a seat is the relevant action feature of the object; such properties as color or texture are irrelevant. These other properties determine only what kind of seat it is, for instance, a chair, a stool, or a bench. An affordance is not perceived by all observers in the same way. A surface that invites an adult to sit may not have this affordance to a child because it is too high above the ground for the child to reach.

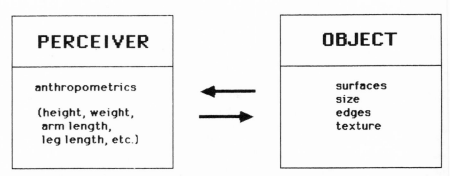

FIG. 3. Diagram illustrating the reciprocal perceiver-object relationship in an affordance situation.

In short, an affordance is anything that a certain object offers to an observer, but its *meaning* to an observer is assessed by the observer's individual metrics (e.g., body weight, height, limb lengths). Gibson proclaimed that his concept of affordances overcame the subject-object dualism of the traditional theories on perception. The affordance is neither a subjective quality of a thing nor its objective property. An affordance of something does not change as the need of the observer changes—the physical properties of the object remain unchanged although the observer's perception of the object can vary over time.

Gibson acknowledged that we can misinterpret an affordance. For instance, we can mistake a closed glass door for an open doorway and attempt to walk through it (Gibson, 1977, 1979). Although all affordances can inherently lead to misperceptions, "the basic affordances of the terrestrial environment are perceivable directly, without an excessive amount of learning" (Gibson, 1977, p. 82).

In a series of experiments with infants, Eleanor Gibson and coworkers attempted to provide evidence that perception of simple affordances does not require extensive perceptual experience (Gibson, Riccio, Schmuckler, Stoffregen, Rosenberg, & Taormina, 1987). They were interested in knowing whether infants who could only crawl acted differently than ones who were already able to walk, when given the choice of traversing two different, supporting surfaces (waterbedlike and rigid). It was hypothesized that the crawlers would perceive the affordance of both surfaces as passable, while the walkers would prefer the rigid surface or would regress to crawling when traversing the soft surface. The experiments revealed that walkers exploited a different behavior than the crawlers toward the waterbed: unlike crawlers, they hesitated longer before crossing it; they preferred the rigid surface as an alternative when it was offered; they engaged in more exploratory activity (visually and haptically) when confronted with the waterbed. Gibson et al. (1987) interpreted these results as indicating that the traversability of surfaces is perceived in relation to the infants' locomotor abilities and their developmental stage. This finding is in line with the concept of affordances. It showed that basic terrestrial features, like support surfaces, are perceived in relation to the motor abilities of the observer.

Gibson's concept of affordances has definite similarities to the Gestalt approach. Eleanor Gibson (1982) pointed out that the concept of affordances had close antecedents in Gestalt psychology. She cited Koffka (1935), who stated that the object in the environment has a *demand character;* that is, it "says what it is and what one ought to do with it: A fruit says, 'Eat me'; water says 'Drink me'; thunder says, 'Fear me'" (Koffka, 1935/1963, p. 7). Lewin (1938) suggested that each object possesses a certain "valence" ["Aufforderungscharakter"], an environmental force that "steers" the perceiver's subsequent behavior. It invites the observer to act on the specific subject.

These terms carry obviously a connotation similar to that of an *affordance,* but Gestalt psychology addressed only the subjective part of the perceptual process.

Lewin's theory implied a psychological force, which drives the observer to an object to satisfy his needs. Gibson (1979) emphasized that the affordance of an object is independent from the observer's needs or desires. It is an inherent feature of the object.

The Perception of Ego-Movement

In earlier works Gibson (1966) strongly criticized the traditional classification of the perceptual system into the categories exteroceptors and proprioceptors. Traditionally, exteroceptors—the eyes, ears, nose, mouth, and skin—were said to receive the external sensory signals, whereas the proprioceptors—receptors of joints, muscles, and inner ear—were responsible for registering the sensations of the body movements (internal, kinesthetic information). In Gibson's (1979) view, the visual system is both exteroceptive and proprioceptive.

The role of vision in the control of movement and its relationship to other proprioceptive sensory systems has been thoroughly researched in recent years. Lee and others conducted several experiments to verify Gibson's claim that vision contains a proprioceptive component (Butterworth & Hicks, 1977; Lee, 1980; Lee & Aronson, 1974; Lee & Thomson, 1982). They agreed with Gibson's critique of the ineffective definitions of the terms *exteroceptive* and *proprioceptive* information. They introduced the new term *exproprioceptive* to account for any information received "about the position, orientation, and movement of the body as a whole, or part of the body, relative to the environment" (Lee & Thomson, 1982, p. 412).

Lishman and Lee (1973) revealed experimentally the importance of vision as an exproprioceptive tool. Human subjects were brought into a situation where their visual information conflicted with the information received through other senses. The apparatus used was a so-called "swinging room," a floorless box that could be moved noiselessly while the subjects stood or moved inside the box on a trolley. In most cases, self-motion within a stable environment provides a changing optic flow field, but theoretically the effect is the same, if the perceiver remains stable and the environment moves. This was the reasoning behind the construction of the moving room. It allowed the researchers to control the direction of the optic vector field, and to test the effect of a changing flow field on the subject's spatial orientation under various conditions. They hypothesized that vision would override the kinesthetic information of the mechanoreceptors— for example, while the mechanoreceptors signaled a stable position, the changing flow field, caused by the room movement, indicated "motion" of the subject. The conflicting information would induce the subjects to adjust their posture according to either one of the two types of information (visual or kinesthetic). In the first condition the subjects walked back or forth in the trolley, or on the fixed floor beneath it (active movement). In the second condition the subjects were still surrounded by the walls of the trolley, but were pulled through the room while standing still on the trolley. The results showed the dominance of vision over kinesthetic input in 75% of the active movement trials and in 86% of the passive-movement trials. That is, when confronted with conflicting visual and kinesthetic information, the subjects tended to rely heavily on the optical information instead of the kinesthetic information from the mechanoreceptors.

Lee and Aronson (1974) conducted a similar study with infants, ranging in age from 13 to 16 months. In 82% of the trials the room movement resulted in enhanced body sway of the subjects. In 33% of the trials the effect was so potent that the children lost their balance. This phenomenon could not be explained as a possible "looming effect" (Schiff, 1965)—that is, as avoidance behavior away from an expected collision as the front wall moved toward the subjects. The effect was also observable when the front wall was moved away from the subjects. The experimenters concluded that vision is a potent source of exproprioceptive information (Lee & Thomson, 1982).

Butterworth and Hicks (1977) replicated these findings with two groups of infants. One group had just managed to achieve a standing position over a longer period of time, while the other group was only able to sit in an upright position. Both groups were tested in a sitting position and the older subjects were also tested while standing. The effect of visual proprioception was observable for both groups with no qualitative or quantitative difference between the groups, but the amount of body sway in the older infants while standing was significantly higher. This finding suggested that, under both test conditions, the infants relied heavily on visual information to control their posture. In the less stable standing position, they were significantly more susceptible to the visual input than to kinesthetic information. Butterworth and Hicks (1977) attributed this effect to the immaturity of the nervous system, not yet capable of using the proprioceptive information provided by the ankle joint receptors.

The moving-room experiments underline Gibson's claim that dynamic optical structures play an important part in controlling human movement. In the three experiments presented here, the manipulation of the optic flow field resulted in disturbances or misperceptions that had a direct impact on the individuals' actions. We also saw that neuromotor development influenced the quality and the usage of visual kinesthetic information in the growing infant.

PSYCHOPHYSIOLOGICAL EVIDENCE FOR DIRECT PERCEPTION

The ecological theory of perception is based on two premises. First, the optic array specifies the variant and invariant features of the visual world. Second, the

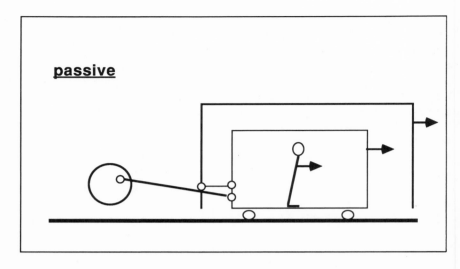

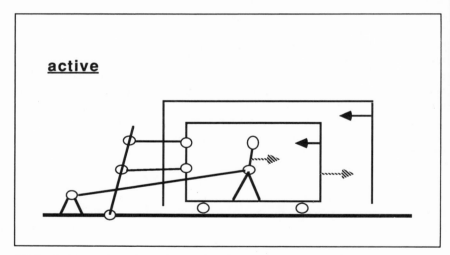

FIG. 4. Examples of passive and active movement experiments.

Passive movement: Solid arrows indicate actual direction of mechanical movement. Broken arrows indicate the corresponding direction of visually specified movement—the movement relative to the room.

Active movement: Solid arrows indicate the mechanical velocities as a result of the subject stepping forward. Broken arrows correspond to the visually specified velocity—the velocity relative to the room. (Redrawn from Lishman & Lee, 1973, pp. 290–291).

perceptual system is able to detect these changes or nonchanges in the optic flow field.

So far I have addressed only the former premise by presenting theoretical and experimental evidence for the flow-field approach to vision. The compelling question posed by the second premise remains unanswered: Is the neurophysiological hardware of the perceptual system actually capable of extracting invariant information from the ambient array of light?

J. J. Gibson's ecological theory proposed a psychophysical model of perception. He makes no statement about the biological properties of the visual system, nor does his theory of information pick-up explain the processing of the visual input. Nevertheless, in recent years physiological research on vision, especially in the area of depth perception, has produced results that are compatible with the views of ecological perception.

For instance, vision research in the last two decades has found evidence for a motion-detecting neural network reaching from the eye to the visual cortex. In the 1950s the West German scientists Hassenstein and Reichardt (1956) detected that insect retinas responded to motion. Barlow and Levick (1965), who experimented with rabbit retinas, and later Stone and Hoffmann (1972) suggested that a specific cell arrangement of the photoreceptors influences the cell response of the motion-detection cells in the retina. They found motion-specific ganglion cells that responded only weakly to a stationary light stimulus, but their neural response increased explosively if the stimulus was moving. The cell response was also dependent on the direction of the movement. A moving stimulus in the preferred direction caused rapid firing; movement in the opposite direction (null-direction) resulted in no cell response. Poggio and Koch (1987) suggested a synaptic mechanism that could account for motion-specific cell responses.

As Figure 5 illustrates, the photoreceptors for each ganglion cell are arranged so that a stimulus moving in the preferred direction activites excitatory receptors before reaching inhibitory receptors. The inhibitory signals are delayed and the excitatory impulse reaches the ganglion cell first. For movement in the null direction, however, the inhibitory signal arrives at the same time as the excitatory signal in the ganglion cell. They negate each other and no action potential is generated.[2]

This example underlines indirectly the Gibsonian notion that basic features of the visual world are perceived directly. The perceptual system is capable of receiving information from the ambient array of light. Motion is not computed or added to the retinal image at higher brain centers, but it is directly recorded via a synaptical network in the retina. Despite the compatibility of psychophysical and physiological research in this case, it would be premature to conclude that the ecological model *in toto* is supported by the findings of electrophysiological and neuroanatomical research on vision.

Although recent attempts have been made to combine the results of these

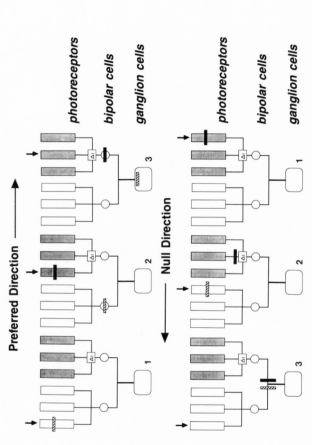

FIG. 5. Simplified wiring diagram of motion-detecting retinal cells. The race between the nerve potentials has different outcomes depending on whether the motion is in the preferred direction (top) or the null direction (bottom). When a stimulus (heavy arrow) is moving in the preferred direction, it activates the excitatory receptors (white) before reaching the inhibitory receptors (grey). The model assumes a delay mechanism, t, that slows down the inhibitory signal (black bar) with repsect to the excitatory signal (gray bar). When the stimulus moves in the preferred direction (left to right), the inhibitory pulses never catch the excitatory impulses, which then generate action potentials at the ganglion cell body. However, for stimulus movement in the null direction (right to left), the inhibitory signal arrives at the same time as the excitatory signal, and no action potential is generated at the ganglion cell. (Redrawn from Poggion & Koch, 1987, p. 50).

different reseach avenues (Livingstone & Hubel, 1988), the adaptation of ecological theory to physiological optics is not without problems. For example, Nakayama (1985) suggested that the biological hardware available for motion processing might impose restrictions on the applicability of the ecological model. He stated that the motion-detection system in the eye possesses only a limited spatial and temporal resolution, thus constraining the possible information flow of the optic flow field. He stressed the fact that the ideas of ecological optics are based on mathematical and physical concepts, not biological ones. The existence of information in the optic array is no guarantee that the perceptual systems of humans or other animals are capable of registering such information (Nakayama, 1985).

ECOLOGICAL MOTOR DEVELOPMENT WITHIN A THEORY OF PERCEPTION AND ACTION

The Principles of a Theory of Ecological Motor Development

The Bernstein perspective on motor behavior and the Gibsonian perspective on visual perception are two complementary parts of a global *theory of perception and action*. The need for an action theory that incorporates perception was originally expressed by Bernstein (1967) and his Russian investigators. Their ideas were later amplified by Turvey (1974, 1977), who argued that the fundamental problems in a theory of action and a theory of perception may be solved by the application of the same concepts and principles. Turvey felt it was not unreasonable to assume that the nervous system solves similar problems in similar ways.

Kugler, Kelso, and Turvey (1982) suggested that a synthesis of physical and biological models with ecological perception could lead to the formulation of a unified *theory of perception and action*. Within such a theoretical framework, motor development could be considered a subdiscipline that studies the developmental patters of human motor coordination within the environment. Developmental research, under a global model of perception and action, would need to adhere to the basic principles of ecological theory.

First, the organism cannot be studied as either perceiving *or* acting. Perception and action are integral parts of *one* organism. Second, the perceptual and action processes take place in an environment in space and time. Research in motor development cannot continue to treat the organism and the environment as distinct parts of a dualism. Finally, the information exchanged between the environment and the organism is unique and specific to the *ecosystem* they constitute.

The last principle addresses the issue of ecological information. One needs to be aware that ecological theory defines the term information differently than information theory. The smallest unit of information in an ecological model are the texture elements in the optic array, whereas information theory describes visual information as a function of semantical descriptors (e.g., bits). Ecological theory defines information as a physical variable in a constantly changing organism—environment system (Kugler et al., 1982). To assess such ecological information the observer needs an intrinsic metric that is specified by the dimensions of the ecosystem. That is, the organism assesses the properties of the environment not in extrinsic units (such as meters, inches, seconds, etc.), but in relation to its body or body parts, its own movement capability, and its relative location to the objects in the environment. For example, a ski jumper requires a metric to analyze the information provided during the approach. Without ecological information it would be impossible for the athlete to determine the accurate time for take-off (Lee & Young, 1985). Such an ability to time interceptive acts rapidly and precisely can be seen in such diverse human activities as running (Warren, Young, & Lee, 1986) and the braking of a car (Lee, 1976). It can also be observed in animals, for instance, in the diving behavior of plummets (Lee & Reddish, 1980).

Body Scaled Information

The study of such intrinsic reference systems bears potential for motor development research. It allows the investigation of changing motor behavior while considering the impact of the perceptual system. Ecological theory provides a framework for studying the development of the perception *and* action system. It suggests experimental hypotheses that focus on the interaction of perceptual and action variables, and how they influence the emergence of new behavior.

Recent research on walking through apertures, sitting, and stair-climbing represent examples of how body scales might be used in visual motor coordination, although few studies have looked at body-scaled information from a developmental perspective.

Warren and Whang (1987) studied the effect of visual guidance on walking through apertures. Tall and small subjects were videotaped while walking through apertures of different widths. The transition from frontal walking to body rotation marked the critical action boundary for each individual, which was intrinsically expressed by the aperture-to-shoulder ratio (A/S). This metric was unique to the ecosystem *walker-aperture,* because it exclusively described the relationship between an environmental variable (aperture width) and an anthropometric property (shoulder width).

The results indicated that tall and small observers perceived the critical point in free walking at approximately A/S = 1.30, independent of static or moving viewing conditions. Further, static monocular information was sufficient to judge the passability of an aperture; kinematic information appeared to be unnecessary. Warren and Whang acknowledged that these findings demonstrate no proof that observers actually use body-scaled information under natural conditions. However, they revealed that the subjects acted in accordance to their body-scaled visual judgments of an environmental property.

In an earlier experiment, Warren (1984) tested the hypothesis that humans assess the climbability of a stair in relation to the length of their legs. He hypothesized that the affordance of a particular stair to an observer can be described as a function of the riser height (R) of the stair and the leg length (L) of the observer: π = R/L. This dimensionless ratio represented an intrinsic metric that was scaled to the dimensions of the *climber-stair system.*

Warren found that tall or short college adults perceived a set of stairs as no longer climbable (in bipedal stair climbing) if the riser height of a stair exceeded 88–89% of the individual's leg length (π = 0.88). A biomechanical model, based on their leg measurements, calculated the maximum riser height they ought to be able to climb. It predicted that the subjects could not climb a stair with a riser height in excess of 88% of their leg length. Thus their perception coincided with their predicted climbing ability. He concluded that short and tall observers judged a particular stair as unclimbable at a riser height that was a constant proportion of their leg length (Warren, 1984).

Konczak, Meuwssen, and Cress (1988) could ot confirm these results in a similar developmental experiment. They studied the affordances of the same stair-climbing task with a young adult and elderly population. In contrast to Warren (1984), they hypothesized that the affordance for climbing a particular set of stairs was not exclusively a function of riser height and leg length. They suggested that other anthropometric variables like trunk flexibility and leg strength played an important role in the perception of climbability at different points in the lifespan. The results revealed that Warren's (1984) biomechanical model corresponded neither to the observer's perception nor to their actual stair-climbing performance. As shown in Table 1, the prediction of the actual critical boundary, using Warren's model, exceeded the perceived critical boundary for both groups. The analysis indicated that strength variables (absolute peak torque) and hip-joint flexibility influenced the affordances in this stair-climbing task, especially for the older group. In the combined group, *peak torque to body weight ratio* for the leg extensors was the single best predictor of climbing performance (r = 0.896) as well as for the perceived critical boundary (r = 0.811).

The experimenters concluded that both perception and the ability to climb are not solely determined by the dimensions of leg segments. Leg strength and flexibilty are also reference scales that are used in assessing affordances of stair-climbing. Further, affordances and the body scales to assess them are not static, but change during the life-span. This finding suggests that the observers'

Table 1
Predicted, Perceived Critical Boundaries

	Predicted	Perceived	Actual
Warren:			
Adults (tall)	0.88	0.89	
Adults (short)	0.88	0.88	
Konczak et al.:			
Young Adults	0.88	0.80	0.96
Older Adults	0.91	0.45	0.52

Values represent the group averages of the affordance variable *pi*.

changing motor development has a direct effect on their perception of affordances.

In another study on stair climbing and sitting, Mark (1987) tested the effect of eye height–scaled information on judging maximum sitting height (SHmax) and maximum riser height (Rmax). The observers, wearing 10-cm blocks under their feet, were asked to determine visually whether the height of an adjustable chair afforded sitting or climbing. When standing on blocks, the subjects initially judged SHmax and RHmax, as if their eye height had not increased from their normal level, but their estimation of these two affordance variables approached their biomechanically predicted value (normal eye height + 10-cm blocks) after the first pair of trials. The author concluded that the change in eye height led to a readjustment of the perceptual boundaries. This would underline Gibson's view that an affordance is a dynamic structure determined by the properties of the observer and the object. In this case, an anthropometric property was manipulated, and the perception of the affordance situation was adjusted according to these changes.

Ulrich, Thelen, and Niles (1990) studied stair-climbing among infants. They tested infants and toddlers at different age groups (*M* age: 13.3 months and 20.3 months) in their perception of affordances, offered by three sets of stairs of varied riser heights (small, medium, large). The results indicated that the younger group selected almost exclusively the stairs of medium and small riser height. In contrast, the older subjects displayed no restriction in their stair choices, but their stair choices were distributed evenly among all three sets of stairs. The authors suggested that the children perceived the climbability of each set of stairs according to their motor abilities and their perceptual experience. No anthropometric variable distinguished the stair choice in the older group, thus refuting the notion of body-scaled information in this case.

The above experiments tested Gibson's (1979) hypothesis of body-scaled information. The results of the experiments are not conclusive in identifying what specific metrics were used in these stair-climbing tasks. Nevertheless, they demonstrate how motor coordination and its development can be studied under a framework of ecological theory. The experiments highlight the close linkage of action and perception variables; specifically, they stress the reciprocal relationship of perception and action. Perception does not only determine the action patterns of the observer, but the observer's motor development has in turn an impact on his or her perception. However, many aspects pertaining to the issue of body-scaled information are not yet fully understood. Several questions that are relevant to the development of coordination remain unanswered.

First, what type of body scales are used in coordinating specific movement patterns and skills? Many other activities of daily living besides stair climbing require visual guidance. If this process is defined by the organism-environment relationship, it must be possible to identify specific body scales that relate to specific activities. The research on stair-climbing behavior represents only a portion of possible metrics used in visual motor coordination.

Second, how do such metrics evolve during the life-span? How do affordances of objects change as the body of the observer changes? A motor development researcher is especially interested in determining what variables control the change in the coordination of visually guided behavior. For example, one variable most likely to exert influence on scaling operations is growth. The bodily dimensions of a growing child are constantly changing. How does a change in height, weight, limb length, and so on affect the perception of environmental objects? Further, how are these changing perceptions of the environment reflected in the observer's action repertoire? All these questions address the interaction of perceptual and motor variables. Ecological theory proposes that motor development research investigates these variables (a) in combination and (b) in an ecologically valid setting, in order to find answers to the above questions.

Finally, does body-scaled equipment aid the acquisitin of motor tasks in children or the retention of skills in an elderly person? If the environment is scaled to the dimensions of the observer's body, it seems plausible that childrens' action capabilities will be enhanced—if household products (e.g., silverware, cups, toothbrush) or sport equipment (e.g., balls, racquets) were scaled to the dimensions of *their* bodies and not to the dimensions of an adult. In the same way, we need to consider the decline in the motor abilities of an older adult, and ask whether many products afford the same use for an older person as they do for a middle-aged adult?

SUMMARY AND CONCLUSIONS

Gibson's psychophysical approach to perception marked a departure from mainstream perceptual theory. Gibson criticized traditional theories for adapting a physical model of the visual input (photon model) that cannot explain the complexity of perceptual phenomena. In contrast, the Gibsonian model specified the dynamic and ecological structures of the visual stimulus (optic array of light), but it stopped short of explaining the physiological mechanisms of perception.[3]

Ecological theory applied to motor development advances a new view of human motor coordination. The phenomenon of changing motor behavior cannot be studied adequately without the consideration of its perceptual basis. The research on body-scaled information represents an attempt to incorporate the Gibsonian paradigm into motor development.

In conjunction with the Bernstein perspective of motor control, the ecological approach to visual perception presents a theoretical framework for studying the development of the human perception-action system. Both theoretical views imply that coordination and perception are not exclusively the result of maturational or learning processes. Moreover, they stress that perception and action are determined by the interaction of the organism with the environment. The Bernstein perspective suggested that the development of movement patterns is governed by organismic and environmental constraints imposed on action.

In complementing such a theory, the concept of direct perception represents a construct that provides a link between a specific set of organismic and environmental constraints. The environmental variables acting upon the action system need to be perceived by the organism, visually or via other sensory modes. Without such information the organism lacks the essential parameters for coordinating its activity in space and time. The consideration of biological and biomechanical constraints on the action system cannot fully explain the development of coordination. Moreover, we need to conceive developmental changes in motor patterns as the results of constraints that are imposed on the perception *and* action system. The experiments of body-scaled information showed that the perception of the environment has a direct impact on our action capabilities, and in turn, our movement repertoire might influence our perception of the visual world. The traditional view of perception and action as two different systems of one organism is no longer valid in the light of ecological theory.

A theory of ecological motor development is just beginning to emerge. One of its bases is the ecological theory of visual perception, which in itself is far from being complete. J. J. Gibson (1959) recognized the immaturity of his psychophysical theory, but he also realized its potential applicability to a wide scope of problems:

> The theory has been extraordinarily fruitful in suggesting to the author hypotheses for experiments and in opening up new ways of experimenting on

old problems. The important question is whether it will serve the same function for others. (Gibson, 1959, p. 499)

Many aspects of his ecological theory appear quite radical and are not universally accepted. Nevertheless, the Gibsonian theory has triggered an array of perceptual research in the last decades. This paper attempted to show that Gibson's theory has heuristic value for motor development. Motor development, as a scientific field, lacks explanatory constructs. Maturation and learning theories provided contrasting models of development. The adaptation of ecological principles to motor development offers an opportunity to overcome this dichotomy.

REFERENCES

Barlow, H. R., & Levick, W. R. (1965). The mechanism of directionally selective units in the rabbit's retina. *Journal of Physiology, 178,* 477–504.

Berkeley, G. (1969). *A new theory of vision and other select philosophical writings.* London: Dent & Sons.

Bernstein, N. (1967). *The coordination and regulation of movements.* London: Pergamon Press.

Butterworth, G. H., & Hicks, L. (1977). Visual proprioception and postural stability in infancy. *Perception, 6,* 256–262.

Fitch, H. L., Tuller, B., & Turvey, M. T. (1982). The Bernstein perspective: III. Tuning of coordinative structures with special reference to perception. In J. A. S. Kelso (Ed.), *Human motor behavior: An introduction* (pp. 271–281). Hillsdale, NJ: Erlbaum.

Frost, B. J., & Nakayama, K. (1983). Single visual neurons code opposing motion independent of direction. *Science, 220,* 744–745.

Gibson, E. J. (1969). *Principles of perceptual learning and development.* New York: Meredith.

Gibson, E. J. (1982). The concept of affordances in development: The renascence of functionalism. In W. A. Collins (Ed.), *The concept of development.* (Vol. 15, pp. 55–81). Hillsdale, NJ: Erlbaum.

Gibson, E. J., Riccio, G., Schmuckler, M. A., Stoffregen, T. A., Rosenberg, D., & Taormina, J. (1987). Detection of the traversability of surfaces by crawling and walking infants. *Journal of Experimental Psychology: Human Perception and Performance, 13,* 533–544.

Gibson, J. J. (1959). Perception as a function of stimulation. In S. Koch (Ed.), *Psychology: A study of science. Vol. 1.* New York: McGraw-Hill.

Gibson, J. J. (1961). Ecological optics. *Vision Research, 1,* 253–262.

Gibson, J. J. (1966). *The senses considered as perceptual systems.* Boston: Houghton Mifflin.

Gibson, J. J. (1977). The theory of affordances. In R. Shaw & J. Bransford (Eds.), *Perceiving, acting and knowing* (pp. 67–83). Hillsdale, NJ: Erlbaum.

Gibson, J. J. (1979). *The ecological approach to visual perception.* Boston: Houghton Mifflin.

Hassenstein, B., & Reichardt, W. (1956). Systemtheoretische Analyse der Zeit-, Reihenfolge und Vorauszeichenauswertung bei der Bewegungsperzeption des Rüsselkafers. *Zeitschrift für Naturforschung, 11b,* 513–524.

Helmholtz, H. von (1925). Physiological optics. In J. P. C. Southall (Ed.) *Helmholtz's treatise on physiological optics.* New York: Optical Society of America.

Helmholtz, H. von (1962). The recent progress of the theory of vision. In M. Kline (Ed.), *Popular scientific lectures by Hermann von Helmholtz.* New York: Dover.

Johannson, G. (1975). Visual motion perception. *Scientific American, 232*(12), 76–88.

Kant, I. (1979). Die Kritik der reinen Vernunft [The critique of pure reason]. In W. Weischedel (Ed.), *Die Kritik der reinen Vernunft* (Vol. 1). Frankfurt am Main: Suhrkamp.

Koffka, K. (1963). *Principles of Gestalt psychology.* New York: Harcourt.

Koffka, K. (1980). *The growth of the mind.* New Brunswick, NJ: Transaction.

Köhler, W. (1942). Kurt Koffka. *The Psychological Review, 49,* 97–101.

Konczak, J., Meuwssen, H., & Cress, E. (1988, August). *Perceiving affordances in stair climbing: A comparison of young adult and elderly women.* Paper presented at the Lolas Halverson Symposium on Motor Development, Madison, WI.

Kugler, P. N. (1986). A morphological perspective on the origin and evolution of movement patterns. In M. G. Wade & H. T. A. Whiting (Eds.), *Motor development in children: Aspects of coordination and control* (pp. 459–525). Dordrecht: Martinus Nijhoff.

Kugler, P. N., Kelso, J. A. S., & Turvey, M. T. (1982). On the control and co-ordination of naturally developing systems. In J. A. S. Kelso, & J. E. Clark (Eds.), *The development of movement control and co-ordination* (pp. 5–78). New York: Wiley.

Ladd, G. T. (1898). *Outlines of descriptive psychology.* New York: Scribner's.

Lee, D. N. (1976). A theory of visual control of braking based on information about time-to-collision. *Perception, 5,* 437–459.

Lee, D. N. (1980). Visuo-motor coordination in space-time. In G. E. Stelmach & J. Requin (Eds.), *Tutorials in motor behavior* (pp. 281–295). New York: North-Holland.

Lee, D. N., & Aronson, E. (1974). Visual proprioceptive control of standing human infants. *Perception and Psychophysics, 15,* 529–532.

Lee, D. N., & Reddish, P. E. (1980). Plummeting gannets: A paradigm of ecological optics. *Nature, 293,* 293–294.

Lee, D. N., & Thomson, J. A. (1982). Vision in action: The control of locomotion. In D. Ingle (Ed.), *Analysis of visual behavior* (pp. 411–433). Cambridge, MA: MIT Press.

Lee, D. N., & Young, D. S. (1985). Visual timing in interceptive action. In D. J. Ingle, M. Jeannerod, & D. N. Lee (Eds.), *Brain mechanisms and spatial vision* (pp. 1–30). Dordrecht: Martinus Nijhoff.

Lewin, K. (1938). Will and need. In E. D. Ellis (Ed.), *A source of Gestalt psychology.* New York: Harcourt.

Lishman, J. R., & Lee, D. N. (1973). The autonomy of visual kinesthetics. *Perception, 2,* 287–294.

Livingstone, M., & Hubel, D. (1988). Segregation of form, color, movement, and depth: Anatomy, physiology, and perception. *Science, 240,* 740–749.

Mace, W. M. (1977). James J. Gibson's strategy for perceiving: Ask not what's inside your head, but what your head's inside of. In R. Shaw & J. Bransford (Eds.), *Perceiving, acting, and knowing— toward an ecological psychology* (pp. 43–65). Hillsdale, NJ: Erlbaum.

Mark, L. S. (1987). Eyeheight-scaled information about affordances: A study of sitting and stair climbing. *Journal of Experimental Psychology: Human Perception and Performance, 13,* 361–370.

Marr, D. (1982). *Vision.* San Francisco: Freeman.

Maunsell, J. H. R., & Newsome, W. T. (1985). Visual processing in the monkey extrastriate cortex. *Annual Review of Neuroscience, 10,* 363–401.

Nakayama, K. (1985). Extraction of higher order derivatives of the optical vector field. In D. J. Ingle, M. Jeannerod, & D. N. Lee (Eds.), *Brain mechanisms and spatial vision* (pp. 59–71). Dordrecht: Martinus Nijhoff.

Nakayama, K., & Loomis, J. M. (1974). Optical velocity patterns, velocity-sensitive neurons, and space perception: A hypothesis. *Perception, 3,* 63–80.

Newell, K. (1986). Constraints on the development of coordination. In M. G. Wade & H. T. A. Whiting (Eds.), *Motor development in children: Aspects of coordination and control* (pp. 341–360). Dordrecht: Martinus Nijhoff.

Pastore, N. (1971). *Selective history of theories of visual perception: 1650–1950.* New York: Oxford University Press.

Poggio, T., & Koch, C. (1987). Synapses that compute motion. *Scientific American. 256*(5), 46–52.

Robertson, M. A. (1977). Stability of stage categorizations across trials: Implications for the "stage theory" of overarm throw development. *Journal of Human Movement Studies, 4,* 167–175.

Rock, I. (1984). *The logic of perception.* Cambridge, MA: MIT Press.

Rogers, B., & Graham, M. (1979). Motion parallax as an independent cue for depth perception. *Perception, 8,* 125–134.

Rogers, B., & Graham, M. (1985). Motion parallax and the perception of three-dimensional surfaces. In D. J. Ingle, M. Jeannerod, & D. N. Lee (Eds.), *Brain mechanisms and spatial vision* (pp. 95–111). Dordrecht: Martinus Nijhoff.

Schiff, K. (1965). Perception of impending collision. A study if visually guided avoidant behavior. *Psychological Monograph, 79*(11), 1–25.

Stadler, M., Seeger, F., & Raeithel, A. (1975). *Psychologie der Wahrnehmung* [The psychology of perception]. Munich: Juventa.

Stone, J., & Hoffmann, K. P. (1972). Very slow conducting ganglion cells in the cat's retina: A major new functional type. *Brain Research, 43,* 610–616.

Torre, V., & Poggio, T. (1978). A synaptic mechanism possibly underlying directional selectivity to motion. *Proceedings of the Royal Society of London: B, 202*(1148), 409–416.

Turvey, M. T. (1974). A note on the relation between action and perception. In M. G. Wade & R. Martens (Eds.), *Psychology of motor behavior and sport* (pp. 307–313). Champaign, IL: Human Kinetics.

Turvey, M. T. (1977). Preliminaries to a theory of action with reference to vision. In R. Shaw & J. Bransford (Eds.), *Perceiving, acting, and knowing—toward an ecological psychology* (pp. 211–265). Hillsdale, NJ: Erlbaum.

Ulrich, B. D., Thelen, E., & Niles, D. (1990). Perceptual determinants of action: Stair-climbing choices of infants and toddlers. In J. E. Clark & J. H. Humphrey (Eds.), *Advances in Motor Development Research* (Vol. 3, pp.). New York: AMS Press.

Warren, W. H. (1984). Perceiving affordances: Visual guidance of stair-climbing. *Journal of Experimental Psychology: Human Perception and Performance, 10,* 683–703.

Warren, W. H., & Whang, S. (1987). Visual guidance of walking through apertures: Body-scaled information for affordances. *Journal of Experimental Psychology: Human Perception and Performance, 13,* 371–383.

Warren, W. H., Young, D. S., & Lee, D. N. (1986). Visual control of step length during running over irregular terrain. *Journal of Experimental Psychology: Human Perception and Performance, 12,* 259–266.

Wässle, H. (1985). Auge und Gehirn: Informationsverarbeitung im visuellen System der Saugetiere [Eye and brain: Information processing in the visual system of mammals]. In P. Karlson (Ed.), *Information und Kommunikation* (pp. 227–241). Stuttgart: Technische Verlagsgesellschaft.

Whewell, W. (1840). *The philosophy of inductive sciences* (Vol. 1.). London: Parker.

NOTES

[1]Helmholtz (1925, p. 295) noted that "in walking along, the objects that are at rest by the wayside appear to glide past us in our field of view. . . . More distant objects do the same way, only more slowly. . . ." He concluded that the movement of the observer, or the movement of objects across the observer's field of view, result in *relative movement* of the images across the retina, a phenomenon he called *motion parallax.*

[2]The actual physiological process is not as simple as I presented here. The interested reader is referred to Torre and Poggio (1978), Poggio and Koch (1987), and Wässle (1984) for a more detailed explanation.

[3]Gibson acknowledged that the completion of his perceptual theory required also a theory of perceptual processing that is compatible with the premises of ecological optics. It was clear to him that one can have direct perception only if the invariants in the optic array can be encoded by one's perceptual system.

AUTHOR NOTE:

I would like to thank Drs. Mary Ann Roberton and Jill Whitall for their valuable comments and their help in editing this manuscript.

11

MOVEMENT CONFIDENCE: AN ELABORATION AND EXPANSION OF THE MODEL

Norma S. Griffin

Michael E. Crawford

ABSTRACT

This paper presents an expanded view of the model for movement confidence as proposed by Griffin and Keogh (1982). Movement confidence is defined and discussed as a construct, and studies of behavioral manifestations and antecedents are reviewed and discussed. Findings of previous studies are elaborated leading to reformulation of the model for movement confidence in the physical dimension. An expansion of the model is proposed, based on theoretical and empirical literatures, for movement confidence in the social and psychological dimensions of human movement performance.

The purpose of this paper is twofold, to provide an elaboration and an expansion of the model for movement confidence (Griffin & Keogh, 1982) in light of theoretical and empirical literatures. This dual purpose seemed best served by utilizing an unusual organization in the structure of the paper. The paper is presented as a set of problem statements with companion argument and need statements that define important research questions and issues related to the construct of movement confidence. This format was selected as a means of presenting, in part one, a summary of the model and previous research and, in part two, a complex reformulation of the model. A brief outline of the contents appears below:

I. PART ONE: An Elaboration of the Model for Movement Confidence
  A. PROBLEM: The Definition of Movement Confidence as a Construct
    1. PROBLEM: Identification of Behavioral Manifestations of Movement Confidence

PART ONE: AN ELABORATION

Problem:

The definition of movement confidence as a construct.

Argument:

The purpose of this paper is to present and discuss movement confidence as a construct with specified antecedents and consequences, not as a unitary concept. That was also the intent of the original model for movement confidence proposed by Griffin and Keogh (1982). Although confidence as used in research is a term connoting probability or sureness, "self-confidence" taken as a generalized concept has been used to mean "self-efficacy" (Bandura, 1977a; Feltz, 1982), to reflect a sense of personal effectiveness (Harter, 1978; Klint & Weiss, 1987) and competence (Duda, 1987; Roberts, Kleiber, & Duda, 1981). Corbin (1981, 1984) and others (Corbin, Stewart, & Blair, 1981; Petruzzello & Corbin, 1988;

Ulrich, 1987; Vealey, 1986) have also studied confidence as a general notion of sureness, efficacy, competence, or sport confidence (Vealey, 1986).

Movement confidence presented as a construct was an attempt to specify testable hypotheses about the nature and impact of perceptions of confidence on involvement and movement performance decisions and behavior. The model for movement confidence posited antecedents of confidence and the interaction and influence of those antecedents. In the model, movement confidence was defined as both a consequence and a mediator of involvement decisions and movement performance behavior. The model, thus, was not an attempt to diminish or duplicate theories or studies of confidence (taken as a unitary concept) as an influence on movement performance or behavior. It was, rather, an attempt to expand the notion of confidence by introducing posited antecedents, consequences and dimensions of influence.

In its initial formulation the model built on and acknowledged extant theories related to an involvement cycle (Coelho, Hamburg, & Adams, 1974), competence (Connolly & Bruner, 1974; White, 1978), cognitive evaluation and motivation (Bandura, 1977b; Harter, 1974, 1978), achievement motivation (Atkinson, 1964), intrinsic motivation (Deci, 1975), and causal attributions (Weiner & Kun, 1974) as related to performance. Since that time, Vallerand's work (1984, 1987), that of Vallerand & Reid (1984) and Vallerand, Colavecchio & Pelletier (1988) has contributed to knowledge of mechanisms of cognitive evaluation of performance, especially cognitions of "emotions—affect."

While the definition of confidence and the formulation of the model were similar to formulations of self-efficacy (Bandura, 1977a) and effectance motivation (Harter, 1978, 1981; White, 1959), a specific intent of the model was to present ways of examining the relationship between competence and confidence and testing the hypothesis that performer cognitions included information about "moving" and the consequences of moving. Although both Bandura (1977) and Harter (1974, 1978) argue for perceptions of efficacy and effectance as cognitions, those concepts are defined as parallel with "self-confidence/competence." In the model for movement confidence, perceptions of movement sensations (sensory experiences) are also treated as cognitions that interact with and modify the influence of competence cognitions. Thus, the model for movement confidence included testable hypothesis about the identity, separability, and interaction of factors that were posited to be antecedent to confidence in the physical domain. The argument from the model is that movement confidence (MC) as a construct is produced by perceptions of the components MOVCOMP (competence factor [C]) and MOVSENSE (enjoyment [E] and harm [H] factors) where the interaction is expected to be: $MC = C + (E-H)$. It was posited that performers would evaluate tasks for both the potential for "enjoying" and the potential for "harm"; thus these two factors were designated as interactive influences within MOVSENSE, as the component representing cognitions of movement sensations.

The delineation of antecedents was grounded in the supposition that competence, as variously defined and described by Bandura (1977a), Connolly & Bruner (1974), White (1978), Harter (1978), Roberts, Kleiber, & Duda (1981), and, more recently, Duda (1987), Feltz & Brown (1984), Roberts & Duda (1984), Ulrich (1987), and Klint & Weiss (1987), is of central importance as an influence on confidence. The influence of sensory experiences as expectations of "enjoyment" has more recently been supported in the literature (Vallerand, 1983, 1984, 1987; Vallerand & Reid, 1984; Vallerand, Colavecchio, & Pelletier, 1988; Wankel & Kreisel, 1985) and as "fun" by Scanlan & Leuthwaite (1986). What then, one might ask, is different about the formulation of the model? Since there were several primary arguments in the model that required testing, one could suggest that these arguments represented differences—hypotheses for which there was no empirical evidence, e.g., (1) that confident and nonconfident movement is observable and describable, (2) that confidence has antecedents that can be identified and their proportional influence determined, and (3) that performer evaluations include cognitions of expected movement sensations as well as competence factors. Testing these hypotheses required a series of studies identifying behavioral manifestations of movement confidence as viewed by observers (Keogh, & Griffin, & Spector, 1981), and of the identity, separability, and proportional influence of competence, enjoyment, and harm as antecedents of confidence (Crawford & Griffin, 1986; Griffin & Crawford, 1989; Griffin, Keogh, & Maybee, 1984).

Currently, the model for movement confidence should be viewed as a "synthesizing" argument, an argument grounded in much that is known about movement performance and one that attempts to expand existing knowledge of causal influences on movement behavior. Defining confidence as a construct is an attempt to move our understanding of the term beyond a generalized sense of competence or effectiveness or efficacy. The model (Griffin & Keogh 1982), for example, posits proportional and differential influence for the three antecedent factors for high and low confidence performers. If these suppositions hold, teachers, counselors, coaches, and others will be able to move beyond a generalized notion of the meaning of the term. We will be able to measure confidence more precisely and to be more precise in designing more effective interventions and performance strategies.

Need:

In order to test the central argument of the model that was for confidence as a construct, not as a general concept parallel to a sense of competence or efficacy, several hypotheses of the model required testing, including the identity of behavioral manifestations of confidence and the identity, separability, and proportional influence of posited antecedents to movement confidence. Appropriate assessment instruments grounded in the model assumptions were needed in order to test these model hypotheses.

Problem:

The identification of behavioral manifestations of movement confidence as described by observers.

Argument:

In a study of observer perceptions of movement confidence, Keogh, Griffin, and Spector (1981) studied the question of observer-defined behavioral manifestations of movement confidence. Because the model presented confidence as a construct, it seemed important to examine the complexity of the behaviors that observers used to describe confidence and nonconfidence in movement. The notion of studying the "reality" of confidence was considered of central importance as a preliminary step in testing assumptions of the model. A fundamental question initially seemed to be whether movement confidence existed only as a "feeling," state, temporary effect, or amorphous notion of skill or whether it could be described by a particular set of observer-described behaviors. In a series of four studies over a period of two years it was found that confident behavior could be described and was generalizable across populations of observers.

In that study, preschool children newly enrolled in a movement development program at the Los Angeles School of Gymnastics were filmed performing three movement tasks. Tasks were novel to the children and designed to minimize the competence (skill) requirement. Task one, for example, required the child to stand on a low vaulting box with back toward a tumbling crash mat and the instructions were to "fall backward straight like a stick."

Over the period of two years the films were rated by four separate populations of observers. The observers included two groups of adults—from California, one group of trained professionls, and from Nebraska, one group of deaf adults accustomed to interpreting nonverbal behavior. Two groups of elementary school children (aged 10–11 years) also viewed and rated the films, one from California (UCLA laboratory school) and one from Nebraska (young gymnasts). Observers were asked to rate the filmed movement performances as to confidence, nonconfidence, or mixed signals of confidence and nonconfidence and then, in a taped, structured interview, to provide the reasons for the ratings. Reasons were stated as descriptions of observed behavior.

Findings revealed that movement confidence was perceived by observers in a consistent manner and was generalizable across populations of observers. Because the rating scale and general instructions permitted personal (observer) rather than imposed notions of the meaning of confidence, it was inferred that movement confidence had some commonality of meaning for observers for both adults and children—it was real.

In a content analysis of information obtained through structured interview, observer perceptions also were examined for behavioral manifestations of confidence and nonconfidence. Observer statements identified two types of confidence indicators, that might be identified as performance and nonperformance behaviors. Nonperformance behaviors were those not required for the task but surrounding the task (e.g., hesitation, foot shuffling). These were identified by observers as important signs and signals of confidence or nonconfidence.

Behavioral manifestations of movement confidence were coded into three categories as follows: (1) performance movements—the implicit question was "did the performance 'look like' it should look," or as presenting signals of nonconfidence such as breaking or tucking while doing the movement; (2) tempo—did the performer move too quickly or too slowly, hesitate, appear uncertain; (3) attention—did the focus remain on task or did body and vision vary inappropriately, "avoiding looking at task," for example.

An additional aspect of this research (and findings of subsequent research to be discussed in the next sections) provided data germane to the question of whether the level of confidence may be expected to match level of performance. In this study it was apparent that changes in the behaviors that appeared to observers to signify nonconfidence might not parallel actual changes in the movement performance itself. For example, there were instances of hesitation or speeding up of the movements preparatory to performance followed by actual movement (task performance) in a "normal, confident" manner. Observers rated the changes in tempo of preparatory moves as evidence of nonconfidence, yet the actual performance itself did not seem to be affected.

It therefore was concluded that important behavioral manifestations of nonconfidence may not be found in the performance itself. Performance may change little even as level of confidence decreases. As we have learned in subsequent studies (Crawford & Griffin, 1986; Griffin & Crawford, 1989), at high levels of competence, performer-perceived confidence may essentially equal perceived competence, with enjoyment and harm variables explaining little of the variance. At mid-levels of competence and confidence, performer perceptions have been found to be quite variable and difficult to interpret in view of performance decisions alone. It may be that it is at this level of competence that nonperformance behaviors of hesitation and so on may be important indicators of nonconfidence. However, at low levels of competence, perceptions of confidence are more likely to be manifest in the performance decisions explained by the interaction of all three factors, i.e., competence + (enjoyment – harm) with enjoyment and harm factors taking on increasing importance in explaining variance in movement confidence. These findings confirm a hypothesis from the 1982 model, that the factor interaction producing movement confidence would explain performance better at low levels than at high levels of competence. Thus the hypothesis of proportional influence of antecedent factors is also supported.

The educational significance of this research is suggested by Griffin and Keogh (1981) in an application of the model to handicapped or developmentally delayed children and by Romance (1985) discussing confidence as a primary consideration in the development of effective movement skills for children. Succinctly stated, "observing for confidence," utilizing both nonperformance and performance behavioral cues identified in this research, may assist teachers and others in recognizing mixed signals of confidence/nonconfidence before extremely low levels of confidence results in withdrawal from activity or involvement. It may well be that nonperformance, refusal to perform, opting out of involvement may be a secondary, tertiary, or even fourth-level indicator of nonconfidence.

Need:

The need is for a better understanding of the manner and mechanisms by which perceptions of movement confidence and movement behaviors may be related. From this study as well as from findings of subsequent studies of performer perceptions of movement confidence (reported in next section of this paper), this is an issue not yet resolved. Although behavioral manifestations of confidence/nonconfidence were found to be generalizable across populations of observers, the question remains as to whether behavioral manifestations of confidence/nonconfidence are generalizable for children across tasks and at what, if any, developmental levels. Duda (1987), in proposing a developmental theory of children's motivation, suggests that differences for the competence factor will be found across developmental levels. A study of behavioral manifestations of confidence/nonconfidence across developmental levels where competence may be expected to vary would be interesting.

Problem:

Examination of posited antecedent factor identity in the physical dimension of performance.

Argument:

A second critical question in the investigation of model assumptions required inquiry into the identity and separability of the three factors—competence, enjoyment, and harm—which had been predicted as antecedent factors to interact and influence the level of confidence for the physical dimension of performance. Of major concern was whether "confidence" represented more than another way of expressing personal perceptions of competence. The initial study of behavioral manifestations had not addressed this important question of whether or not confidence really was another way of expressing efficacy or competence.

Utilizing a Movement Confidence Inventory (Griffin, Maybee, & Keogh, 1981), college-age performer perceptions of movement confidence were studied by Griffin, Keogh, and Maybee (1984). In that study movement confidence was found to be more than perceptions of competence. Responses obtained in the inventory describing 12 separate movement tasks/sport skills were quite variable across tasks. Although competence, as a factor, was the major contributor to perceived level of confidence across tasks, for some tasks both factor and regression analyses indicated that the interaction of the enjoyment and harm variables contributed more of the response variance than did competence. The large number of tasks and variables in this study resulted in much variance of response across tasks and, thus, the inability to describe the precise contributions of factors producing confidence across tasks in a definitive way.

As a way of defining movement confidence as a construct, this study expanded the general definition of confidence to suggest that it "is a complex personal quality which includes personal perceptions of more than skill and that it varies for individuals and by situations." In the 1982 model delineation, Griffin and Keogh had stated that the general definition of movement confidence as a sense of adequacy does not differ greatly from the general definitions of a sense of personal (self) efficacy (Bandura, 1977a), effectiveness (Harter, 1978, 1981, 1982), or competence (Connolly & Bruner, 1974). What did differentiate movement confidence from those theoretical positions was the notion that, as a construct, it (1) was "more than a sense of personal competence" and (2) that it included performer cognitive evaluation of self for expected sensory experiences as well as for performance competence requirements. The outcome of personal evaluation of self in relation to task demands and expected sensory experiences was likened to Rotter's (1982) notion of personal formulation of expectancies.

One of the findings of this study of performer perceptions confirmed findings of the behavioral manifestations study (Keogh, Griffin, & Spector, 1981) that is, that level of movement confidence appears to be task and situation specific. While generalizable behavioral manifestations for movement confidence were obtained in the Keogh, Griffin, and Spector (1981) study and identifiable and separable factors interacting to produce confidence in the Griffin, Keogh and Maybee (1984) study, individual responses were *not* found to be predictable across tasks or situations.

In summary, movement confidence as measured by the Movement Confidence Inventory (MCI) did seem to be more than perceptions of competence, although competence variables dominated the factor and regression analyses for most tasks. It was produced by interactions of the predicted variables of competence, enjoyment, and harm in varied arrangements across tasks. It was found to vary widely by task and situation, both as to level and to factors interacting to produce it, thus confirming individual cognitive evaluation for each task.

Need:

Out of this study grew the need for other, improved measures to study performer perceptions of movement confidence. Subscales representing the independent variables (factors) of competence, enjoyment, and harm were, therefore, created and two additional inventories, the *Playground Movement Confidence Inventory* (PMCI; Crawford & Griffin, 1983a) and *Stunt Movement Confidence Inventory* (SMCI; Crawford & Griffin, 1983b), suitable for upper elementary age children were designed. In these inventories fewer questions were asked about fewer tasks, and subscales comprising fewer variables were created. These design features were incorporated in hopes of achieving more definitive answers regarding the identity and separability of the posited antecedent factors. Thus was created the need for both validation of the measures and the study of perceptions of confidence of children for whom the inventories were developed. Studies of two different populations of elementary children involving tests of factor identity, separability, and posited interaction are reported in the following section.

Design and validation of measures is an incessant need. McAuley and Gill (1983) comment on the need to develop a scale (measure) for "general," not situation specific, self-efficacy. In their study a situation-specific measure was found to be more powerful than a more general measure. (Theirs was a replication study of one reported by Ryckman et al. [1982]). The McAuley and Gill study did not confirm the validity of the measure they were testing. Sherer et al. (1982) also report construction and validation of a self-efficacy scale with the creation of two subscales, that is, "general" self-efficacy and "social" self-efficacy. The goal of that study was to develop a general, not situation-specific, measure. Items on the social scale, however, were expressed exclusively as behaviors with friends or as "making friends." Even though described as general, it appears to be limited. Tyron (1981) offers a critique of Bandura's methodology and suggests that lack of control for social context in experimental design and its effect on behavioral assessment are problematic.

Harter's Perceived Competence Scales for Children (1982) were validated to measure competence in four domains: physical, social, cognitive, and self-esteem. Feltz and Brown (1984), however, found situation specific measures to be more powerful than more general measures (Harter, 1982) in their study of young soccer players. While such findings are understandable, they do present measurement, and therefore research, problems. Yet they do not argue for the design of endless numbers of sport- and situation-specific measures. A present need in human movement studies is the design and validation of a battery of measures with confidence, including (but not necessarily limited to) antecedent factors of competence, enjoyment, and harm as a central assessment focus. Harter (1978), Harter and Connell (1984), and Duda (1987) argue persuasively for consideration of developmental level in measurement design.

Problem:

Testing construct validity by examining factor identity, separability, and posited interaction in the physical dimension of performance.

Argument:

Another major research question—the validity of the model for movement confidence as a construct—was the focus of two studies involving upper elementary age children. The two inventories designed by Crawford and Griffin (1983a; 1983b) were utilized to examine the movement confidence of children for playground and stunt activities. While previous studies had confirmed key assumptions about the behavioral manifestations (Keogh, Griffin, & Spector, 1981) and identity of antecedents and cognitive evaluation of performance demands (Griffin, Keogh, & Maybee, 1984), those studies did not provide sufficient evidence to confirm the argument for interactive antecedents as precursors to movement confidence.

In separate studies of playground movement confidence (Crawford & Griffin, 1986) and stunt movement confidence (Griffin & Crawford, 1987, 1989), involving two separate, validated inventories, the PMCI and SMCI, factor identity, and interactions as postulated in the model for the physical dimension were verified. Findings of these studies confirmed previous findings that competence dominated the factor structure, particularly for the high competent child as well as for tasks that were perceived by all children to be simple and physically nonthreatening. Nonconfident children also perceived themselves to be noncompetent, but to have a perceived level of confidence produced by the interaction of all model factors: $C + (E - H)$.

In both these studies, however, the harm subscale was found to subdivide, with two aspects of perceived harm exerting negative influence in the equation. What will be called Harm One (H1) in the model-reformulation section of this paper interacted directly with competence (C) to reduce the level of perceived competence, and Harm Two (H2) interacted directly with enjoyment (E) to diminish perceived potential for enjoying the movement. The H1 subscale comprised variables related to the potential for physical harm—getting hurt. H2 was defined by subscale statements that described not liking the expected/

anticipated moving sensation. As a result of these findings, which held for both the study of playground movement confidence and of stunt movement confidence, the influence of harm on performance decisions could be expressed as: $MC = (C - H1) + (E - H2)$.

For both of these studies, the finding that the inventory subscales representing the three factors accurately identified and classified confident and nonconfident children and interacted as predicted to produce confidence provided verification of the validity of confidence as a construct. Elaborating the specificity of the interaction of harm with the other two factors contributes significantly to an understanding that children perceive harm in various ways and also differentiate between harm expressed as "getting hurt" and harm expressed as "not liking the sensations produced by moving."

This elaboration of the movement-confidence equation verifies the importance of perceptions of sensory experiences as important influences in level of confidence and performance decisions, a crucial element in arguing for movement confidence as a construct. Findings of these two studies provide additional, persuasive evidence of the validity of the model for movement confidence in the physical dimension, while at the same time suggesting a complexity of interaction not originally theorized by Griffin and Keogh (1982).

Need:

With these research findings that supported model hypotheses about the identity, separability, and interaction of posited antecedents to movement confidence in the physical dimension, one need was to incorporate information about confidence antecedents and their proportional influence into the conceptualization of the model for the physical dimension of movement performance. Since research findings also supported the notion of confidence defined for the physical dimension as a construct, a second need was to extend model hypotheses to the definition of antecedents of movement confidence in the social and psychological dimensions of human movement performance.

The following discussion identifies the question and argument for a comprehensive perspective of movement confidence delineated as a multi-dimensional influence on movement performance. It argues for a multi-dimensional confidence where antecedents (C, E, and H) are identified for each of the three dimensions of physical, social, and psychological (parallel to Harter's cognitive dimension).

Problem:

The delineation of multidimensional movement confidence.

Argument:

Confidence has consistently evaded definition and even recognition except as a generalized sense of "sureness." It is invoked as a mediator, modifier, and motivator in human movement performance, yet both its antecedents and impact are generally unspecified. It is surely multidimensional in nature with multi-variate antecedent factors and complex, proportional influence on performance. Yet it is generally treated, both in language and in the literature, as a univariate, generalized concept. This reiteration may seem redundant, yet the continuing need seems to be for a better understanding of confidence as a complex construct that is significant to the movement domain. Some important questions seem to be:

> Is there a constant meaning to confidence as it is applied to movement performance? Is there a constant meaning that can be generalized across performance levels and dimensions? Across developmental levels? Can we identify antecedent or precursor factors that interact to produce confidence for the social and psychological as well as physical dimensions? How is multidimensional confidence defined, and how does it impact performance?

Seeking to rescue the concept of confidence from its generalized application to everything from climbing a tree to winning a pennant, Griffin and Keogh (1982) posed the Model for Movement Confidence and in it hypothesized movement confidence as a construct with specified antecedents and influence, a consequence, and a mediator of movement decisions and behavior. Understanding that no model or single set of variables explains the total of human movement performance fully, it seemed important at the time to attempt to understand the influence of variables other than skill—ability—competence, which is of unquestioned importance to performance. Thus, for the physical dimension of movement performance, the model for movement confidence set out several hypotheses about components and factors that were postulated to be antecedents of movement confidence. In a series of studies just summarized (Crawford & Griffin, 1986; Griffin & Crawford, 1987, 1989; Griffin, Keogh, & Maybee, 1984; Keogh, Griffin, & Spector, 1981) these hypotheses werte tested systematically and the identity and proportional influence of factors antecedent to movement confidence described. In each of these studies deliberate designs were invoked to control for influences of factors in the social and psychological dimensions, all the while understanding that it is ultimately impossible to control for such influences completely.

Need

The need is for a better understanding and definition of a multidimensional movement confidence, one that comprehends the nature and influence of factors in the social and psychological as well as physical dimensions of human movement performance. The need is for increased knowledge of antecedents of confidence in three dimensions and their proportional influence on performance decisions and behavior. The need is for development of multidimensional, multifactor measures of movement confidence. This represents a complex design problem and a set of needs that will not be met quickly or easily.

A measurement design that will permit study of dimension and factor interaction, for example, is crucial to the study of multidimensional confidence. Harter (1982) developed multidimension measures, but as individual scales that were validated as measures of competence. The social dimension scale operationalized social competence, and so on. Bandura (1977a, 1985) argues for the importance of social and personal comparison as references in the judgmental process. Yet the self-efficacy scale reported by Sherer et al. (1982) for "social" self-efficacy appears to be limited to one aspect of "social" behavior, that of "making friends."

If this argument is persuasive, there is a need to define a multidimensional movement confidence, to expand the model in order to study multiple-factor, multiple-dimension influence. As a beginning of this process, this paper presents reformulated hypotheses for the physical dimension based on studies that have been reported in the literature and summarized briefly in this paper. The discussion is then extended to present definitions and arguments to expand the model for movement confidence to the social and psychological dimensions of performance.

PART TWO: AN EXPANSION

Model Semantics

In the original model conceptualized for the physical dimension of movement performance, the terms MOVCOMP and MOVSENSE were used to describe the factors posited to be antecedent to confidence. For the model reformulation, MOV is used as a prefix for terms denoting the three *dimensions* rather than as descriptors of antecedent factors. Since the overriding purpose of the model for movement confidence is to establish a set of questions and assumptions to guide research contributing to a better understanding of movement performance decisions and behavior, one way of stressing that relationship of the consistent use of the prefix MOV. Thus, in the expanded model formulation, MOVSOC is to social dimension as MOVPHYS is to physical dimension, while MOVPSYC represents the psychological dimension.

The competence factor in a definition or equation will continue to be represented by "C" where "E" will connote the enjoyment factor and "H" the harm factor. Any number contained in a factor definition—such as one (1) as in H1 or

E1—specifies which of multiple variables defined for that factor is expected to be operational as described in the context of the discussion. Both enjoyment and harm are defined as multivariate in the reconceptualized model.

In summary, with the introduction of hypotheses for multidimensional influences on movement confidence, it was assumed that it would be confusing to continue use of the MOVCOMP and MOVSENSE terms, which were used as factor definitions in the original model. Those terms were appropriate when discussing factor interaction within the single dimension (physical). In this paper, however, in order to avoid confusion, the prefix MOV is *not* used in factor designation. This represents a semantic change, not a conceptual change in the model. Examination of confidence in movement performance including cognitions of competence and of moving sensations remains the focus that is implied.

Problem

Definition of a reconceptualized movement confidence in the physical dimension.

Argument

Competence. For the physical dimension (MOVPHYS) competence (C) factor is assumed to be the perception of the skill/ability to perform the task. In the various movement confidence inventories reported in the literature (Crawford & Griffin, 1986; Griffin & Crawford, 1989; Griffin, Keogh, & Maybee, 1984) this variable has been described by such terms as "can do/cannot do, skilled/unskilled, expert/clumsy" (Griffin, Maybee, & Keogh, 1981) and such phrases as "Some kids can do this cause they are good climbers . . . other kids aren't very good at climbing" (Crawford & Griffin, 1983a).

In the reconceptualized model, definition of the competence factor in the physical dimension has not changed substantially. The body of literature defining and describing competence and perceptions of competence has provided a varied and very good perspective of its nature and influence in performance (Alderman & Doverspike, 1988), sport (Brody, Hatfield, & Spalding, 1988; Feltz & Brown, 1984; Weiss, Bredemeier, & Shewchuck, 1984) and competition (Ulrich, 1987; Vealey, 1986).

For the enjoyment and harm factors, however, findings of previous research, reported in the literature and summarized in part one of this paper, have influenced the reconceptualized definitions. Both enjoyment and harm factors (across dimensions) have been "partitioned" and defined as being represented by two variables. The criterion for variable definition was that of whether the influence was a result of (1) the moving itself or (2) anticipated as a consequence of moving—the performance. Thus "enjoying moving, e.g., the sensation of speed" is an example of E1 (MOVPHYS), and "enjoying the consequences of moving, for example, runner's high," an example of E2 (MOVPHYS).

Enjoyment. Performer perceptions of enjoying movement sensations continues to be posited as a positive influence on movement confidence. For the physical (MOVPHYS) dimension, E1 is specified as performer perceptions of potential for enjoying moving sensations, For E2, enjoyment is defined as potential for liking the sensory consequences of moving. One of the reasons for elaborating the definition of enjoyment in the physical dimension is to provide a set of hypotheses that will permit investigation of the differential influence of perceptions of "sensations while moving", for example, breathlessness, speed, and so on, as contrasted to "expected sensory consequences" of moving, for example, muscle relaxation, runner's high, and so on. Although the enjoyment factor did not partition as did harm in the factor analyses reported earlier (Crawford & Griffin, 1986; Griffin & Crawford, 1989), the descriptors of H2 (harm two) were descriptions of the negative aspect of moving sensations, that is, being upside down, going too fast, and so on. With the expanded definitions for enjoyment, the study of harm and enjoyment factor interaction can now be examined with greater specificity.

Harm. In the physical (MOVPHYS) dimension, H1 is defined as performer-perceived potential for physical injury, "getting hurt." H2 is defined as disliked consequences of moving, for example, feelings of speed, muscle soreness, breathlessness, fatigue, pain. Expanding the definition of harm to include both the potential for physical harm or injury and the perceived potential for disliked movement sensations is based on research on movement confidence reported in earlier sections of this paper. These findings were particularly significant since they not only identified harm as a multivariate factor but also provided a way of identifying the influence of undesired consequences of moving, that is, the negative influence of movement sensations. Harm was identified as a generally negative influence interacting directly with both competence and enjoyment variables and diminishing the positive influence of both. The definition of antecedent factors for confidence in the physical dimension of performance has, therefore, been reconceptualized to incorporate this evidence and to define a revised set of assumptions about harm as an antecedent, its influence and interaction.

For the physical dimension of movement confidence (reconceptualized as MOVPHYS), the equation for predicting movement confidence (MC) is proposed as follows:

$$MC = MOVPHYS (PhysC1 - PhysH1 + PhysE1 + [PhysE2 - PhysH2])$$

Where:

PhysC1 = Perceptions of competence/skill/ability in physical performance

PhysH1 = Perceived potential for physical harm, personal injury
PhysE1 = Perceptions of potential for enjoying moving sensations
PhysE2 = Perceived potential for sensory consequences of moving
PhysH2 = Perceived potential for physical discomfort while moving

Need:

The need in the physical dimension is for continued study of the nature, interaction, and proportional influence of factors posed as antecedents of movement confidence. The factors posited to be antecedents of movement confidence in the physical domain have been reconceptualized based on findings of previous studies (Crawford & Griffin, 1986; Griffin & Crawford, 1989; Griffin, Keogh, & Maybee, 1984; Keogh, Griffin, & Spector, 1981). Factor identity and interactions posited in the reconceptualized model thus require additional testing and verification.

Because the H variable was found in previous research to interact and diminish both C and E in the movement confidence interaction, it cannot be inferred directly that harm will continue to influence confidence perceptions as found in the first several studies. There is a need, therefore, to reexamine movement confidence in the physical dimension with a particular focus on the reconceptualized harm factor. Viewing harm as a multivariate factor having negative influence on both competence and enjoyment is considered a hypothesis worthy of test.

While it was not clear from research in the physical dimension whether the enjoyment factor (E) might also be a dichotomous or multivariate factor, that hypothesis was also considered worthy of test. In the reconceptualization enjoyment is also posited as multivariate with generally positive influence on involvement decisions and movement behavior. Studies along the lines of confidence as (1) perceived potential for enjoying moving during performance and (2) expectations for enjoying the consequences after the performance can, thus, focus on the nature of enjoyment in relation to "moving" vs. postperformance sensations as well as on the interaction of E2 with H2. This latter question is particularly inviting, since performers have described undesired sensations of moving as within the scope of "harm" in previous studies.

Problem:

The definition of movement confidence in the social dimension.

Argument:

Factor identity and interactions for the social dimension have been inferred and posited based on constructs from the literature. There is no empirical precedent from previous movement confidence research to support the specific definitions and interactions that are proposed. However, based on parallel social science paradigms and the research bases for those theories, they appear intuitively appropriate to the general factor definitions that have been developed for the movement confidence construct.

Competence. In the social (MOVSOC) dimension, competence (C) is defined as the personal perception of social appropriateness of task, influenced by social learning history. Influences are defined as a sense of age, gender, social group, status order, appropriateness of movement, and expected outcomes.

Enjoyment. For the social dimension (MOVSOC), enjoyment as E1 is defined as the perceived potential for social interaction, stimulation, and/or competition during performance. Enjoyment as E2 is defined as perceived potential for positive social sanctions following performance, and as satisfaction derived from postperformance social effect.

Harm. For the social dimension (MOVSOC), harm as H1 is defined as the potential for failure to meet social group standards as identified by social group comparison/evaluation by important others during performance. Harm as H2 is posited to be perceived potential for longer-term negative consequences of failing to meet group standards resulting in exclusion from personal, social network because of performance.

Interaction. In the social dimension, MOVSOC, predicted interactions of factors to influence movement confidence are:

$$MC = MOVSOC (SocC1 - SocH1 + SocE1 + [SocE2 - SocH2])$$

Where:

SocC1 = Perceptions of social appropriateness of participation
SocE1 = Perceived potential for social facilitation through group interaction, stimulation, competition
SocE2 = Perceived potential for postperformance positive social sanctions
SocH1 = Perceptions of potential for negative social evaluation by important others; negative social comparison
SocH2 = Perceived potential for negative consequences for failing to meet group standards

Discussion:

Review for the formulation of posited definitions in the social dimension focused on attentional, behavioral, intrapersonal, social, and stress-anxiety variables. Major theoretical positions and papers were reviewed, including effectance motivation (Harter, 1978, 1986; Stott & Sharp, 1975; White, 1959), achievement motivation (Atkinson, 1964; Weiner, 1972; Weiner & Kun, 1974), self-efficacy theory (Bandura, 1977a, 1977b, 1985), as well as varied developmental play, sport, and social psychology models and papers (Blaylock, 1981; Brustad, 1986; Corbin, 1981, 1984; Corbin, Stewart, & Blair, 1981; Cottrell, 1972; Festinger & Aronson, 1975; Greendorfer, 1977; Greendorfer & Ewing, 1981; MacCracken & Stadulis, 1985; Petruzzello & Corbin, 1988; Ruble, Parsons, & Ross, 1976; Scanlan & Lewthwaite, 1986; Vallerand, 1983, 1987).

Social competency is defined within this model as a perception of social "appropriateness." One of the more compelling influences for this definition came from Bandura's work on personal mastery (1977b). He proposed the term "social persuasion" to describe an interactive influence of the social dimension on self-efficacy. The phenomenon of "social persuasion" poses the need for development of social competency. Attributional models in psychology also suggest this need. The achievement motivation model seeks to explain causes of success and failure. One of its major proponents and theorists (Weiner & Kun, 1974), for example, has written of "the urgent need to explore the effects of social context upon the causal evaluations of achievement outcomes" (p. 428). Similarly, effectance motivation psychology with its focus on individual striving for effectiveness and control of environment has recognized what had been referred to as "an intruding social motivation" on individual thought processes (Stott & Sharp, 1975). While it was the attributional psychologists that were convincing as to the need to propose a definition of social competency, it was the work of Blaylock (1971), Greensdorfer (1977), and Greensdorfer & Ewing (1981) that helped to ground the definition in terms of variables central to "personal social history" to define social appropriateness. Harter (1978) also comments on the variation in motivation depending on personal history of experience and socialization. Cheron and Ritchie (1982) provided further empirical support of the confirmatory power of the social experiences on self-worth.

These theoretical arguments are often viewed to take the general position on information synthesis that holds that social variables serve principally as inhibitors or blockers. Within the movement confidence model, it is assumed that these variables also offer rich potential as outcome and process goals and so the social psychology, sport, and play literatures were examined seeking support for the hypothesis of social enjoyment through movement.

The ideas on social enjoyment were shaped by arguments on social bonding and social support in conjunction with empirical results from sport and play research. Social support is usually considered to be the presence of others on whom one can rely, those who know, value, and care for us. The presence of a supportive social network (family, friends, coach, teammates) may directly affect engagement and performance decisions or it may serve to buffer negative effects of participation (stress, injury, failure). It is this social interaction process that drives our definition for E1. Brown's (1978) work on positive inclusion and enjoyment through social interaction was an influence, as was Duda's research (1986), which found that social participation was a major goal of individual engagement. Klint & Weiss (1987) found motivation influenced by affiliation aspects of sport. Scanlan & Lewthwaite (1986) operationalized "enjoyment" as (1) amount of fun experienced and (2) degree of liking, and found important predictors of enjoyment to be "significant adults." "Important other" satisfaction, positive interactions with parents and coaches, and lack of negative reaction from parents were all found to be predictors of enjoyment. Smith et al. (1979, 1983) identified the shaping influence of coaches' behaviors on children's attitudes about youth sport participation.

The definition for social E2, perceptions of positive social outcomes, was influenced by several arguments. From the literature on group conformity and social bonding, it was suggested that some individuals are inspired to form relationships with groups for the self-defining nature of this identification. With identification follows certain group expectancies or pressures for certain behaviors. Kelman (1975) found that certain behaviors are adopted not because of their own value but to gain or maintain specific reward or approval of the group. Satisfaction is thus derived from the "social effect" following behavior. Such a chain of events, if found consistently, would contribute to an explanation of why some stunt/dare activities may take place among children and adolescents and is parallel in concept to Bandura's views of "social persuasion." Other supportive literature for the definition of E2 included Kelman's (1975) identification of the strength of the peer-group influence in this regard and Iso Ahola's (1980) research findings that children's playground performances serve to create strong bonds of loyalty and friendship and that the major mechanism children invoke to distinguish themselves in this process is creative movement performances. Similarly, Brustad (1986) found for children involved in competitive youth sports that social outcomes and pressures from significant others were among the most important determinants of enjoyment outcomes. Duda (1986) has shown that for many adults it is the social comparison component of sport participation that is one of the major goals of intramural participation. Finally, Wankel and Kreisel (1985) also found social items of "being with friends" and "being on a team" were of moderate importance for children's rankings of enjoyment in sport participation.

While the social bonding literature presents a compelling rationale for the enjoyment (E) potential of social influence, it is cognitive dissonance theory that provides primary support for the potential for social harm. The core of dissonance theory holds that interaction with people and groups is dissonance arousing because an individual does not have good control over the greater environment (Festinger & Aronson, 1977; Pitman & Pitman, 1980). As choices of behavior are made, dissonance is produced because seldom are chosen alternatives entirely positive and the unchosen alternatives entirely negative. The conceptualization of harm as H1, the performance or process experience of discomfort, is related closely to Cheron and Ritchie's 1982 work on social comparison and evaluation. Siegleman's work (1983) on interpreting major factors in personal risk helped to cement this definition with the findings on the specificity of personal perception in evaluating ongoing social expectations. Short-term anxiety, embarrassment, and discomfort related to anticipated performance feedback represents the influence of this inhibitor.

For harm as H2, defined as more long-term or permanent social consequences, the power or influence of important others is perceived to last beyond the immediate context of the performance. Within the sport context, coaches, teammates, parents and/or others may comprise the "significant other" group. For the individual participant the engagement question may be something like—"If I blow this performance will my peers think less or make fun of me?" or, "Will I be excluded from the group or kicked off the team?" Griffith, Steel, and Vaccaro (1982) have confirmed the nature of this influence within a risk-recreation context. They found the major source of participation anxiety for femal scuba divers not to be physical danger, but perceived social evaluation by other class participants. The findings of Scanlan and Lewthwaite (1986) also confirm the influence of negative reactions from important others to diminish enjoyment.

Need:

With the conceptualization of antecedents of movement confidence in the social dimension, the needs are to operationalize the posited factors, to develop measures and to study their interactional influence on perceptions of movement confidence and movement performance decisions. As with any model or theory development, there is also a continuing need to examine postulations in light of development of related theories and arguments from the research literature.

Problem:

The definition of movement confidence in the psychological dimension.

Argument:

Factor definitions for MOVPSYC have been posited and inferred from the literature to fit the general factor definitions that are identified for the construct. As with the social dimension, there is no empirical research precedent for specifying the psychological dimension influence on movement confidence for either factor definition or predicted interaction other than the intuitive "best fit" of persuasive arguments that are found in the literature.

Competence. In the psychological dimension, MOVPSYC, competence (C) is defined as the perception or ability to understand task demands as well as a sense of "being willing to learn/do," thus accepting the motor learning/performance challenge of the task—a constellation of cognitions producing a "psychological hardiness."

Enjoyment. In the psychological dimension, MOVPSYC, enjoyment as E1 is posited to be perceived potential for performance achieving, being successful during performance. Enjoyment as E2 in the psychological dimension is defined as momentary recall and prizing-valuing the movement experience or achievement; achieving personal movement goals as consequences of performance.

Harm. For the psychological MOVPSYC dimension, harm as H1 is defined as perceived potential for frustration, confusion, and failure during moving, resulting in decreased feeling of personal control. Harm as H2 is defined as perceived potential for outcome state of anxiety, cognitive dissonance, awareness of personal inadequacy, and lowered self-efficacy.

Interactions. For the psychological dimension, MOVPSYC, factors and their predicted interactions have been proposed as follows:

$$MC = MOVPSYC (PsycC1 - PsycH1 + PsycE1 + [PsycE2 - PsycH2])$$

Where:

PsycC1 =   Personal understanding of task demands and a sense of "being willing to learn/do," accepting movement challenge (psychological hardiness)
PsycE1 =   Perceived importance of being successful, achieving
PsycE2 =   Recall, prizing movement performance, achieving personal movement goals
PsycH1 =   Perceived potential for frustration, confusion, failure, loss of personal control
PsycH2 =   Potential for outcome state of anxiety, dissonance, diminished personal adequacy

Discussion:

Cognitive theories of motivation generally maintain that the intensity of arousal or motivation is directly related to the power of the outcome or goal attractiveness for each individual, that performance is a function of expectancy (Harter, 1974; Nicholls, 1978, 1984; Nicholls & Miller, 1983; Rotter, 1982; Ruble, Parsons, & Ross, 1976). Thus, the influence of psychological incentive (value) and the linkage of value with performance outcomes may logically be a relationship of great importance to a comprehensive model of movement confidence. In research related to this postulated relationship, Vallerand (1983, 1984) has proposed an intuitive-reflective appraisal model for what he describes as "self-related affects" in achievement situations. This model is grounded by the notion that it is the cognitive evaluation of events and not the events themselves that produce emotions. Deci and Ryan (1980) also provide strong support for the cognitive evaluation theory.

Examples of these relationships and linkages within cognitive psychology may be found in literatures related to perceived ability and effort (Alderman & Doverspike, 1988; Nicholls, 1978; Nicholls & Miller, 1983; Roberts, 1984; Roberts & Duda, 1984), locus of contirol (Rotter, 1982), causal attributions (Weiner & Kun, 1974), personality influences on emotional responsiveness (Harter, 1974), and causes of internal arousal (Ruble, Parsons & Ross, 1976). Within this extensive body of literature, several constructs appeared appealing as foundation arguments to define psychological competence within a movement model. In this conceptualization, psychological competence is assumed to be defined as a willingness to accept challenge and task demands—a willingness to do, to use Kobasa's (1979) phrase—a psychological "hardiness."

In the psychological literature, the concept of challenge is central to several theories of motivation, among them achievement motivation (Atkinson, 1964), intrinsic motivation (Deci, 1975), and Harter's (1978, 1981, 1986; Harter & Connell, 1984) explanations of White's (1959) theory of effectance motivation. In all of these theories, the doing or persisting in performance is suggested to be driven by "need to achieve, to be competent" or an intrinsic drive to be "effective" in interacting with one's environment. Vallerand and Reid (1984) found support for the hypothesis of Deci and Ryan (1980) for the mediating effects of perceived competence on intrinsic motivation. As movement tasks are evaluated by performers, the decision to perform, according to these theories, would be fueled in part by motivation to achieve, to become more competent and/or effective. Achievement motivation holds that persons high in achievement needs will initiate, persist, and work with heightened intensity even in the face of failure. If this sense of what Kobasa (1979) refers to as "psychological hardiness" has a parallel form within movement environments, it would help to explain disparities in performance among individuals with similar abilities or competence.

For the psychological enjoyment variable E1, which was paired with the process of moving, Atkinson's work (1964) on the importance of achieving along with Deci's (1975) study regarding the pleasure of problem solving were important cornerstones of the definition. For Bandura's (1977a) work on self-efficacy, corollaries in the movement environment seem plausible. Several studies (Feltz & Landers, 1977; Feltz & Petlichoff, 1983; Roberts & Duda, 1984; Siedentop, 1976 [perceived ability]) have confirmed the relationship of self-efficacy to decisions and performance in the movement context.

Bandura (1977a) postulates that cognitive events are induced/altered most readily by experiences of mastery arising from effective performance. PSYC E1 represents the enjoyment experience that would result from this sense of mastery during performance and it is thus specified as the perceived importance of achieving, being successful in movement performance. Direct support for this may be found in the youth sport motivation literature. Wankel and Kreisel (1985) found that factors intrinsic to sport activity such as personal accomplishment and a sense of improving one's skills were consistently rated as a most important aspect of enjoyment. Harter's work (1981) relates "joy" and achievement. Passer (1981) put participation motives of children in categories and identified excitement/challenge as important. (Other categories were affiliation, skill development, success/status, fitness, and energy release. Klint and Weiss [1987] added "fun" to this list.)

To the extent that expectant states or anticipated outcomes may be considered desirable, the enjoyment factor E2 in the model may take on facilitation qualities for the participant. Enjoyment as E2 is defined as a sense of recalling or "prizing" the movement experience. Conceptualization for this outcome variable was guided initially by arguments from the play literature. Sutton-Smith (1970) found that children's movements on playgrounds were often driven by mental play-fantasy experiences that represent the child's attempts to achieve psychological closure or synthesis of external events or influences. In another, ethological study of play, Gabbard and LeBlanc (1980) coined the phrase "view of the world" to describe the cognitive outcome state of mastery, importance, and control over the environment that children sought on playgrounds by physically conquering (climbing) high structures.

A somewhat different pleasurable cognitive state as a result of movement is described by Welch (1987). Her definition of "grace" within a movement context refers to prizing or recalling past, perfect movements. The concept of grace as an expression of perfect personal action or power has an intuitive, powerful appeal as a potential desired outcome that individuals might seek to experience.

Clearly, failure with its attendant anxiety to be either effective or to achieve represents the harm component in the psychological dimension. For harm as H1, the process variable, the locus of control literature that seeks to describe individual perceptions of events in terms of personal control is relevant (Rotter, 1982). Lack or loss of personal control while performing has the power to generate attendant feelings of frustration, confusion, and disorientation (Pitman & Pitman, 1980). Cheron and Ritchie (1982) describe this as a form of "functional risk" whereby strong feelings or personal inadequacy are generated by poor performance. Siegelman's work (1983) on the power of personal risk in producing discomfort (anxiety) in conjunction with Blaylock's work (1981) on the subjective perception of personal risk helped to define the dimensions of PSYC H1. Their arguments that individuals make engagement decisions regarding tolerance or avoidance based on questions of personal appropriateness reinforces the proposal that subjective perceptions of failure and accompanying cognitions of discomfort can have a strong inhibitor effect.

The psychological harm H2, outcome variable, refers to the potential for more permanent or serious psychological discomfort beyond the immediacy of the performance. For example, it is one thing to be frustrated and uncomfortable within the process of a game (H1); it is yet another to be left with the cognition that because of your performance, the team lost the championship or your country the cup, and so on (H2). Within the psychology literature, Bandura (1977a) writes that negative cognitive appraisals provide incentives for disengagement and lowered efficacy. Siegelman (1983) asserts that personal risk is often seen as a test of self-worth. Finally, Festinger and Aronson (1975), in researching issues of control, found that loss of personal control resulted in the creation of dissonance and psychogenic pain.

Need:

With the conceptualization of antecedents of movement confidence in the psychological dimension, the needs are to operationalize the posited factors, to develop measures, and to study their interactional influence on perceptions of movement confidence and movement performance decisions. As with any model or theory development, there is also a continuing need to examine postulations in light of development of related theories and research.

Problem:

The posited interactional influence of multidimensional factors on movement confidence.

Argument:

Across dimensions, the general influence of factor interactions to produce movement confidence is assumed to be summative, according to the following equation:

$$MC = MOVPHYS (PhysC1 - PhysH1 + PhysE1 + [PhysE2 - PhysH2]) + \\ MOVSOC (SocC1 - SocH1 + SocE1 + [SocE2 - SocH2]) + \\ MOVPSYC (PsycC1 - PsycH1 + PsycE1 + [PsycE2 - PsycH2]).$$

As postulated in the original model (1982), extremely high or low levels for any factor or variable in any dimension may act to imbalance the equation such that factor influences are not expected to be "even" or easily predicted. For example, assume that a task decision involves whether or not to parachute from a plane. Your perceptions of physical competence are that you have the skill to parachute from a plane; the cognition of social competence evaluation for age, gender, and so on is positive; and your psychological competence evaluation is that you understand the task and are eager to accept the challenge. Your sense of physical harm (H1), however, is identified by the personal cognition, "But the last time you did this, you broke your leg!" As a performer you may choose to ignore this cognition; its existence, however, is expected to reduce overall confidence for performing the task. If perceived potential for physical injury is enormous, this may override other cognitions and, thus, reduce confidence so that the decisions may be to withdraw or not to perform.

Discussion:

To recapitulate the assumed general interactions that have just been specified: in the cognitive evaluation leading to a performance decision, perceptions of competence (C) would be expected to interact with perceptions of potential for harm during performance, C—H1 representing that interaction. Either C at very low levels or H1 at extremely high levels would be expected to produce low perceptions of competence with the posisbility of blocking further evaluation or involvement.

Enjoyment is expected to enhance the level of confidence and be additive to competence in the interaction. E1 is identified as perception of potential for enjoying moving sensations—enjoying moving. E1 in the equation is postulated to add to (enhance) perceptions of confidence. E2 is defined as expectations of enjoying the consequences of moving, the way you feel (consequences of) after the performance, and is postulated to further enhance (add to) the level of movement confidence. It may, however, be diminished by the influence of H2 (perceived potential for harm as consequence of performance). In previous movement confidence research in the physical dimension, cognitions of disliked movement sensations were perceived as negative and, thus, loaded on the harm factor in those studies.

The factor H2 (harm), defined as the potential for not liking movement sensations, is hypothesized to interact with E2 to diminish the overall additive effect of enjoyment on confidence. Thus, if E2 evaluation "tells" you that you will be sore and fatigued after the performance and H2 tells you that you do not like that feeling, your performance decision will be negatively affected.

Potential for harm (H) in all dimensions represents a potential "blocking," or negative influence. Where H is high, the effect would subtract in the overall equation. Where H is low or neutral, the effect would be moot. It may function in one or all dimensions as all or none, rather than a graded influence. Harm, across dimensions, is defined for two related but separate variables. H1 represents the perceived potential for harm/injury during performance and interacts negatively with perceived competence across dimensions. The impact of H1, in fact, appears to be similar to a concept expressed in the psychological literature. Wherry and Curran (1966) identified the concept of "Anticipatory Physical Threat Stress (APTS)" to describe the detrimental effect that fear has on motor performance. According to Wherry's (1966) research, the effects of APTS on performance and the effect of H1 (as defined in the model) on making performance decisions seem parallel. Both exhibit a detrimental, or "blocking," effect for performance. Expressed as interactions across dimensions:

For physical C: H1 represents potential for physical injury, "getting hurt"
For social C: H1 represents potential failure to meet social group standards
For psychological C: H1 represents potential frustration, failure, loss of personal control

Harm as H2 has been identified as the perceived potential for "not liking the moving sensations or movement consequences," which interacts directly with and reduces the influence of enjoyment. Expressed as interactions across dimensions:

For physical E2   H2 represents potential for "not liking moving sensations—consequences"
For social E2:   H2 represents potential for negative social sanctions—exclusion from personal, social network
For psychological E2: H2 represents potential for anxiety, dissonance, loss of personal esteem.

If for the competence interaction influence of H1 is moot ("moving is not the problem, it is what will happen as a consequence!"), then H2 may reduce confidence through perceptions of undesirable sensory experiences or consequences of moving, potential for negative social sanctions, or potential for anxiety, dissonance, loss of personal esteem.

Summary:

Assumptions. For the reconceptualized model, the following major assumptions are either explicitly stated or implicit in the definition and predicted interaction of postulated factors for the physical, social, and psychological dimensions.

One: Performers make an individual cognitive evaluation of self in relation to movement task demands for three dimensions of influence—physical, social, and psychological. This evaluation is not linear or hierarchical, but parallel and circular—that is, cognitions in all dimensions occur more or less simultaneously, although they are not at all times equal in their influence.

Two:

Results of evaluation produce cognitions of personal adequacy that is the composite of perceptions formed by the factor interactions of competence, enjoyment, and harm, across the three dimensions. This is the personal cognition of adequacy by which movement confidence is defined and includes cognitions of both competence and sensory experiences.

Three:

Personal perceptions of competence (C) for all dimensions are the foundation, dominant factor in interactions producing level of movement confidence.

Four:

The enjoyment factor (E), as personal perception of potential for enjoying moving and the consequences of movement performance, is postulated to be an additive or facilitating influence on movement confidence. Enjoyment has been redefined for this model as E1, representing the perceived potential for enjoying some aspect of moving or movement sensations during performance, and E2, defined as potential for enjoying the consequences of moving, that is, movement.

Five:

The harm (H) factor, defined as perceived potential for harm or injury, is presumed to subtract from level of confidence in factor interactions. Across dimensions, harm is expected to interact with both the competence and enjoyment factors to reduce level of movement confidence. H1, as the potential for harm or injury during performance, is expected to interact directly and negatively with competence. H2, defined as the potential for harm or injury as a consequence of performance, is expected to interact directly and negatively with E2 (potential for enjoying consequences of movement).

SUMMARY

To recapitulate briefly, the purpose of this paper was twofold: first, to provide an elaboration of the original model for movement confidence in the physical dimension, and second, to extend the theoretical arguments of the model to the social and psychological dimensions. Both the reformulated model for the physical dimension and the posited extension to the social and psychological dimensions continue to be greatly influenced by related and parallel theories and constructs in the literature.

The duality of this paper in presenting both an elaboration and extension of the model rests upon the theory-guided approach to model building. That approach has been to to identify the important arguments that appear to be critical to understanding the cognitive evaluation—involvement decision cycle for movement performance and also to consider the nature and influence of interdependent structures of multidimensional movement confidence in light of both empirical and theoretical literatures.

Reformulation of the model for movement confidence represents an attempt to define a construct with testable properties that is ultimately comprehensive enough to embrace a range of critical variables and dimensions of influence. Because the reformulation of the model has been based in part on theoretical intuition and in part on empirical research, its value as a construct continues to be dependent on generation of an empirical data base needed to test model hypotheses. Thus the reconceptualized model for movement confidence has been generated as a theoretical argument to guide further research aimed at improved understanding of confidence as it relates to movement.

REFERENCES

Alderman, M. K., & Doverspike, J. E. (1988, April). *Perceived competence successful experience, expectations and achievement differences among seventh-, eighth-, and ninth-grade students.* Paper presented at American Research Association, Washington, D.C.

Atkinson, J. W. (1964). *An introduction to motivation.* Princeton, NJ: Van Nostrand.

Bandura, A. (1977a). Self-efficacy: Toward a unifying theory of behavioral change. *Psychological Review, 84,* 191–215.

Bandura, A. (1977b). *Social learning theory.* Englewood Cliffs, NJ: Prentice-Hall.

Bandura, A. (1982). Self-efficacy mechanism in human agency. *American Psychologist, 37,* 122–147.

Bandura, A. (1985). *Social foundations of thought and action.* Englewood Cliffs, NJ: Prentice-Hall.

Blaylock, B. K. (1971). Method for studying perception of risk. *Psychological Reports, 49,* 899–902.

Brody, E. B., Hatfield, B. D., & Spalding, T. W. (1988). Generalization of self-efficacy to a contininuum of stressors upon mastery of a high-risk sport skill. *Journal of Sport and Exercise Psychology, 10,* 32–44.

Brown, B, R. (1978). Human factors analysis of injuries associated with public playground equipment. *U.S. Consumer Product Safety Commission,* Oct. (5). (Supt. of Documents, 20402). Washington, DC: U.S. Government Printing Office.

Brustad, R. J. (1986, June). *Affective outcomes in competitive youth sports: The influence of intra-personal and socialization factors.* Paper presented at North American Society for the Psychology of Sport and Physical Activity, Scottsdale, Az.

Carmack, M. A., & Martens, R. (1979). Measuring commitment to running. *Journal of Sport Psychology, 1,* 25–42.

Cheron, E. J., & Ritchie, J. R. (1982). Leisure activities and perceived risk. *Journal of Leisure Research, 14,* 139–154.

Coelho, G. V., Hamburg, D. A., & Adams, J. E. (Eds.). (1974). *Coping and adaptation.* New York: Basic Books.

Corbin, C. B. (1981). Sex of subject, sex of opponent and opponent ability as factors affecting self-confidence in a competitive situation. *Journal of Sport Psychology, 3,* 265–270.

Corbin, C. B. (1984). Self-confidence in females in sports and physical activity. *Clinics in Sports Medicine, 3,* 895–907.

Corbin, C. B., Stewart, M. J., & Blair, W. O. (1981). Self-confidence and motor performance of preadolescent boys and girls studied in different feedback situations. *Journal of Sport Psychology, 3,* 30–34.

Connolly, K., & Bruner, J. (Eds.). (1974). *The growth of competence.* New York: Academic Press.

Cottrell, N. B. (1972). Social facilitation. In C. G. McClintock (Ed.), *Experimental social psychology* (pp. 185–236). New York: Holt, Rinehart & Winston.

Crawford, M. E., & Griffin, N. S. (1983a). *Playground movement confidence inventory.* (Available from authors.)

Crawford, M. E., & Griffin, N. S. (1983b). *Stunt movement confidence inventory.* (Available from authors.)

Crawford, M. E., & Griffin, N. S. (1986). Testing the validity of the Griffin/Keogh model for movement confidence by analyzing self-report playground involvement decisions of elementary school children. *Research Quarterly for Exercise and Sport, 57,* 8–16.

Deci, E. L. (1975). *Intrinsic motivation.* New York: Plenum Press.

Deci, E. L., & Ryan, R. M. (1980). The empirical evaluation of intrinsic motivational processes. In L. Berkowitz (Ed.), *Advances in experimental social psychology* (Vol. 13, pp. 38–47). New York: Academic Press.

Duda, J. L. (1986, June). *Variations in goals among intercollegiate and recreational athletes.* Paper presented at the Annual Meeting of the North American Society for the Psychology of Sport and Physical Activity, Scottsdale AZ.

Duda, J. L. (1987). Toward a developmental theory of children's motivation in sport. *Journal of Sport Psychology, 9,* 130–145.

Feltz, D. L. (1982). Path analysis of the causal elements in Bandura's theory of self-efficacy and in anxiety-based model of avoidance behavior. *Journal of Personality Social Psychology, 42,* 764–781.

Feltz, D., & Brown, E. W. (1984). Perceived competence in soccer skills among young soccer players. *Journal of Sport Psychology, 6,* 385–394.

Feltz, D. L., & Landers, D. M. (1977). Informational-motivational components of a models demonstration. *Research Quarterly, 48,* 525–533.

Feltz, D., & Petlichkoff, L. (1983). Perceived competence among interscholastic sport participants and dropouts. *Canadian Journal of Applied Sport Sciences, 8,* 231–235.

Festinger, L., & Aronson, E. (1975). Arousal and reduction of dissonance in social contexts. In E. Krupat (Ed.), *Psychology is social* (pp. 141–147). Glenview IL: Scott and Foresman Co.

Gabbard, C. P. & LaBlanc, E. (1980). Movement activity levels on traditional and contemporary play structures. (ERIC Document Reproduction Service No. 198-082).

Greendorfer, S. L. (1977). Role of socializing agents in fitness and sport involvement. *Research Quarterly, 43,* 304–310.

Greendorfer, S. L., & Ewing, M. E. (1981). Race and gender differences in children's socialization into sport. *Research Quarterly, 52,* 301–310.

Griffin, N. S., & Crawford, M. E. (1987). Development of a valid and reliable inventory to assess self-perceptions of movement confidence in involvement decisions in sport and movement activity. *ACTES Proceedings,* IV International Congress of Sport Psychology (pp. 459–472). Brussels, Belgium.

Griffin, N. S., & Crawford, M. E. (1989). Measurement of movement confidence with a stunt inventory. *Journal of Sport and Exercise Psychology, 11,* 26–40.

Griffin, N. S., & Keogh, J. K. (1981). Movement confidence and effective movement behavior in adapted physical education. *Motor Skills: Theory into Practice, 5,* 23–25.

Griffin, N. S., & Keogh, J. K. (1982). A model for movement confidence. In J. A. S. Kelso & J. E. Clark (Eds.), *The development of movement control and coordination,* (pp. 213–236). New York: Wiley.

Griffin, N. S., Maybee, R., & Keogh, J. K. (1981). *Movement confidence inventory.* (Available from N. S. Griffin.)

Griffin, N. S., Keogh, J. K., & Maybee, R. (1984). Performer perceptions of movement confidence. *Journal of Sport Psychology, 6,* 395–407.

Griffiths, T. J., Steel D. H., & Vaccaro, P. (1982). Anxiety of SCUBA divers: A multidimensional approach. *Perceptual and Motor Skills, 55,* 611–614.

Harter, S. (1974). Pleasure derived by children from cognitive challenge and mastery. *Child Development, 45,* 661–669.

Harter, S. (1978). Effectance motivation revisited: Toward a developmental model. *Human Development, 21,* 34–64.

Harter, S. (1981). The development of competence motivation in the mastery of cognitive and physical skills: Is there still a place for joy? In G. Roberts & D. Landers (Eds.), *Psychology of motor behavior and sport—1980* (pp. 3–29). Champaign, IL: Human Kinetics.

Harter, S. (1982). The perceived competence scale for children. *Child Development, 53,* 87–97.

Harter, S. (1986). Cognitive-developmental processes in the integration of concepts about emotions and the self. *Social Cognition, 4,* 119–151.

Harter, S., & Connell, J. P. (1984). A model of children's achievement and related self-perceptions of competition, control and motivational orientation. *Advances in Motivation and Achievement, 3,* 219–250.

Iso-Ahola, S. E. (1980). *The social psychology of leisure and recreation.* Dubuque: W. C. Brown.

Kelman, H. C. (1975). Compliance, identification and internalization: Processes of attitude change. In E. Krupat (Ed.), *Psychology is social* (pp. 98–106). Glenview IL: Scott & Foresman Co.

Keogh, J. K., Griffin, N. S., & Spector, R. (1981). Observer perceptions of movement confidence. *Research Quarterly for Exercise and Sport, 52,* 465–473.

Klint, K. A., & Weiss, M. R. (1987). Perceived competence and motives for participating in youth sports: A test of Harter's competence motivation theory. *Journal of Sport Psychology, 9,* 55–65.

Kobasa, S. C. (1979). Stressful life events, personality and health: An inquiry into hardiness. *Journal of Personality and Social Psychology, 37,* 1–11.

MacCracken, M. J., & Stadulis, R. E. (1985). Social facilitation of young children's dynamic balance performance. *Journal of Sport Psychology, 7,* 150–165.

Maehr, M. L., & Braskamp L. A. (1986). *The motivational factor: A theory of personal investment.* Lexington, MA: Heath & Co.

McAuley, E., & Gill, D. (1983). Reliability and validity of the physical self-efficacy scale in a competitive sport setting. *Journal of Sport Psychology, 5,* 410–418.

Murphy, I. B. (1962). *The widening world of childhood.* Chicago: Basic Books.

Nicholls, J. G. (1978). The development of the concepts of effort and ability, perception of attainment, and the understanding that difficult tasks require more ability. *Child Development, 49,* 800–814.

Nicholls, J. G. (1984). Striving to demonstrate and develop ability: A theory of achievement motivation. In J. G. Nicholls (Ed.), *The development of achievement motivation* (pp. 328–346). Greenwich, CT: JAI Press.

Nicholls, J. G., & Miller, A. (1983). The differentiation of the concepts of difficulty and ability. *Child Development, 54,* 951–959.

Passer, M. (1981). Children in sport: Participation motives and psychological stress. *Quest, 33,* 231–244.

Petruzzello, S. J., & Corbin, C. B. (1988). The effects of performance feedback on female self-confidence. *Journal of Sport and Exercise Psychology, 10,* 174–183.

Pitman, T, S., & Pitman, N. L. (1980). Deprivation of control and the attribution process. *Journal of Personality and Social Psychology, 39,* 377–389.

Roberts, G. C. (1984). Toward a new theory of motivation in sport: The role of perceived ability. In J. M. Silva & R. S. Weinberg (Eds.), *Psychological foundations of sport* (pp. 214–228). Champaign IL: Human Kinetics.

Roberts, G., & Duda, J. (1984). Motivation in sport: The mediating role of perceived ability. *Journal of Sport Psychology, 3,* 312–324.

Roberts, G. C., Kleiber, D., & Duda, J. (1981). An analysis of motivation in children's sport: The role of perceived competence in participation. *Journal of Sport Psychology, 3,* 206–216.

Romance, T. J. (1985). Observing for confidence. *Journal of Physical Education, Recreation and Dance, 56* (8), 47–49.

Rotter, J. B. (1982). *The development and application of social learning theory.* New York: Praeger.

Ruble, D. N., Parsons, J. E., & Ross, J. (1976). Self-evaluative responses of children in an achievement setting. *Child Development, 47,* 990–997.

Ryckman, R. M., Robbins M. A., Thornton, B., & Cantrell, P. (1982). Development and validation of a physical self-efficacy scale. *Journal of Personality and Social Psychology, 42,* 891–900.

Scanlan, T. K., & Lewthwaite, R. (1986). Social psychological aspects of competition for male youth sport participants: IV. predictors of enjoyment. *Journal of Sport Psychology, 8,* 25–35.

Sherer, M., Maddux J. E., Mercandante B., Prentice-Dunn S., Jacobs, B., & Rogers, R. (1982). The self-efficacy scale: Construction and validation. *Psychological Reports, 51,* 663–671.

Siedentop, D. (1976). Self-control. In *Personalized learning in physical education* (pp. 44–54). Washington, DC: AAHPERD Publications.

Siegelman, E. (1983). *Personal Risk.* New York: Harper & Row.

Smith, R. E., Smoll, F. L., Hunt, E., Curtis, B., & Coppel, D. B. (1979). Psychology and the bad news bears. In G. C. Roberts & K. M. Newell (Eds.), *Psychology of motor behavior and sport—1978,* (pp. 109–130). Champaign, IL: Human Kinetics.

Smith, R. E., Zane, N. W. S., Smoll, F. L., & Coppel, D. B. (1983). Behavioral assessment in youth sports: Coaching behaviors and children's attitudes. *Medicine and Science in Sport and Exercise, 15,* 208–214.

Sonstroem. R. J. (1978). Physical estimation attraction scales: Rationale and research. *Medicine and Science in Sports, 10,* 97–102.

Stott, D. H., & Sharp, J. D. (1975). Effectiveness motivation in pre-school children. *Educational Research, 18,* 117–123.

Sutton-Smith, B. (1970). A psychologist looks at playgrounds. *Educational Product Reports, 3* (8), 13–18.

Tryon, W. W. (1981). A methodological critique of Bandura's self-efficacy theory of behavioral change. *Journal of Behavior Therapy and Experimental Psychiatry, 12,* 113–114.

Ulrich, B. D. (1987). Perceptions of physical competence, motor competence and participation in organized sport: Their interrelationships in young children. *Research Quarterly in Exercise and Sport, 58,* 57–67.

Vallerand, R. J. (1983). On emotion in sport: Theoretical and social psychological perspectives. *Journal of Sport Psychology, 5,* 197–215.

Vallerand, R. J. (1984). Emotion in sport: Definitional, historical and social psychological perspectives. In W. F. Straub & J. M. Williams (Eds.), *Cognitive sport psychology* (pp. 65–78). Lansing, NY: Sport Sciences Associates.

Vallerand, R. J. (1987). Antecedents of self-related affects in sport: Preliminary evidence on the intuitive reflective model. *Journal of Sport Psychology, 9,* 161–182.

Vallerand, R. J., Colavecchio, P. G., & Pelletier, L. G. (1988). Psychological momentum and performance inferences: A preliminary test of the antecedents-consequences of psychological momentum model. *Journal of Sport and Exercise Psychology, 10,* 92–108.

Vallerand, R. J., & Reid, G. (1984). On the causal effects of perceived competence on intrinsic motivation: A test of cognitive evaluation theory. *Journal of Sport Psychology, 6,* 94–102.

Vealey, R. S. (1986). Conceptualization of sport-confidence and competitive orientation: Preliminary investigation and instrument development. *Journal of Sport Psychology, 8,* 221–246.

Wankel, L. M., & Kreisel, S. J. (1985). Factors underlying enjoyment of youth sports: Sport and age group comparisons. *Journal of Sport Psychology, 7,* 51–64.

Weiner, B. (1972). An attributional analysis of achievement motivation. *Journal of Personality and Social Psychology, 15,* 1–20.

Weiner, B. (1979). A theory of motivation for some classroom experiences. *Journal of Educational Psychology, 71,* 3–25.

Weiner, B., & Kun, A. (1974). The development of causal attributions and the growth of achievement and social motivation. In S. Feldman & D. Bush (Eds.), *Cognitive development and social development* (pp. 426–447). Potomac, MD: Erlbaum Press.

Weiss, M., Bredemeier, B. J., & Shewchuck, R. (1984). *The dynamics of perceived competence, perceived control and motivational orientation in youth sports: A causal analysis.* Paper presented at the Olympic Scientific Congress, Eugene, OR.

Welch, D. J. (1987). Power beyond performance: The experience of grace in movement. *Journal of Physical Education, Recreation and Dance, 58* (2), 82–84.

Wherry, R. J. (1966). Model for the study of psychological stress. *Aerospace Medicine, 87,* 495–499.

Wherry, R. J. & Curran, P. M. (1966). A model for the study of some determiners of psychological stress: Initial experimental research. *Organizational Behavior and Human Performance, 1,* 226–251.

White, B. L. (1978). *Experience and Environment* (Vol. 2). Englewood Cliffs, NJ: Prentice-Hall.

White, R. W. (1959), Motivation reconsidered: The concept of competence. *Psychological Review, 66,* 297–323.

INDEX

6/2004
DVD 2014